FREEDOM
ENCYCLOPEDIA

Pledge of Allegiance *(see page 134)*

FREEDOM ENCYCLOPEDIA
American Liberties in the Making

BY FRANCES CAVANAH

in collaboration with

ELIZABETH L. CRANDALL

Illustrated by LORENCE F. BJORKLUND

RAND McNALLY & COMPANY

Chicago   New York   San Francisco

Other Rand McNally Books
by Frances Cavanah

OUR COUNTRY'S STORY

OUR COUNTRY'S FREEDOM

ABE LINCOLN GETS HIS CHANCE

ADVENTURE IN COURAGE:
The Story of Theodore Roosevelt

TRIUMPHANT ADVENTURE:
The Story of Franklin Delano Roosevelt

Copyright© 1968 by RAND MCNALLY & COMPANY

Copyright 1968 under International Copyright Union
by RAND MCNALLY & COMPANY

All rights reserved. Printed in U. S. A.

Library of Congress Catalog Card Number 68-11646

Manufactured in the United States of America
by RAND MCNALLY & COMPANY

First printing, September, 1968

GUIDE TO

Freedom Encyclopedia

The main entries, which appear in alphabetical order in this book, are classified according to subject in the following Guide. For more detailed references and cross-references, the Index, beginning on page 193, may be consulted.

Colonial Quest for Freedom, and a New Nation

The same desire for freedom that brought many early settlers to the New World caused later colonists to declare the United States a free and independent nation.

America, Discovery and Exploration of
American Revolution
Boston Tea Party
Bunker Hill, Battle of
Charter Oak
Colonial Self-Government
Committees of Correspondence
Constitutional Convention
Constitutional Ratifying Conventions
Continental Congress
Declaration of Independence
Declaration of Rights, Virginia
Declaration of Rights and Grievances
Huguenots
Independence Day
Lexington and Concord
Mayflower Compact
Pilgrims
Sons of Liberty
Stamp Act
Town Meetings

Documents and Declarations

The progress made by man in his struggle for liberty can be traced through the written documents handed down from generation to generation.

American Declaration of Human Rights

Articles of Confederation
Atlantic Charter
Bill of Rights, American
Constitution of the United States
Declaration of Independence
Declaration of Rights, Virginia
Declaration of Rights and Grievances
Declaration of Sentiments (antislavery)
Declaration of Sentiments (women's rights)
Emancipation Proclamation
Mayflower Compact
Monroe Doctrine
Northwest Ordinance
United Nations Charter
United Nations Declaration
Universal Declaration of Human Rights
Virginia Statute for Religious Freedom

Fundamental Rights of Americans

The American people have shown their belief in the inalienable rights of man by including these rights in their policies and laws.

Assembly, Right of
Bill of Rights, American
Civil Liberties and Civil Rights
"Democracy in a Republic, A"
Dissent, Right of
Due Process of Law
Expression, Freedom of
Four Freedoms
Freedom Amendments
Freedom from Want
Freedom of Thought
Government by Consent
"Government of the People . . ."

Habeas Corpus, Writ of
Jury Trial
Law, Liberty Under
Minority Rights
Petition, Right to
Press and Other Forms of Communication
Religion, Freedom of
Self-Determination
Separation of Church and State
Suffrage

Government, Law, and Politics

Changing interpretations of the laws of the United States to meet the changing needs of the people and provide for their welfare prove "there is no quarrel between government and liberty."

Articles of Confederation
Bill of Rights, American
Constitution of the United States
Constitutional Convention
Constitutional Ratifying Conventions
Democracy
"Democracy in a Republic, A"
Dissent, Right of
Due Process of Law
Federalist, The
Government by Consent
Government by Consent v. Dictatorship
Habeas Corpus, Writ of
Jury Trial
Law, Liberty Under
Mayflower Compact
New Deal
Northwest Ordinance
Political Parties
Progressive Movement
Separation of Church and State
Suffrage
Supreme Court of the United States
Town Meetings
Woman Suffrage Movement

Heritage of Liberty from the Old World

Americans had a head start in their quest for human rights because of the ideas early settlers brought from the Old World.

"Areopagitica," by John Milton
Bible, The
Bill of Rights, English
Brotherhood of Man

Civil Wars, English
English Heritage of Freedom
Glorious Revolution
Greek and Roman Heritage of Freedom
Habeas Corpus, Writ of
Levellers, The
Magna Carta
Natural Law
Natural Rights
Petition, The Right to
Petition of Right
Reformation
Runnymede

Landmarks and Museums

The United States has preserved landmarks and created museums that provide a vivid picture of the nation's heritage of freedom.

Charter Oak
Faneuil Hall
Independence Hall
Liberty Bell
National Archives
Statue of Freedom
Statue of Liberty
Williamsburg

Organizations

Group effort has frequently been necessary to advance human rights.

American Civil Liberties Union
American Colonization Society
Committees of Correspondence
Continental Congress
Freedmen's Bureau
League of Nations
National Association for the Advancement of Colored People (NAACP)
Political Parties
Sons of Liberty
Underground Railroad
United Nations

Problems and Progress in an Expanding America

With the nation's expansion westward, the increase in its population, and its development into a great industrial giant, new problems arose that were a challenge to man's quest for freedom.

Antislavery Movement
Civil War, American
Education in a Democracy
Equal Rights in Schools
Immigration
Indians, American
Labor Movement
Negro Rights Movement
New Deal
Progressive Movement
Suffrage
Texas, Republic of
Westward Movement
Woman Suffrage Movement

Songs, Poems, Creeds, and Speeches

Authors, poets, and statesmen have given eloquent expression to American ideals of liberty.

"America," by Samuel Francis Smith
"America the Beautiful," by Katharine Lee Bates
American's Creed, by William Tyler Page
"Concord Hymn," by Ralph Waldo Emerson
Four Freedoms, by Franklin D. Roosevelt
Freedom Pledge
Gettysburg Address, by Abraham Lincoln
"Liberty Song," by John Dickinson
Pledge of Allegiance, by Francis Bellamy
"Star-Spangled Banner," by Francis Scott Key

Responsibilities of Freedom

The welfare of his fellowmen is the responsibility of the individual in a free society.

American Civil Liberties Union
American's Creed
American Declaration of Human Rights
Antislavery Movement
Bill of Rights, American
Brotherhood of Man
Civil Liberties and Civil Rights
Constitution of the United States
Declaration of Independence
Declaration of Rights, Virginia
Declaration of Sentiments (antislavery)
Education in a Democracy
Equal Rights in Schools
Freedmen's Bureau
Freedom Amendments
Freedom from Want
Freedom Pledge

Gettysburg Address
Labor Movement
Law, Liberty under
Liberty, Limitations on
Liberty of the Community
New Deal
Progressive Movement
Suffrage
Universal Declaration of Human Rights
Woman Suffrage Movement

The United States in War and Peace

When the American people have gone to war, their hope—as in time of peace—has been to extend freedom and democracy.

American Declaration of Human Rights
American Revolution
Civil War, American
League of Nations
Lexington and Concord
Texas, Republic of
United Nations
United Nations Declaration
Universal Declaration of Human Rights
World War I
World War II

Leaders in Liberty

The story of freedom is, in large part, the story of the men and women whose ideals and efforts have advanced human rights.

Adams, Abigail
Adams, John
Adams, John Quincy
Adams, Samuel
Altgeld, John Peter
Anthony, Susan B.
Baltimore, Lord
Blackstone, Sir William
Brandeis, Louis D.
Brown, John
Burke, Edmund
Clay, Henry
Coke, Sir Edward
Douglass, Frederick
Eisenhower, Dwight D.
Emerson, Ralph Waldo
Franklin, Benjamin
Garrison, William Lloyd
Gompers, Samuel

Definition of Terms

Certain terms are defined because they are frequently used in discussions of freedom and democracy.

Introduction

SOMETHING NEW
UNDER THE SUN

"We can no longer say there is nothing new under the sun," wrote Thomas Jefferson the year that he became President of the United States. "For this whole chapter in the history of man is new. The great extent of our Republic is new. . . ."

The citizens of that republic were the first people who, as a nation, had ever had an opportunity to choose the kind of government under which they wished to live. They had been entrusted with the success of a unique experiment, as President George Washington had pointed out in his First Inaugural, and he knew the way would not be easy. "It is a strenuous thing," he said, "this living the life of a free people."

Each succeeding generation has learned the truth of that statement. The principle of "government of the people, by the people, for the people," as stated by Abraham Lincoln, was put to a severe test during the Civil War. The nation survived that test. Since then there have been other crises, for not every American has always enjoyed the same rights. Through the years, many of them have had to struggle for their fair share of freedom's benefits; and in seeking equal rights for themselves, they have guaranteed more liberty for their countrymen.

And the process still goes on. It will continue to go on, for ideas change and needs change with the changing times. The young people who will live on into the twenty-first century will have new challenges to meet, new problems to solve, a new chapter to contribute to a story that is never finished—the story of American liberties in the making. Since the present must build on the past and pave the way for the future, a knowledge of earlier struggles and triumphs is important, and never more so than today.

One purpose of *Freedom Encyclopedia* is to furnish a glimpse into the past in the hope of providing a better understanding of some of the liberties and rights too often taken for granted. Among the numerous entries are those that tell of the Old World heritage that gave Americans a head start in their quest for human rights and of early struggles to establish those rights in the new nation.

Other entries tell of the continuing efforts to expand freedom in the United States and of groups and individuals, past and present, that have played a part in those efforts. In the sketches of individuals, emphasis has been placed on their contributions to liberty; and their words have been quoted, when such quotations seemed appropriate, so the reader may share in their wisdom. Still other entries in *Freedom Encyclopedia* are concerned with great freedom documents and books; with landmarks that have been the scene of important events in the story of liberty; and with terms that are frequently used in discussions of liberty and human rights.

Since a single volume can serve only as an introduction to such a vast topic as "freedom," books for further reading have been listed on page 191—books, it is believed, that will deepen an appreciation of our heritage. About this subject, so fascinating in its history and so vital to our present and future happiness and well being, certainly none of us can ever read enough.

For her help in compiling this list, the authors are deeply grateful to Virginia Haviland, head of the Children's Book Section at the Library of Congress. They are grateful to Dr. Louise Austin, Chairman of Social Studies, South Side Senior High School, Rockville Centre, N.Y., for her excellent suggestions and aid in compiling the Guide that begins on page 5.

Acknowledgment also is due several publishers for permission to quote from copyrighted material: Friendship Press, for the quotation on page 82 by Hiamovi, a Cheyenne chief, from *Indians Are People, Too,* by Ruth Bronson (a book now out of print) ; Curtis Publishing Company, for the quotation on page 76 by Kenneth Has-

brouck, president of the Huguenot Society of New Paltz, N.Y., from an article, "The Durable Huguenots," by Ernest O. Hauser, in the *Saturday Evening Post,* September 29, 1962; Random House, Inc., for the quotation on page 86, Column 2 from *My Hope for America,* by Lyndon B. Johnson; Viking Press, Inc., for the quotation on page 117 from *How Far the Promised Land,* by Walter F. White; Harper & Row, Inc., for the quotation on page 91 from *Where Do We Go From Here?* by Martin Luther King, Jr.

The number of volumes consulted, including standard textbooks and encyclopedias, general histories, biographies, and reminiscences, available to the public in many schools and libraries, are too numerous to be listed. The authors have also made use of government records and newspaper accounts of the activities and public utterances of government and other leaders, especially those of recent years, who have contributed to the freedom story.

FRANCES CAVANAH
ELIZABETH L. CRANDALL

Adams, Abigail Smith (1744–1818), wrote to her husband, John Adams (March, 1776), when he was serving in the Continental Congress:

I long to hear that you have declared an independency. And, by the way, in the new code of laws which I suppose it will be necessary for you to make, I desire that you would remember the ladies. Be more generous and favorable to them than your ancestors.

Abigail Adams believed in freedom for women as well as men, but she was a woman ahead of her time. Many years were to pass before women would be allowed to vote and share in other privileges enjoyed by their husbands and brothers. Mrs. Adams had to be content to make her contribution to the cause of liberty as a devoted wife. When the American Revolution began, and even before, she took all the responsibility for running the little farm in Braintree (later a part of Quincy), Mass., during her husband's frequent absences on business for his country. During the occupation of Boston by enemy troops (1775–76), many residents fled from the city. Any of these refugees and any American soldiers who passed by Abigail's home were made welcome. If they asked for lodging, she took them in. If they were hungry, she fed them.

After the United States became an independent nation, Abigail Adams shared her husband's triumphs and difficulties, and she was the first wife of a President to live in the "President's Palace," as the White House was then called. Seven years after her death, her son, John Quincy Adams, became the sixth President. It was he who wrote the inscription for one of the walls of the church in Quincy where his parents lie buried. In this inscription he spoke of how Abigail Adams had met undaunted "the terrors and trials of that Revolution" which made secure the freedom of her country and "brightened the prospects of . . . man upon earth."

Adams, John (1735–1826), proved his mettle as a patriot when, as a rising young lawyer just ten years out of Harvard, he protested against the Stamp Act (1765). In other events preceding the American Revolution, Lawyer Adams of Braintree, Mass., and later of Boston, played a leading part. He was a delegate to the Continental Congress (1774–77), and after war broke out at Lexington and Concord, it was John Adams who nominated George Washington to be commander in chief of a new Continental Army. In June, 1776, he was appointed to a committee to draft a Declaration of Independence, but he insisted that another member, Thomas Jefferson, do the actual writing. In the stormy debates that followed, when Jefferson's manuscript was presented to Congress, Adams argued eloquently for its adoption. He said:

We may not live to the time when this Declaration shall be made good . . . But while I do live let me have a country and that a free country . . . live or die, survive or perish, I am for the Declaration.

After Congress voted for independence, Adams was sent to France and to Holland to obtain help for the struggling new nation. He then became a member of the commission that worked out the terms for a treaty of peace, whereby the British

government recognized the independence of the United States (1783).

Later, as the first Vice President of the new nation (1789–97) and as President (1797–1801), he was very unpopular, partly because he had become more conservative. He was believed to prefer a government by "the rich, the well born and the able," an expression he himself had once used, and dislike for him increased after Congress passed the Alien and Sedition Acts (1798). The Alien Act gave the President power to deport aliens if he considered them dangerous, and the Sedition Act made it a crime to criticize any federal law or government official. Under this latter law, for example, one newspaper editor who wrote about "the ridiculous pomp" of President Adams was fined $1,000 and spent four months in jail. Indignant citizens protested that the Sedition Law violated the right of free speech guaranteed by the First Amendment to the Constitution. The Federalist political party became very unpopular because it had been responsible for the law, and President Adams, the party's candidate, had to take most of the blame.

Adams, after being defeated in his bid for a second term, retired to the home he had purchased in Quincy, Mass., embittered by the thought that his countrymen failed to appreciate him. Yet even his enemies admitted that, though he might be vain and stubborn, he was brilliant and honest; nor could they forget his part in making the United States an independent nation. A short time before he died, on July 4, 1826, the fiftieth anniversary of the first Independence Day, when his countrymen were preparing to celebrate that great event, John Adams was asked to suggest an appropriate toast. "I give you," he said, "independence forever."

Adams, John Quincy (1767–1848), eldest son of John and Abigail Adams, was not quite eight years old in the early days of the American Revolution when he stood on a hill beside his mother and watched the battle of Bunker Hill (June 17, 1775) in the distance. In the days that followed, several other battles were fought close by, and the family's little house in Braintree, Mass., would rattle and shake whenever the big guns started firing. Growing up in such a dangerous time gave Mr. Johnny, as his mother called him, a greater sense of responsibility than most boys, and he helped care for many of the refugees who stopped at their house to rest.

Later, after his graduation from Harvard (1787), John Quincy Adams studied law and held several important offices in government. As Secretary of State he was principally responsible for the Monroe Doctrine (1823). Then he became President (1825), but like the elder Adams, failed to win a second term. Two years later he was elected to Congress.

It was here, in the House of Representatives, where the former President served for seventeen years (1831–48), that he made his great contribution to the cause of freedom. There was a growing feeling in the United States that slavery was wrong, and petitions poured into Congress, signed by people who wished to see slavery abolished. Due to the influence of pro-slavery members, the House of Representatives then passed several resolutions known as "gag rules," which forbade discussion in the House of any antislavery petitions. John Quincy Adams, in speech after speech, declared that the right of the people to petition their government was guaranteed to them by the U.S. Constitution. His arguments were so forceful that he came to be known as "Old Man Eloquent." Though he made many enemies, he never gave up, and after eight years the gag rules were finally repealed (1844).

In defending the right of Americans to petition Congress, John Quincy Adams also became a champion of freedom for the slaves. It was a great cause, he insisted, but he knew he would not live to see the end of the struggle.

"My career must close," he said toward the end of his long life, "leaving the cause at the threshold. To open the way for others is all that I can do."

Adams, Samuel (1722–1803), probably did more than any other man to plant a desire for independence in the minds and hearts of the American colonists. Even as a student at Harvard, when young Sam was asked to select a subject for discussion, he chose "Liberty." After graduation (1740) he studied law and went into business in Boston, but business did not interest him. Instead, he turned to public affairs.

More radical than his second cousin, John Adams, Sam Adams was an agitator and a master of propaganda. In numerous pamphlets and newspaper articles, he condemned the harsh measures of the men then in control of the British government. In speeches before the Boston Town Meeting and the Massachusetts Legislature, of which he was a member, he tried to arouse his listeners to resist those measures.

No man in the colonies protested against the Stamp Act more vigorously than did Sam Adams, and he was among the first Americans to declare that Parliament had no legal right to tax them. He then helped to organize the Sons of Liberty and the Committees of Correspondence, and he was primarily responsible for the Boston Tea Party.

"Let us remember," he said in one speech, "that if we suffer tamely a lawless attack upon our liberty, we encourage such attack."

Sam Adams was convinced that, in order to preserve their liberty, the colonies must form a separate nation. In his single-minded determination to make them independent, he neglected his own interests. Money was of no concern to him, and when he became a delegate to the Continental Congress (1774), his clothes were so shabby that some of his friends bought him a new outfit. He arrived in Philadelphia wearing a claret-colored coat, ruffles at the

wrist, a new wig, and a new cocked hat, as elegantly dressed as any of his fellow congressmen.

As a delegate, Sam Adams opposed any compromise with the British government. Later, during the Second Continental Congress, he took part in the debate concerning a motion that the colonies should declare their independence. His voice was heavy, his gestures awkward, but his arguments were convincing.

"I always considered him as, more than any other member," said Thomas Jefferson later, "the fountain of our important measures."

Though Samuel Adams later served as Governor of Massachusetts, it is as "the father of the American Revolution" that he is most gratefully remembered.

Altgeld, John Peter (1847–1902), sat at his desk one day in 1893, soon after he had taken office as Governor of Illinois, looking at a huge pile of documents. They included affidavits and court records of the notorious Haymarket trial seven years earlier. During a meeting of labor sympathizers in Haymarket Square, Chicago, a bomb had gone off, killing six policemen and injuring forty other people. The man who threw the bomb was never found, but eight anarchists were arrested.

The city of Chicago had seemed gripped by hatred and fear, and it was in this atmosphere that the men were tried for murder. All were convicted, and those who were not executed were sent to prison. When the new governor, John Peter Altgeld, reviewed the evidence, he

Haymarket Riot

concluded they were innocent of murder and the trial had been unfair. No one was even sure that the accused men were anarchists, and the governor decided to pardon the three who were in prison.

When his political friends learned of the governor's decision, they warned that the public would turn against him. They tried to convince him that, if he issued the pardons, he could never be reelected as governor, and he might as well forget his ambition to be elected to the Senate.

"No man's ambition," he replied, "has a right to stand in the way of performing a simple act of justice."

As Altgeld had been warned, there was a storm of protest after the pardons were granted. He was burned in effigy and overwhelmingly defeated for reelection. Not until years later did his countrymen come to appreciate his sacrifice in giving up a promising political career to make sure that justice was done.

When the centennial of Altgeld's birth (Dec., 1947) was observed in Chicago, William O. Douglas, associate justice of the Supreme Court, was the principal speaker. It took courage, he said, to stand up for the rights of an unpopular minority and insist, as the late Governor of Illinois had insisted, that the Bill of Rights was designed for all people. But it was men like John Peter Altgeld, the justice continued, who "win greatness even in defeat and leave behind a rich heritage for those who later rebuild on our lost hopes."

"America," by Samuel Francis Smith. Such phrases as "sweet land of liberty" and "let freedom ring" from this song (also known as "My Country 'Tis of Thee") have become a part of the nation's patriotic literature. The author, a graduate of Harvard College, was studying for the ministry at Andover (Mass.) Theological Seminary when he came across the tune in an old song book. He set words to it and did not realize until later that the

Park Street Church

tune was the same as the one for "God Save the King," the British national anthem.

The first performance of Smith's song was at a Fourth of July celebration (1832) at Park Street Church in Boston. Later that year it was published and immediately became popular. By the time Smith returned to Harvard for his thirtieth reunion (1859), he had published other poems and was a successful college professor and Baptist minister. "Fate tried to conceal him by naming him Smith," joked his classmate, the poet Oliver Wendell Holmes, in a poem celebrating the class reunion. Smith's real fame, though, has always rested on his song, "America."

America, Discovery and Exploration of. Neither Christopher Columbus who found the New World by accident in 1492, nor most of the explorers who sailed across the Atlantic during the next century, ever grasped the real significance of their discoveries. Such explorers and adventurers as John Cabot, Hernando de Soto, and Francisco Vásquez Coronado came seeking riches. Some of them succeeded, but their more important accomplishment was the opening of a vast new area for settlement. What they never realized was that the land they had explored was to become the scene of the world's first great experiment in freedom and democracy.

The first explorer who seemed aware of the real possibilities of the new, almost empty land was the bold English adventurer, Captain John Smith. He joined an expedition and helped found a settlement called Jamestown (1607) in that part of the New World the English called Virginia. Before returning to England, he explored some of the rivers close by and made maps of the regions he visited. Later he came back to America to lead an exploring expedition (1614) along a coast much farther north—a coast he named New England.

It was John Smith's dream to found a colony where English families could come and make new homes, start farms, and build towns and cities, but he lacked financial backing to carry out his plans. What he did was probably even more important, for he wrote several books about Virginia and New England that stirred the imagination of his readers.

He knew that in England few people ever had a chance to rise above the class into which they had been born. Few of them owned any land, but in America, John Smith pointed out, there was more land than the natives could ever use. With this land going to waste, why should people stay in England and work for greedy landlords who paid them a mere pittance? There were many who could find no work at all.

"Here [in America] by their labor," said John Smith, "they can live exceedingly well."

Captain Smith's statement that in America "every man may be master" and his belief that all men should be permitted "as much freedom as may be" continued to inspire and encourage his discontented countrymen and others in Europe for years to come. Thousands took his advice and crossed the Atlantic. Some came, as had the Pilgrims, in search of religious freedom. Others wanted to escape the harsh rule of kings, or to find something better than the grinding poverty that had always been their lot. John Smith never realized how well his plan would succeed in years to come.

See WESTWARD MOVEMENT.

"America the Beautiful," which is probably America's favorite patriotic hymn, was written by Katharine Lee Bates, author and professor at Wellesley College, during her first trip to the West. After stopping in Chicago to see the Columbian Exposition (1893), she spent several weeks in the Rocky Mountains. It was while she was standing on Pikes Peak that the words of her famous poem began to come to her, and it was doubtless the breathtaking view of the surrounding countryside that inspired the second stanza:

> *O beautiful for pilgrim feet*
> *Whose stern, impassioned stress*
> *A thoroughfare for freedom beat*
> *Across the wilderness ...*

Later the poem was set to music, and it has appeared in collections of the author's verse as well as in a number of anthologies.

American Civil Liberties Union (ACLU) was founded in 1920. Roger Baldwin, reformer and civic leader, one of the founders, and its first director, once described himself as "the only man who ever made a professional career out of defending the Bill of Rights." During the thirty years in which he served as director (1920–1950), the ACLU grew into a nationwide, nonpartisan organization, with headquarters in New York City and a number of affiliated chapters throughout the United States. It is supported by dues and voluntary contributions of thousands of members.

From the beginning, the organization's purpose has remained the same: to preserve and defend the rights and freedoms guaranteed by the American Bill of Rights. The conviction that free speech, press, and assemblage and all other civil rights should apply to everyone alike was summed up by John de J. Pemberton, Jr., who had been appointed the executive director in 1962. He said:

We think of our [governmental] system as one in which the subjects of government are at the same time the rulers. It's essential that their society treat them as it would the rulers . . . . We have constitutional guarantees. If they work they must work for everyone. Otherwise they're not constitutional guarantees. The protection of the rights of every individual, we believe, including the most despised and feared and hated, is essential to being a free nation.

The ideas of liberty were revolutionary in 1776, and they're still pretty revolutionary today. For that reason, there's often a wide gap between the liberties America proclaims and the things America does. The union's purpose is to close that gap.

In pursuit of this ideal the central organization and its affiliated chapters have helped to alert the public to the need for constant vigilance in maintaining civil rights. Both in the U.S. Congress and in state legislatures, members of the American Civil Liberties Union have lobbied against proposed laws that might threaten the rights guaranteed by the Constitution, and they have urged the passage of bills that would strengthen those rights.

Among other measures, the organization has supported anti-discrimination laws, a fair deal for Indians, and the right of teachers and all other persons to believe what they wish and to express their beliefs. It has insisted that accused persons must always be given a fair trial.

Much of the work of the Union, therefore, centers in the courts, and there are usually several hundred cases pending at the same time in various parts of the United States. More than 800 lawyers, who contribute their services, furnish legal counsel for men and women whose civil rights are believed to have been violated. The ACLU does not welcome the support of Communists, Fascists, members of the Ku Klux Klan, or others who adhere to totalitarian doctrines. Yet so long as such persons or groups do not break the law, the organization stands ready to defend their constitutional rights.

Recent Presidents and many other leading Americans have endorsed the work of the ACLU. President Lyndon B. Johnson said:

The American Civil Liberties Union has an essential role at this critical time. It defends the rights of even the most despised to speak, to assemble, and to petition for redress of grievances. It protects the individual's constitutional guarantees of the right to counsel, to confrontation and to due process of law. It has come to symbolize racial justice and religious freedom.

American Colonization Society. This organization, founded (1817) to provide free Negroes with a home in Africa, was financed by church and other philanthropic groups. A site was purchased on the west coast of Africa, and the colony started there was called Liberia after the word "liberty." The town of Monrovia, named for President James Monroe, was established (1822) as the capital when the first group of Negro colonists arrived.

Estimates vary as to the number of Negroes transported to Liberia before the Civil War through the efforts of the society, but the number was probably under 12,000. One reason why the enterprise was not more successful was lack of funds. A more important reason was that few Negroes wanted to go.

"We were stolen from our country and brought *here*...," said Richard Allen, well-known Negro minister and leader. "This land which we have watered with our tears and our blood is now our mother country; and we are well satisfied to stay where wisdom abounds ..."

Liberia, an independent Negro republic since 1847, has a Constitution modeled after that of the United States. The country today is inhabited by a number of native African tribes, but about 5 percent of the population is made up of descendants of the original Negro colonizers. This group, which lives in Monrovia and other coastal towns, furnishes most of the native leaders in business and government.

"American's Creed." This creed was written by William Tyler Page, clerk of the House of Representatives, and submitted in a nationwide contest (1917). Before setting to work, Page consulted a number of important historical sources, including the Declaration of Independence, the U.S. Constitution, the Bill of Rights, the Federalist Papers, and speeches by Washington, Jefferson, and Lincoln. In finished form the creed was what he had hoped to make it: "a summary of the fundamental principles of American political faith as set forth in its greatest documents, its worthiest traditions and by its greatest leaders."

Page's 100-word essay was selected as the winner out of thousands of manuscripts submitted. At a special ceremony in April, 1918, in the House of Representatives, he was awarded a $1,000 prize which had been offered by the city of Baltimore. A more satisfying reward was the acceptance of the Creed by the House on behalf of the American people.

The Creed reads as follows:

I believe in the United States of America as a government of the people, by the people, for the people, whose just powers are derived from the consent of the governed; a democracy in a Republic; a sovereign Nation of many sovereign states; a perfect Union, one and inseparable; established upon those principles of freedom, equality, justice and humanity, for which American patriots sacrificed their lives and fortunes.

I therefore believe it is my duty to my country to love it; to support its Constitution; to obey its laws; to respect its flag, and to defend it against all enemies.

See also PLEDGE OF ALLEGIANCE.

American Declaration of Human Rights was adopted at a conference of representatives of the United States and twenty other American republics in Bogotá, Colombia (1948). The Preamble reads: "All men are born free and equal..., and they should conduct themselves as brothers one to another."

Following the Preamble is a list of twenty-seven articles concerning rights and duties. These include the right of each person in the Americas to "life, liberty and the security of his person"; "the equality of all persons before the law"; the right to profess a religious faith; to have an education; to work under proper conditions; to assemble peaceably with others; and not to be deprived of liberty, "except in the cases and according to the procedures established by pre-existing law."

The final article reads: "The rights of man are limited by the rights of others, by the security of all, and by the just demands of the general welfare and the advancement of democracy."

The Bogotá Declaration was adopted several months before the adoption of the Universal Declaration of Human Rights by the UN General Assembly.

American Revolution. When the English colonists in America first took up arms against the mother country, very few wanted independence. Most of them had come from England or were descendants of English settlers, and they thought of themselves as English, entitled to the traditional rights of Englishmen (see ENGLISH HERITAGE OF FREEDOM).

But England was more than 3,000 miles away, and Americans had grown accustomed to having their own colonial legislatures make most of their laws. When, in the 1760's, the British Parliament began to pass new laws and enforce old ones —laws taxing the Americans and interfering with their trade—feeling ran high throughout the colonies. In Massachusetts, resentment against the British troops sent across the Atlantic to enforce the laws led to outright revolt at Lexington and Concord—and the American Revolution had begun.

Even then most Americans did not want to cut their ties with the mother country. They did want freedom from oppression and the right to continue to control their own colonial governments. When General George Washington took command of the Continental Army, he said his only wish was for the reestablishment of "peace and harmony between the mother country and the colonies." Most of the colonists agreed, but this feeling began to change after several months of bitter warfare against a superior foe. More and more Americans came to feel that they could not hope for justice and liberty as long as they remained in the British Empire.

In early July, 1776, the delegates to the Second Continental Congress resolved to separate from Great Britain. What until then had been a revolution now became a War for Independence. The adoption of the Declaration of Independence made it clear that a new nation, called the United States of America, had come into being.

But had it? The American troops, ragged and ill-fed, and a few scattered bands of militia, seemed no match for the enemy, and the Americans had only a few warships to oppose the most powerful navy

in the world. Declaring independence was a dangerous step to take in 1776, for even while Congress had been debating the question, fresh detachments of enemy troops were crossing the Atlantic.

Not only then, in 1776, but during the next five years of fighting, the American forces were greatly outnumbered, and to many discouraged patriots it seemed they could not possibly win. General Washington dared not risk many open battles. He would attack and harass the enemy, then retreat—tactics that won him the nickname "the old fox."

A time of special hardship was the winter of 1777–78, when the general and about 10,000 men went into camp at Valley Forge near Philadelphia. These difficult days were made somewhat easier by the presence of two foreigners who had recently arrived to help the Americans. The young Marquis de Lafayette from France was commissioned a general. He cheerfully endured the hardships and became known as "the soldier's friend." Baron von Steuben, a former German army officer, drilled the raw, inexperienced

troops, and by spring there was a well-trained army ready to take the field again.

Spring also brought the welcome news that France had signed a treaty of alliance with the new United States. At last there seemed a good chance that the patriots would win, yet the war went on and on. It was fought on land and on the ocean. There was fighting in the wilderness west of the Appalachian Mountains and along the Atlantic seaboard, both in the north and in the south.

"We fight, get beat, rise and fight again," said General Nathanael Greene, commander of the American Army of the South.

October, 1781 found a large part of the British army, under the command of Lord Cornwallis at Yorktown, Va., penned up on a peninsula jutting out into Chesapeake Bay. Washington marched his main army southward to join American forces in Virginia. With the aid of French troops and a French fleet, they besieged Cornwallis for nearly three weeks until he surrendered (Oct. 19).

Yorktown was the last important battle of the war. Nearly two years passed before the final treaty of peace was signed, but the independence of the new nation was assured. American freedom had been won against what had once seemed impossible odds.

It was won not only by Washington and other American soldiers and officers, but by officers from other lands, such as General Lafayette and Casimir Pulaski, a patriot from Poland who was mortally wounded before the war was over. It was won by financiers, like Robert Morris, a successful businessman, and Haym Salomon, a Polish refugee who spent the last years of his life raising money for "the cause," as he called the American struggle for liberty. It was won by Samuel and John Adams, Thomas Paine, Benjamin Franklin, and Thomas Jefferson, whose ideas had stirred the patriots to action and had given them a cause to fight for.

"Posterity! You will never know how much it costs the present generation to preserve your freedom," John Adams once said. "I hope that you will make good use of it."

See AMERICAN REVOLUTION in the INDEX for a list of related entries.

Anthony, Susan B. (1820–1906), of whom it has been said, "She changed the mind of a nation," was one of the early crusaders in the woman suffrage movement. The words "We the people," in the U.S. Constitution, she said, did not refer exclusively to "white male citizens" (as many Americans then thought), but to "the whole people who formed the Union— women as well as men."

For more than half a century Miss Anthony waged an unrelenting fight against prejudice, making speeches and writing articles to convert the public to her views. For eight years (1892–1900) she served as president of the National American Woman Suffrage Association. Before the end of her term, four western

states had granted women the franchise, but Susan Anthony's main objective was the enactment of an amendment to the federal Constitution. Year after year, she and her co-workers appeared before committees of Congress to present an amendment and to urge its adoption. Year after year, Congress refused to act.

In spite of many disappointments, Susan B. Anthony never lost faith in the worthiness of her cause. Toward the end of her life, at the age of eighty-six, she attended a woman's rights convention in Baltimore. When she rose to speak, looking ill and frail, the members of the audience broke into prolonged applause. After it finally subsided, the pioneer suffrage leader had a final plea to make. "The fight must not cease," she said. "You must see that it does not stop."

The fight went on for another sixteen years. In 1920, the centennial of Miss Anthony's birth, the Nineteenth Amendment, granting women citizens throughout the nation the right to vote, was finally added to the U.S. Constitution.

Antislavery Movement. The first African slaves to reach the English colonies that later became the United States arrived in Jamestown, Va., aboard a Dutch slave ship in 1619. After the need for cheap labor in the new country increased, captains of Spanish and English slave vessels also began to do a thriving business. They captured the Negroes in Africa, or bought them from African tribes that had captured members of weaker tribes. Later some New England vessels also were used to bring the captives to America.

The traffic in "black gold," as the slave trade was called because it proved so profitable, was carried on for years, at a terrible human cost to the unfortunate victims. Slavery, which was to bring much misery to the American people in time to come, spread throughout the colonies.

Almost from the first, though, there

were some white colonists who considered it a great wrong to enslave Negroes just because their skin was dark. In Germantown, Pa., a resolution was adopted (1688) by a group of settlers who belonged to a religious sect known as Mennonite. "Here [in America] is liberty of conscience, which is right and reasonable," the resolution read. "Here ought to be likewise liberty of the body."

The same position was taken by the Society of Friends, or Quakers. Long before the American Revolution, many Quakers freed their slaves and often saw to it that Negro youths who had been freed were taught a trade, and that those who were too old to work were provided for. A number of early antislavery societies were formed by Quakers, and they were always among the most dedicated members. It was through the Pennsylvania Society for the Abolition of Slavery that Philadelphia's leading citizen—Benjamin Franklin— though not a Quaker, became more aware of the evils of slavery. He spoke of it as "an atrocious debasement of human nature."

Other leaders of Revolutionary days, besides Franklin, felt uncomfortable about "the peculiar institution," as slavery came to be called. They realized it was inconsistent to fight a war for the sake of liberty and then deny liberty to several million of their fellow human beings. General George Washington had inherited a large number of slaves, and sometimes there were more Negro servants at Mt. Vernon than he could afford to support. Unlike some plantation owners, he refused to separate slave families by selling any of the members, and in his will he provided that all of the Negroes at Mt. Vernon should be given their freedom.

He hoped that someday laws would be passed for the gradual emancipation of the slaves. Such laws, he said, might prevent much "future mischief." He seemed to sense, years before the Civil War, the danger that the slavery issue might break

up the Union he had fought and worked to establish.

Another antislavery slave owner— who also had inherited his slaves—was Thomas Jefferson. "Nothing is more certainly written in the book of fate, than that these people are to be free," he said.

Jefferson's friend, George Mason, author of the Virginia Declaration of Rights, agreed. When he attended the Constitutional Convention (1787), he made an eloquent plea that the Constitution under consideration should forbid "the infernal traffic," as he called the slave trade. His plea was not heeded, but a compromise was reached. It was decided that the trade could continue until 1808, but after that date no more slaves could be brought into the country.

There were some delegates to the Constitutional Convention who doubtless shared the general feeling of the late 1700's that it was only a matter of time before all slaves would be emancipated by law. Slave labor had not proved profitable in the North, and the Northern states passed laws freeing their slaves. In parts of the South, also, many people believed slavery was not only morally wrong but no longer profitable. In several Southern states, there were more slaves than were needed, and sometimes a plantation owner was forced to sell a few of them in order to buy food for the others.

And then the cotton gin came into general use. This machine, invented in 1793, made it possible to separate the cotton fibers from the seeds in much less time than had been possible when the work was done by hand. English factories, as well as factories in the North, wanted cotton in ever-increasing quantities for the manufacture of cloth. To supply all the cotton that could now be sold, the plantation owners said slave labor was a necessity.

During this same period there was a growing feeling, especially in the North, that big profits could not justify the ownership of one human being by another. Men and women, called Abolitionists because they favored the immediate abolition of slavery, were very active during the thirty years preceding the Civil War. They flooded the country with pamphlets, books, and posters denouncing slaveholders for their cruel treatment of the Negroes.

Southerners, including many who had once hoped for the gradual emancipation of the slaves, replied hotly that the accusations were neither just nor true. Agitators in both sections of the country shared the responsibility for increasing the bitterness between North and South—a bitterness that was to end in Civil War.

Many years before the war began there were numerous antislavery people in the North, equally sincere, who denounced slavery but did not approve of the methods sometimes used by Abolitionists. Among those who deplored the acts of extremists such as John Brown was a rising Illinois lawyer and politician named Lincoln.

No one was ever more opposed than Abraham Lincoln to exploitation in any form, and this included exploitation of the Negro. Yet he knew the problem had no easy solution, for the Constitution at that time did not forbid slavery. There was no legal way of abolishing it in states where it already existed, but this fact did not alter his belief that it was wrong—terribly wrong. In speech after speech, he urged that slavery not be allowed to spread into the Western territory then being opened up for settlement, and he had little patience with those people who maintained that Negroes were better off as slaves.

"Whenever I hear anyone arguing for slavery," he once said in his wry way, "I feel a strong impulse to see it tried on him personally."

Because of the firm stand Abraham Lincoln had taken against the extension of slavery into the territories, he was very unpopular in the South and, after his election as President, seven Southern states seceded from the Union, to be joined later by four others. Secession led to the Civil War which—though it was not fought primarily for that purpose—led finally to the abolition of slavery.

Yet even the amendments added to the Constitution after the war, forbidding slavery and granting the Negroes the privileges of citizenship, did not bring them complete liberty. The fight for Negro Rights still lay ahead.

See NEGRO RIGHTS MOVEMENT on page 119; also see ANTISLAVERY MOVEMENT in INDEX for a list of related entries.

"Areopagitica" is the title of John Milton's great essay, published in pamphlet form (1644), in defense of freedom of the press. The word is based on "Areopagus," the name of the high court of ancient Athens, where matters of the gravest importance were discussed. By titling his essay as he did, Milton implied that the questions it dealt with were important enough to deserve the attention of Parliament, the "Areopagus" of England.

Areopagitica was published during the course of a political and religious struggle in England. The essay apparently made little impression at the time, but in future years its splendid prose and forceful arguments would be used again and again to support the cause of freedom of expression.

See MILTON, JOHN.

Articles of Confederation. The plan of government adopted by the Continental Congress (1777), after the colonies had declared their independence, was called the Articles of Confederation. By March, 1781, the plan had been ratified by all the states which agreed to "enter into a firm league of friendship with each other, for the common defense, the security of their liberties, and their mutual and general welfare."

The Articles provided for a Congress, but granted the Congress no real power

and no authority to levy taxes to carry on the government. After independence was assured, quarrels developed among the states which threatened the freedom won at such great cost and, in 1789, the Articles of Confederation were superseded by a new and stronger plan of government, the U.S. Constitution.

Assembly, Right of. "Congress shall make no law . . .," reads the American Bill of Rights, "abridging . . . the right of people peaceably to assemble." This provision, in the First Amendment to the U.S. Constitution, guarantees the legal right of the people to meet in public places (which would include the right to take part in marches and demonstrations) for the purpose of protesting governmental or other policies when it is felt such protest is called for. Such meetings and such marches must be peaceable and no law may be broken.

Decisions as to what is lawful and what is not must necessarily be left to local authorities, and their decisions in many instances have been a subject of controversy. Local authorities accused of violating the constitutional rights of a citizen may legally be brought to trial, but many cases of alleged violations have never reached a courtroom.

Atlantic Charter. Four months before the United States was drawn into World War II, President Franklin Delano Roosevelt and Winston Churchill, prime minister of Great Britain, held a secret meeting at sea off the coast of Newfoundland (Aug. 14, 1941). Britain was then fighting for its existence against the Nazis, and Roosevelt, realizing his own nation was seriously threatened, joined Churchill in issuing a statement known as the Atlantic Charter. This charter was neither a treaty nor an agreement for an alliance, but a statement of the kind of world the two leaders wanted to see established when the war was won.

Both heads of state went on record with the statement that neither of their countries sought any additional territory and reaffirmed the principles President Roosevelt had mentioned in his Four Freedoms speech. Other articles in the charter expressed the hope that after the Nazis were defeated a peace could be established that would "afford to all nations the means of dwelling in safety within their own boundaries," and that this could best be accomplished by "a wider and more permanent system of general security."

This last provision foreshadowed the formation of the United Nations as a peacekeeping organization in 1945.

Baltimore, Lord. George Calvert (1580?–1632), the first Lord Baltimore, was a prominent English Catholic who was distressed by the manner in which many members of his faith were persecuted. In 1632 King Charles I named him proprietor of a large tract of land north of Virginia in the New World, where Catholics might find refuge, but Lord Baltimore died before the plan could be carried out. Instead, it was his son, Cecilius Calvert, the second Lord Baltimore (1605–75), who became the owner of the colony. Toward the end

"Ark" and "Dove"

of 1633 he sent two ships, the *Ark* and the *Dove*, to the New World with several hundred colonists. Under the leadership of a younger brother, Leonard Calvert (1606–47), they established the first settlement in Maryland. After Leonard's death, Lord Baltimore appointed other governors to take charge. Though he himself never visited his colony, he remained its proprietor for more than forty years.

As proprietor, he proved to be more broad-minded than some of the leaders of his time, and all Christians were welcomed to his domain. In a few years Protestants outnumbered Catholics and then tried to gain control of the colony. There was so much dissension that Lord Baltimore urged the Maryland Assembly to pass The Act Concerning Religion (1649), usually called the Toleration Act. It read:

> For the more quiet and peaceable government of this province, and the better to preserve the mutual love and unity among the inhabitants here, it is enacted . . . that no person . . . professing to believe in Jesus Christ shall henceforth be in any ways troubled, molested or discountenanced for or in respect to his or her religion . . . .

This Toleration Act did not grant freedom of worship to non-Christians, and it was repealed after a few years. Even so, in an intolerant age, it marked a step forward in establishing the principles of religious freedom in a country one day to be called the United States.

Bible, The. Though the Bible was read by many people in all the colonies for moral and spiritual inspiration, in Puritan New England it also served as a source of political guidance. The principles of good government, the Puritans believed, could be found in the Old Testament, which contained most of the laws needed in their communities.

Since most of the Puritans had come to America to escape the religious and political persecutions of arbitrary rulers, they thought of kings as tyrants. And tyrants need not be obeyed if their laws conflicted with the commands of God, the Puritans insisted. They often quoted a passage from the Bible to show that God himself did not approve of kings.

This Biblical passage was from I Samuel, where it is told how the people of Israel decided that they wanted to be ruled by a king, like all other nations, instead of by God. The Lord granted their request, but first asked the prophet Samuel to warn the people of the consequences.

So Samuel spoke to the people, and said:

This will be the manner of the king that shall reign over you: He will take your sons, and appoint them for himself, for his chariots, and to be his horsemen . . . And he will take your fields, and your vineyards, and your olive-yards, even the best of them, and give them to his servants. . . . He will take the tenth of your sheep: and ye shall be his servants.

Surely in the minds of the Puritans this was strong justification for their frequent protests against royal tyranny.

Bill of Rights, American. After the U.S. Constitution was drawn up by the Constitutional Convention, a copy was sent to Thomas Jefferson, then serving as American minister to France. On the whole he approved of the document, but felt it had one serious weakness. There were no specific provisions guaranteeing such fundamental rights as freedom of religion and freedom of the press.

"A Bill of Rights," Jefferson wrote his friend James Madison, "is what the people are entitled to against every government on earth."

This same opinion was voiced by many of the delegates to the state conventions called to decide whether their states should ratify the Constitution. They wanted to make certain the liberties for which Americans had fought during the American Revolution could never be taken away from the people by officers in the government. Several state conventions voted to ratify the Constitution only on condition that it be amended to include a Bill of Rights.

After the Constitution became the law of the land, a new Congress was elected to replace the old Continental Congress. One of the first acts of James Madison, a member of the first House of Representatives, was to urge the adoption of a number of amendments to be submitted to the state legislatures for approval. By Dec. 15, 1791, ten of these amendments, now called the Bill of Rights, had been ratified by the States and were added to the Constitution.

Amendment I states:

Congress shall make no law respecting an establishment of religion, or prohibiting the free exercise thereof; or abridging the freedom of speech, or of the press; or the right of the people peaceably to assemble, and to petition the government for a redress of grievances.

Other provisions of the Bill of Rights guarantee to the American people other fundamental rights and freedoms. These include protection against government officials who might invade their homes and seize property without legal permission (Amendment IV); protection against having to "be a witness against himself" in any criminal case, or of being "deprived of life, liberty, or property, without due process of law" (Amendment V); the right of a person accused of a crime "to a speedy and public trial by an impartial jury" (Amendment VI); and protection against "cruel and unusual punishments" (Amendment VIII).

The provision in Amendment V that no person shall be forced "to be a witness against himself" has been the subject of much controversy. Though it has probably enabled some guilty persons to evade the law, it also has served to protect the freedom of the innocent.

Since 1791 a number of other amendments have been added to the Constitution. Several were needed to make the government more efficient. Several others, sometimes considered extensions of the Bill of Rights, were passed to extend the privileges of citizenship to more Americans and to offer safeguards for their liberties.

The original document of the American Bill of Rights may be seen in the Exhibition Hall of the National Archives building in Washington, D.C.

See FREEDOM AMENDMENTS and other related entries under BILL OF RIGHTS in INDEX.

Bill of Rights, English (1689). More than a hundred years before a Bill of Rights was adopted in the United States, a Bill of Rights was passed by the English Parliament. During the 1700's the colonists in America considered the English document an important guarantee of their rights as Englishmen. And after the War for Independence some of its principles were woven into the American Bill of Rights that was added to the Constitution of the United States in 1791. These principles included the right to trial by an impartial jury, and the right to petition the government.

Even the wording of one section of the American document is practically the same as that used a century before in England. The English Bill reads: "Excessive bail ought not to be required, nor excessive fines imposed, nor cruel and unusual punishments inflicted." Except for the words "ought" and "to" (instead of "shall") the same sentence appears in the American Bill of Rights as the Eighth Amendment to the Constitution (see GLORIOUS REVOLUTION).

Bill of Rights, Virginia, *see* DECLARATION OF RIGHTS, VIRGINIA.

Blackstone, Sir William (1723–80), was an English legal writer whose *Commen-* *taries on the Laws of England* (4 vols., 1765–69) strongly influenced the development of the common law in the United States during the 1800's. His clarity of style and the simplicity of his explanations made his writing much more popular than the earlier, more profound, works of Sir Edward Coke, the other great English authority on common law. Today Blackstone's *Commentaries* are seldom read except for their historic and literary value. But the fact that American law is based on the great principles of English law is owing in large degree to the respect in which the *Commentaries* were held by many generations of Americans.

See ENGLISH HERITAGE OF FREEDOM.

Boston Tea Party (1773). One of the most important events leading to the American Revolution was known as the Boston Tea Party. Following the repeal of the Stamp Act in 1766, other attempts by the British government to levy taxes on the colonies had also been resisted and had to be repealed. By 1770, only a small tax on tea remained, because some of the leaders in the British government wished to prove that they had the *right* to tax the colonies. The tea was priced so low that Americans could well afford to buy it, tax and all, but the "tea trick," as it was called, did not work. Colonial patriots still refused to pay any tax not levied by their own legislatures.

The most violent reaction was in Boston. On the night of December 16, 1773, a band of Mohawk "Indians"—Sons of Liberty in disguise—boarded three English ships in the harbor. The cargo was 342 cases of tea. As the "Indians" ripped open case after case and dumped the tea overboard, only the sharp sound of their hatchets disturbed the quiet of the winter night. Crowds watching from the wharf were orderly, but their thoughts might well have been summed up by a popular ballad written to celebrate the occasion:

Then overboard she goes, my boys,
  In darkling waters roar,
We love our cup of tea full well,
  But we love freedom more.

Care was taken that the ships should not be damaged and that no tea should be stolen. Its destruction was intended as a protest against the unjust policies of the British government, and even such law-abiding citizens as John Adams admired the daring patriots. Their bold action would have lasting consequences, he confided to his diary that same night. "I cannot but consider it an epoch in history," he wrote. "This is the most magnificent movement of all."

With a few exceptions, leaders in the British Parliament did not agree. To them the Boston Tea Party was a "criminal act," and four additional regiments were sent to Boston to keep order. Several new laws were passed, designed to punish the city—laws so severe they were called the "Intolerable Acts." One of the laws—the Boston Port Bill—closed the port of Boston and brought special hardship to the people, many of whom made their living through trade and shipping. No boat—not even a fishing boat—was allowed to enter or leave the harbor. Business came to a standstill, and men were thrown out of work. Poor and rich alike were threatened with famine, since the inhabitants depended on ships to deliver much of their food and other supplies.

News of what was happening in Boston was carried by riders for the Committees of Correspondence to the farthest corners of the colonies. Elsewhere indignation was aroused by the news that an entire city should be made to suffer for what only a few citizens had done.

It was still possible to reach Boston by land, even after the harbor was closed, and gifts of food, clothing, and money poured in. Fear that what was happening in Massachusetts might happen elsewhere united the colonists, who felt that a threat to liberty in one colony was a threat to liberty in all the others. There was a growing feeling that some united action was necessary, and the result was the calling of a meeting in Philadelphia to discuss the mutual problems of the colonies.

See CONTINENTAL CONGRESS.

Brandeis, Louis D. (1856–1941), is considered one of the U.S. Supreme Court's most brilliant associate justices (1916–39). Unlike earlier justices, he often used medical, economic, and sociological data in support of legal arguments. He and his good friend Associate Justice Oliver Wendell Holmes, Jr. often concurred in minority opinions in the interest of democracy and social justice.

In Boston, where Brandeis had practiced law before his appointment to the Court, he was known as the "people's attorney" because of the public causes he had championed. At that time, some more conservative members of the bar considered him a radical, yet no one had ever believed more fervently in the principles that had guided the founders of the nation.

"Those who won our independence by revolution," Brandeis once said, "were not cowards. They did not fear political change. They did not exalt order at the cost of liberty."

Brotherhood of Man. "All human beings are free and equal in dignity and rights. They are endowed with reason and conscience and should act towards one another in a spirit of brotherhood." These words appear in Article I of the Universal Declaration of Human Rights adopted in 1948 (see separate entry). The ideas they express are remarkably similar to the views held by the Roman lawyer Cicero more than 2,000 years ago. Cicero believed that all men are endowed with reason and that all had the ability to comprehend a universal law of nature that was itself based on reason and righteousness. (See NATURAL LAW.) Since the law applied to everyone, all human beings were bound together like brothers, and as brothers they had the duty to help one another. This belief in the brotherhood of the human family was an important element in the Stoic philosophy that had spread through the Roman world from Greece, where it had originated about 300 B.C.

Even earlier, by several hundred years, belief in the brotherhood of man had taken root among the Jews, and it became a basic precept of their religion, Judaism. Later the belief became an important part of the teaching of the Christian religion. After the fall of the Roman Empire, the Judeo-Christian ideals of the brotherhood of man, influenced to some extent by Stoic ideals, spread through western Europe.

These theories, though not always honored, persisted through the Middle Ages and later became part of the heritage of the United States of America. The standards of equality and social justice of civilized people in the world today, both in America and elsewhere, owe a debt to ancient teachings about the brotherhood of man.

Brown, John (1800–1859), fanatical Abolitionist reformer, by the time he was thirty-seven determined to devote the rest of his life to the destruction of slavery. "These men are all talk," he said after attending an antislavery convention. "What we need is action—action!"

John Brown meant what he said. The year after the Kansas-Nebraska Act was passed (1854) by Congress, he and his sons and their families emigrated to the territory of Kansas. The new law had provided that the voters in Kansas should decide if it was to enter the Union as a free state or a slave state, and settlers from both North and South poured into the new territory. The men in the Brown family took a leading part in the bloody civil war that broke out between anti-slavery and proslavery residents. It did not seem to bother John Brown's conscience that on one occasion he was the leader in a cold-blooded murder of several slavery sympathizers. Another time he raided a farm in Missouri, the state to the east of Kansas, captured several slaves without the firing of a gun, and led them to freedom in Canada.

As soon as John Brown felt confident that antislavery forces would win in Kansas and that it would enter the Union as a free state, he turned his attention to a fantastic scheme for making war on the

entire South. His plan was to raise a small force and capture the U.S. government arsenal at Harpers Ferry, then still a part of the state of Virginia. Here he would be able to seize—or so he thought—the guns and ammunition needed to arm the slaves for a rebellion.

A number of Abolitionists, including some highly respected men in New England and New York, responded to his secret appeals for financial aid. Few of them knew the extent of John Brown's activities in Kansas, or else they refused to believe the reports they had heard. Certainly, some of his backers did not realize the true nature of his latest scheme.

During the summer of 1859, Brown and two sons rented a farmhouse in Maryland across the river from Harpers Ferry, where they were joined by a small band of volunteers. On the night of October 16, they attacked Harpers Ferry. The arsenal was captured and several leading citizens from the town and surrounding countryside were seized and held as hostages. The Negroes of the region evidently realized that the plan was doomed to failure, for much to Brown's chagrin none of them rose in revolt.

Instead, the Virginia militia, reinforced by U.S. troops, arrived and surrounded the engine house where John Brown's men had taken cover. They refused to surrender until several of their number had been killed. Their leader had been badly wounded by the time he was carried off to jail.

At the trial, which Brown admitted was fair, he was convicted of treason against the state of Virginia and criminal conspiracy to incite a slave insurrection. He was sentenced to hang, and even his enemies admired his fortitude. At the end of the trial he asked to say a few words. His intention, he told the court, had been to do, only on a larger scale, what he had

done in Missouri—namely, to free the slaves. He said:

I believe that to have interfered as I have done . . . in behalf of the despised poor, was not wrong but right. Now if it is deemed necessary that I shall forfeit my life for the furtherance of the ends of justice and mingle my blood . . . with the blood of millions in this slave country whose rights are disregarded by wicked, cruel and unjust enactments—I submit; so let it be done.

During the trial, interest throughout the nation had been at fever heat. Many Northerners considered him a madman and condemned his violent methods, but there were others who acclaimed him a martyr and a hero. The Governor of Virginia was urged to commute the death sentence but refused. Southerners who lived in fear of slave uprisings were understandably alarmed by what might have happened had John Brown been successful.

Before Brown was led to his death, he warned that, though he would soon be disposed of, the Negro question was still to be settled. "The end of that is not yet," he said.

He was right; it took the tragic Civil War to settle the slavery problem. Within two years after John Brown's death, Union soldiers were marching to battle singing the words of a popular song that was sweeping the Northern states:

John Brown's body lies a mouldering in the grave . . .
But his soul goes marching on.

Bunker Hill, Battle of (June 17, 1775). This second battle of the American Revolution, though technically a British victory, greatly strengthened the morale of the Americans. The new and inexperienced recruits proved they could stand up against some of the best trained troops in the world.

After war began at Lexington and

Concord in April, the Massachusetts Provincial Congress had voted to raise an army and called for enlistments from the New England states. Thomas Gage, the British general, occupied Boston with a force of more than 10,000 men, and in the hope of driving them away, the Americans decided to fortify one of the hills that overlooked the city. Their first choice was Bunker Hill, but later it was decided to fortify Breed's Hill instead, since it was a little nearer Boston.

The work was carried on under cover of darkness, and on the morning of June 17, when General Gage saw the fortifications that would bring his troops in range of the enemy guns, he ordered an assault on the hill. Twice the British attacked, and twice they were driven back by American fire. The third time they succeeded, for the American supply of ammunition was exhausted. Finally the Americans were

forced to retreat, leaving the British in possession of the hill, but not until they had inflicted heavy losses on the enemy.

"A dear bought victory," exclaimed one officer. "Another such would have ruined us."

Meanwhile, the Continental Congress, meeting in Philadelphia, had voted to adopt the military forces that had gathered outside of Boston and call them the Continental Army. Colonel George Washington was appointed general and commander in chief, and in the company of two of his officers he started north to take over his new duties. On the road they met another horseman riding toward Philadelphia. He explained he was carrying a message to the Continental Congress—a message concerning the battle now usually referred to as the battle of Bunker Hill. When General Washington learned how bravely the Americans had stood up under fire he was much encouraged.

"That is well," he said. "If our men can fight like that, the liberties of our country are safe."

Today a granite shaft, the Bunker Hill Monument, marks the site of Breed's Hill (now a part of Boston). The cornerstone of the monument was laid in 1825, on the fiftieth anniversary of the battle. Participating in the ceremony was an aged visitor to America—the Marquis de Lafayette who, as a young man, had joined the Revolutionary forces to help a new nation in its struggle for freedom.

Burke, Edmund (1729–97). During the events leading up to the American Revolution, the colonists had several friends in the British Parliament who championed their cause. None was more eloquent than Edmund Burke, who realized the colonies might revolt unless the government permitted them more freedom in directing their affairs. In his speech, "On Conciliation With America" (1775), he reminded Parliament that most of the Americans

were of English descent, and had carried with them the English love for freedom.

"This fierce spirit of liberty," he said, "is stronger in the English colonies probably than in any other people of the earth."

Burke warned that the Americans might revolt, unless they were given more freedom in directing their own affairs. His plea went unheeded, with the result that in the end Great Britain lost her American colonies. For many years thereafter he continued to serve in Parliament, where he was involved in numerous controversies. He opposed the slave trade and—to the dismay of many former admirers—he also opposed the French Revolution. Burke, outraged by the violence of the French rebellion, set forth his reasons in his book *Reflections on the Revolution in France*. His opinions, he contended, came "from one, almost the whole of whose public exertion had been a struggle for the liberty of others."

Calvert Family. *See* BALTIMORE, LORD.

Charter Oak. A large oak tree, that once stood in Hartford, Conn., served as a hiding place for the royal charter that permitted the colony of Connecticut the right of self-government. This charter, granted by King Charles II (1662), preserved for the people the same liberties they had enjoyed earlier under the Fundamental Orders, a plan of government they had set up for themselves. All went well until the despotic James II came to the throne of England and appointed Sir Edmund Andros governor of all New England. He arrived in Hartford (Oct., 1687) with an armed escort and, in the name of the king, demanded that the Provincial Assembly turn over the charter to him.

The members dared not refuse, and the cherished document lay on a table in its case as they discussed the matter with the new governor. According to one version of the story, the meeting went on until after dark and, when a door was opened, a sudden gust of wind blew out all the candles. By the time they were relighted, the charter had disappeared.

Not until several years later was it discovered, still safe in its case, inside a hollow tree. By then James had been forced to give up his throne, and there had been a change in the policies of the British government. It was thought safe to bring the charter out of its hiding place, and once more it was recognized as the law of the colony. Some of its provisions were so well liked that they were preserved in a state constitution adopted (1818) by the state of Connecticut more than a century and a quarter later.

According to tradition, on the historic evening when the charter had disappeared, a soldier named Joseph Wadsworth took advantage of the darkness to escape with it through a window. Once outside, he hid the document in a hollow tree that was to become known as the Charter Oak. Many years later the tree was blown down in a storm, and a granite column now marks the spot. Part of the famous charter has been preserved in the Connecticut Historical Society at Hartford.

Civil Liberties and **Civil Rights** are two terms often used interchangeably, but there is a shade of difference. "Civil liberties" protect individuals from the abuse of governmental power by placing limitations on the government. This means that certain rights can never be taken away from the people. The First Amendment to the U.S. Constitution specifies that no law may be passed that interferes with the individual's right of freedom of speech, press, and religion, or with the rights of people to assemble in a peaceable manner.

"Civil rights" means that each individual has the same right as all other individuals to share in the benefits of government. These benefits, which include equal protection under law, may not be legally denied because of race, color, or creed.

Though the demand for civil rights has not been confined to one race, in recent years the term has been used most often in connection with the struggle of Negroes for equality under the law.

Civil War, American (1861–65). This war between North and South marked the most tragic period in American history, the more tragic because both sides were convinced they were fighting for liberty. The differences between the two sections went back almost to the time of the founding of the nation.

One difference was over slavery. Slavery in the North had not proved profitable, and most of the Northern states had freed their slaves. Southerners, though, were dependent on slave labor to work on the big sugar and cotton plantations and, when new territory was added to the Union, Southerners who went there to live wanted to be able to take their slaves with them. Also, since each state had the same number of Senators, Southerners wanted to make sure they would not be outvoted in the Senate.

Then Abraham Lincoln, who had vig-

orously opposed the spread of slavery into territory that was still free, was elected President, and several Southern states passed ordinances of secession. In February, 1861 they sent delegates to a convention in Montgomery, Ala., and adopted a constitution for a new nation they called the Confederate States of America. In their opinion this action was justified because of their doctrine of state sovereignty. They believed that each state had the right to decide about its own affairs and that states' rights were in danger. A state that had voluntarily joined the Union, it was claimed, had a right to withdraw, if its legislature so decided.

The new President was convinced that just the opposite was true. Abraham Lincoln told his secretary:

> We must settle the question, whether in a free government, the minority have the right to break up the government whenever they choose. If we fail, it will go far to prove the incapability of the people to govern themselves.

The South had already begun to raise an army, and the Civil War began (Apr. 12, 1861) when Confederate troops fired on Fort Sumter, a U.S. fort in the harbor at Charleston, S.C. President Lincoln called for 75,000 volunteers to put down what Northerners called an insurrection.

In the Civil War that followed, eleven Confederate states were arrayed against twenty-three states that had remained loyal to the United States. It wasn't altogether a matter of North against South. Several border states (Delaware, Maryland, Kentucky, and Missouri) did not secede, and the fifty western counties of Virginia withdrew from the parent state. Later (1863) these counties were admitted to the Union as the state of West Virginia.

Also, in nearly every section of the country, there were some individuals who did not agree with the majority of their neighbors. A number of Southerners served in the Union forces, and a number of

Northerners supported the Confederate cause. Even families were often divided in their loyalties, especially in the border states. For many it was an agonizing decision to have to make—whether their first allegiance was to their own state or to the national government.

Whatever they decided, the great majority of soldiers in both armies—the Union men in blue uniforms and the Confederates wearing the gray—were fighting for a cause they believed in. Both sides endured hardship, and pain, and death. Since the South was invaded, Southerners resisted with the firm determination that comes to men who are defending their homes, and one of their favorite war songs ended with the words:

> *God save the South,*
> *Now that the war is nigh,*
> *Chanting our battle cry,*
> *Freedom or death.*

Men from the North, fighting far from their own firesides, also sang to keep up their spirits. One of their favorite songs was:

> *Yes, we'll rally around the flag, boys,*
> *We'll rally once again,*
> *Shouting the battle cry of freedom.*

The soldiers in blue and those in gray had great leaders to encourage them. In the South the most popular hero was Robert E. Lee, an able general who inspired a devotion in his men that kept them fighting against impossible odds. The Union soldiers had President Lincoln, whom they affectionately called "Father Abraham." On a visit to the army in 1864, he told one regiment why it was so important to win the war:

It is not merely for today, but for all time to come, that we should perpetuate for our children's children this great and free government which we have enjoyed all our lives . . . The nation is worth fighting for, to secure such an inestimable jewel.

No one was more saddened than the kind and gentle man in the White House by the news, day after day, of mounting casualties in both armies. Yet he kept firmly to his purpose: to preserve the Union so the precious right of self-government might be maintained. When it became clear by early April, 1865, that the South, for all its gallant defense, must soon surrender, Abraham Lincoln expressed great relief that the war was over.

"Thank God, that I have lived to see this day," he said. "It seems I have been dreaming a horrid dream for four years, and now the nightmare is gone."

The President, never having recognized the right of secession, took the position that the chief problem was to help the seceded states—as speedily and kindly as possible—to resume their proper places in the Union. One of the great misfortunes of the war was that he did not live to carry out his policies. After his assassination, vindictive leaders in Congress passed measures that worked unnecessary hardship on the South. The result was great bitterness that made many problems, both old and new, more difficult to solve. There were also short-sighted Southerners who failed to heed General Lee's wise counsel to "bury contention with the war."

Yet in spite of the difficult years that followed, the Union had been preserved; and the United States, instead of breaking up into two smaller countries, was able to grow into one strong united nation.

The Civil War, said one famous Southerner, President Wilson, "created in the country what had never existed before— a national consciousness. It was not the salvation of the Union; it was the rebirth of the Union."

Civil Wars, English (1642–46; 1648). In January, 1642, Charles I, king of England, strode into the House of Commons and demanded the surrender of five of its leading members whose actions had displeased him. The five men had escaped, and the other members refused to give out any information. Charles left, empty-handed and angry, but his anger was more than matched by the fury of the House of Commons.

Charles's seventeen-year reign had been one of devious extortion of money from his subjects, religious intolerance, injustice, and evaded promises. In his high-handed attempt to arrest members of the House of Commons, the king had finally gone too far. His action was a threat to the independence of Parliament, which soon began to raise an army, and before long England was engulfed in civil war.

After four years the war was won by Parliament's army, largely because of the military skill of its most famous commander, Oliver Cromwell. But the army, alarmed that Parliament itself was showing signs of religious intolerance, refused to disband, and in 1648 another civil war broke out. This was a short but complicated struggle, from which Cromwell emerged victorious. The army then purged Parliament of all members who favored a reconciliation with Charles, and the remaining fragment of Parliament appointed a court to try the king. Charles was condemned to death as a tyrant and enemy of his country, and was beheaded (1649).

Parliament then declared that England was no longer a kingdom, but a commonwealth, or republic. Within a few years it was transformed into a military dictatorship under Oliver Cromwell as Lord Protector. After Cromwell's death (1658) and a short period of inefficient government, the fugitive son of Charles I was welcomed back to England as King Charles II (1660).

This long period of unrest in England had a profound influence on the English colonies in the New World. Under despotic Charles I, ever-increasing numbers of Puritans left for America in well-founded fear of civil and religious persecution. By the time the civil wars started, more than 20,000 of them were settled in new homes across the Atlantic Ocean. After the execution of Charles I, great numbers of Royalist sympathizers emigrated to Virginia during the time of the Commonwealth and Cromwell's Protectorate.

The disturbances that had led so many Englishmen to settle in America had kept the leaders in the mother country too busy to pay much attention to the colonies. As a result, the colonists were able to run things very much as they pleased, with little interference from the home govern-

ment. They acquired a strong liking for managing their own affairs, a liking that persisted through the years. When the British government finally clamped down on the colonies in the 1760's, the situation became explosive, and by 1775 the American Revolution had begun.

Clay, Henry (1777–1852), a popular American politician, was known as "the great peacemaker," because of his efforts to settle the slavery quarrel without violence. He served in both houses of Congress, and used his influence for the passage of several bills which, it was hoped, would conciliate both North and South in the increasingly bitter quarrel about slavery. He undoubtedly played a leading role in postponing the Civil War—a tragedy that he felt must be avoided at all costs. The preservation of the Union, he once said, had been the paramount object of his public life.

Coke, Sir Edward (1552–1634), was an English lawyer and judge whose writings were greatly admired by many of the English colonists in America during the 1700's. From his works they gained much of their knowledge of the laws and rights to which, they insisted, they were as much entitled as Englishmen living in the mother country.

Coke, a vigorous champion of the common law, served as lord chief justice of England (1613–16). His belief that the law was superior to the will of the king brought him into frequent fiery conflict with James I. Coke's firm refusal to allow the tyrannical king to influence judicial decisions finally led to his dismissal from office.

Later, as a member of Parliament, Coke played the leading role, at the age of seventy-six, in drawing up the Petition of Right (1628). This famous document was designed to limit the power of the new king, Charles I, who had inherited his father's despotic ways along with the crown. The Petition called attention to various "rights and liberties" that Coke and his colleagues believed had been granted to Englishmen in earlier times. Soon after King Charles had reluctantly agreed to abide by the terms of the Petition, Coke retired from politics to devote all his time to his legal writing.

Coke's books in praise and explanation of the English legal system were written at the time of the first great migration from England to the colonies in America. The crusty, courageous old lawyer would have been astonished had he known that, in the next century, colonial claims to the rights set forth in the Petition and in his books would help bring on a revolution against the mother country.

American admiration for Coke's immense legal knowledge survived the break with England. For many years after the Revolution, American law students still studied Volume I of his *Institutes of the Laws of England* to learn about English common law upon which American common law is based.

Coke indirectly influenced the American legal system in still another way. He believed that even an act passed by Parliament was invalid if it conflicted with the basic principles of common law.

"When an Act of Parliament is against common right and reason," he once wrote, ". . . the common law will control it, and adjudge such Act to be void."

This conviction that legislation must not violate basic principles is reflected in the American system of judicial review. Sometimes, for example, a charge will be made that an act passed by Congress trespasses on rights guaranteed by the Constitution. In such event, the Supreme Court has the authority to review the case and, if warranted, to declare the act of Congress to be void.

See SUPREME COURT OF THE UNITED STATES.

Colonial Self-Government. Long before the American colonies declared their independence, they began the practice of self-government. Twelve years after a little English settlement was founded at Jamestown, Va., a new governor arrived with the news that the colonists were to have a part in making some of their own laws. The London Company, a trading company that had backed the enterprise, had found governing the colony no easy matter, and it was decided it might be more efficient to permit the colonists to handle some of their own affairs.

Accordingly, each of the eleven settlements in the Jamestown area was instructed to elect two members to represent them in a General Assembly called the House of Burgesses (citizens). It was quite an occasion the first time they came together (July 30, 1619) in the little wooden church which, according to one old account, "the governor caused to be kept passing sweet and trimmed up with divers flowers."

The Burgesses, in cooperation with the governor and a council appointed by the company, passed a number of laws for the colony. Their first sessions marked the beginning of representative government in America.

During the next 113 years, twelve other English colonies were founded along the Atlantic Coast. Some of them were permitted a greater measure of self-government than others, but as time passed all of the colonies demanded the right to have an assembly or legislature to make some of their own laws. The English Parliament was more than 3,000 miles away, and the colonists, faced with the difficulties of living in a wild, new land, had to solve most of their own problems. A legislature that could levy taxes to meet local expenses and to decide on other local matters was an absolute necessity. Though usually only white men with property could vote, the colonists had had a taste of freedom.

The result was that when Parliament, in the 1760's, tried to tax the colonies and enforce laws regulating their trade, there were protests all the way from Massachusetts to Georgia. As the protests grew more bitter, they helped to bring on the American Revolution.

Some years later, when a veteran of that war was asked why he had fought against the British, he had a ready answer. "We always had governed ourselves," he said, "and we always meant to. They didn't mean we should."

Committees of Correspondence. In colonial days, when it took a week or more to send a letter from Boston to New York and a month for mail to reach Georgia from Massachusetts, the Committees of Correspondence helped to unite the colonies and hasten the coming of the American Revolution. The first committee (November, 1772) was suggested by Samuel Adams of Boston in order to inform people in other parts of Massachusetts about the threats to freedom in his own city. The following March, the Virginia House of Burgesses voted to make the committees intercolonial, so patriots in widely scattered places could keep in closer touch.

When British authorities closed the Boston port as punishment for the Boston Tea Party, express riders on fast horses spread the news of the city's desperate situation from colony to colony. Later, couriers for the Committees of Correspondence carried the messages that resulted in the calling of the First Continental Congress.

See CONTINENTAL CONGRESS.

"Concord Hymn," by Ralph Waldo Emerson. "Here once the embattled farmers stood/And fired the shot heard round the world," are lines from a poem written to commemorate the beginning of the American Revolution. The occasion was the completion of a granite obelisk (1836) to mark the spot where the first British soldiers had fallen during the skirmish between British and Americans at the bridge in Concord, Mass. On the one hundredth anniversary (1875) of the battle the same words were inscribed on the base of the bronze statue of "The Minuteman," the first important work of a young sculptor, Daniel Chester French.

Constitution of the United States, which has been the supreme law of the land since 1789, consists of a Preamble (see below); seven Articles, or major parts; and a number of amendments that have been adopted from time to time as the need for change arose.

PREAMBLE: *We the People,* the opening words of the Preamble of the U.S. Constitution, mean that the people *are* the government. This Preamble, a source of pride to Americans today, reads as follows:

We the People of the United States, in order to form a more perfect union, establish justice, insure domestic tranquility, provide for the common defense, promote the general welfare, and secure the blessings of liberty to ourselves and our posterity, do ordain and establish this Constitution for the United States of America.

The first three Articles of the Constitution provide for three branches of government: the Legislative, consisting of a Congress to make the laws; the Executive, headed by a President whose duty it is to execute the laws; and a Judiciary, consisting of a Supreme Court and "such inferior courts as the Congress may from time to time ordain and establish." Under a system called separation of powers, or checks and balances, each branch of government has certain powers that balance the powers of the other two, and each has the power to restrain or check the other two branches. The purpose of this system was to make sure that no one person or group of persons in the government could ever become powerful enough to endanger the liberties of the people.

Americans today can be grateful to the framers of the Constitution, not only for planning an efficient system of government, but for providing several built-in guarantees to protect individuals against tyranny. These include the right of *habeas corpus* and trial by jury in criminal cases (see separate entries). Article I of the Constitution also states: "No bill of attainder or *ex post facto* law shall be passed." The first of these two provisions means that no person can be punished without a judicial trial; the second that no person can be punished under a law that was passed after the offense was committed.

Article IV of the Constitution defines the relationship between the states and provides for the admission of new states. Article V provides for adding amendments as the need for them arises, and Article VI that the Constitution shall be "the supreme law of the land." The Constitution was to go into effect after it was ratified

by nine of the thirteen original states
(Article VII).

In urging his own state to ratify the
proposed new plan of government, James
Wilson, a well-known Pennsylvania lawyer, pointed out that in the past most governments had been the result of force,
fraud, or accident. But the men responsible for the Constitution, he said, had
assembled voluntarily, deliberated, and decided on a system of government under
which they would wish that they and their
posterity should live.

The consensus today is that the Constitution, the first important written instrument of government that has endured,
is a remarkable document framed by one of
the most remarkable groups of statesmen
ever assembled. Its success has far ex-
ceeded their hopes. One reason for this is
that they realized that the plan of government they had prepared with such care
would doubtless have to be amended from
time to time, as conditions changed, in
order to meet the needs of a free people.

In the beginning the Constitution was
called "the new roof," after the title of a
popular song. It has proved to be a sturdy
roof, and it is the power of amendment
that has kept it in repair.

See BILL OF RIGHTS, AMERICAN; and
FREEDOM AMENDMENTS.

Constitutional Convention, once known as
the Federal Convention (May 25–Sept. 17,
1787), was held in the Pennsylvania State
House. This was the same red brick building in Philadelphia in which the Declaration of Independence had been signed
earlier and which today is known as Independence Hall. Twelve of the thirteen states
(Rhode Island was the exception) sent
delegates, most of them men of education
and property. Among the delegates were
some remarkable leaders, including George
Washington, who had won victory in the
American Revolution against what had
seemed impossible odds; Alexander Hamil-

ton, who had been the first to suggest the
convention; and the venerable Benjamin
Franklin, ill and feeble at eighty-one, but
with a mind still rapier-quick.

The delegates had been instructed by
the Continental Congress to amend the
Articles of Confederation, which had
served as the central, or federal, government for the new nation since 1781. Now
that same nation was in difficulty. Trade
was almost at a standstill, due to quarrels
among the states. There was much grum-
bling, and in one state an actual uprising
among former soldiers who had never been
paid. Many of them were in need, but Congress could not pay them because it had
no power to levy taxes. The new nation
was heavily in debt, and the American experiment in self-government seemed
doomed to failure.

To prevent such a tragedy, such leaders as George Washington, who was elected chairman of the convention, were convinced that a stronger federal, or central, government was needed. Some of the delegates, however, feared that the people of the country would oppose any but minor changes in the Articles of Confederation.

"If to please the people, we offer what we ourselves disapprove," Washington was later quoted as saying, "how can we afterwards defend our work. Let us raise a standard to which the wise and honest can repair. The event is in the hand of God."

This remark doubtless helped to convince the convention that the plan to revise the old Articles of Confederation must be abandoned. Several new plans were suggested. The one presented by the Virginia delegation was principally the work of James Madison, and he worked tirelessly for the adoption of some of its essential features. Posterity can also be grateful to him for keeping a daily journal of the proceedings. No one was admitted to the meetings except the delegates, since they had decided it would be better to have a completed plan ready before it was presented to the public.

Many times during that sultry summer, it seemed that a completed plan never would be ready. There were heated arguments and disagreements, particularly between the delegates from the large states and those from the smaller ones. Finally Ben Franklin suggested they compromise.

"When a broad table is to be made," he said, "and the edges of planks do not fit, the artist takes a little from both, and makes a good joint. In like manner here both sides must part with some of their demands."

Franklin's counsel prevailed. The Constitution of the United States, when finally approved, was a result of many compromises. Though it did not completely satisfy any of the delegates, it contained a provision (Article V) for amending it in the future. On September 17, a copy engrossed on parchment lay on the chairman's desk, and all but three of the delegates present came forward to sign.

Ben Franklin glanced at the picture of a sun carved on the back of the chair in which Washington had presided. During the stormy sessions, the elderly philosopher remarked, he had often wondered if the sun was rising or setting.

"Now at length," he said, "I have the happiness to know that it is a rising and not a setting sun."

The final Article of the Constitution stated that it was to go into effect after it was ratified, or approved, by nine states. That part of the struggle still lay ahead.

See CONSTITUTIONAL RATIFYING CONVENTIONS.

Constitutional Ratifying Conventions. The new U.S. Constitution adopted by the Constitutional Convention meeting in Philadelphia (1787) was to go into effect after it was ratified by nine states. Copies were sent to the Continental Congress which was then meeting in New York City, and Congress forwarded copies to the different state legislatures. Each legislature then issued a call for a special state convention made up of delegates chosen by the voters in the state. The task of the delegates in each convention was to decide if their state would ratify the new plan of government.

"We exhibit at present," George Washington wrote in a letter to a friend, "the Novel and astonishing Spectacle of a whole people deliberating calmly on what form of government will be most conducive to their happiness."

The deliberations to which Washington referred were calm in the sense that there was no physical violence, but there was what has been called "a war of words." People who opposed the federal Constitution were known as Antifederalists because they feared that a strong central government would not only weaken the power of the state governments, but would also be a threat to the freedom of the people. Some of the back country farmers and working men believed that the members of the Constitutional Convention, including a number of men of wealth, had been chiefly interested in the protection of property rights. Unless human rights and political liberty also could be guaranteed, the delegates in some of the state conventions were determined to vote against the proposed plan.

In order to defend and explain the Constitution to the people, Alexander Hamilton and James Madison, with some help from a well-known American lawyer and diplomat, John Jay, wrote a series of brilliant essays. These essays, published first in newspapers and later as a two-volume work called *The Federalist,* called attention to some of the disorders that the Constitution was intended to correct. Many of its readers, who had once been skeptical, were convinced that the Constitution would provide the cure that was needed.

"These moneyed men," said one farmer, "are all embarked in the same cause with us, and we must sink or swim together."

In the end this point of view prevailed, though several of the state conventions ratified the Constitution only on condition that a Bill of Rights be added. By the Fourth of July, 1788, ten states had voted to come in under "the new roof," as the new plan of government was called. Later the three remaining states, out of the original thirteen, agreed to ratification.

See BILL OF RIGHTS, AMERICAN.

Continental Congress. The suggestion originated with Sam Adams of Boston that delegates from the different American colonies meet in Philadelphia to "determine upon wise and proper measures for the recovery and establishment of their just rights and liberties." Georgia was too far away to send delegates, but patriots representing the twelve other colonies met (Sept. 5 to Oct. 26, 1774) in Carpenters' Hall, Philadelphia, to discuss the threats to their freedom. It was their contention that the Parliament had no right to make laws for the colonists, inasmuch as the colonists had no representatives in the British lawmaking body.

One of the most important steps taken by the Congress (later to be called the First Continental Congress) was the adoption of the Declaration of Rights, which asserted that the colonists were entitled to the same rights and liberties as subjects born in England. "The foundation of English liberty," the declaration read, "and of all free government, is a right in the people to participate in their legislative council."

Copies of the resolutions were sent to England, and a respectful petition was addressed to King George III, asking for a redress of the grievances of which the colonists complained. The delegates passed another resolution stating that there should be no more trade with the mother country until certain objectionable laws were repealed. Before adjourning, it was decided to meet again the following spring unless the situation had improved.

Delegates to the Second Continental Congress came together (May, 1775) in the Pennsylvania State House, later to be renamed Independence Hall. By that time fighting had broken out in Massachusetts at Lexington and Concord, and Massachusetts patriots had begun to enlist an army to drive the British out of Boston. Congress voted to take charge and call it the Continental Army. Colonel George Washington, one of the delegates from Virginia, was elected "General and Commander-in-Chief to take Supreme Command of the forces raised and to be raised in defense of American liberty."

In the years that followed, the Congress, which had first assembled to consult about mutual problems, had a war to fight.

Carpenters' Hall about 1790

During the second year of that war it issued the Declaration of Independence (1776). The thirteen colonies were now called states (the United States), but there was no single authority over all of them. Out of necessity, Congress took over what authority it could. An army and later a navy had to be equipped and paid. The Continental Congress had no legal right to levy taxes, but it issued paper money called "Continentals." It also borrowed large sums and negotiated treaties with foreign governments.

Of special importance was a treaty with France (1778) whereby the French agreed to enter the war on the side of the Americans. Several years later, agents appointed by Congress signed a treaty with Great Britain (1783), which finally brought the war to an end. In this treaty the most powerful nation in the world recognized the independence of the new United States.

Philadelphia was not the permanent meeting place for the Continental Congress. On several occasions it had been obliged to flee before advancing British armies. From time to time it met in a number of different towns, sometimes with fifty-five members in attendance, sometimes with only twenty. Its influence declined after the war, and it went out of existence when a new Congress took office (1789) under the new Constitution.

Though the Continental Congress made mistakes and was bitterly criticized, it carried on its work under great difficulty. Certainly it had played a significant role in creating a new nation dedicated to the cause of freedom. Among the patriots who served as delegates from time to time were such outstanding Americans as John and Samuel Adams, Benjamin Franklin, John Hancock, Thomas Jefferson, James Madison, Robert Morris, Benjamin Rush, and George Washington.

Declaration of Independence. On June 7, 1776, Richard Henry Lee, a delegate from Virginia, stood up before the Continental Congress which was meeting in Philadelphia. "Resolved," he said, "that these united colonies are and of right ought to be free and independent states."

Lee was acting on instructions from a special convention of Virginians then meeting in Williamsburg. The American Revolution had been going on for nearly fourteen months, but in the beginning the majority of the patriots had declared they were only fighting for their rights. Later, many people, not only in Virginia but in several other colonies, had decided that if they wanted to keep their liberties, the colonies must separate from Great Britain.

Not all the delegates to the Continental Congress shared this point of view, for some felt they should remain loyal to the mother country. Others, though they believed in independence, argued that the time had not yet come to declare it. If the colonies lost the war, as seemed all too likely at that time, every man who signed such a declaration would probably be condemned as a traitor.

Finally it was decided to delay a decision on the Lee resolution for three weeks, so the delegates might return home and talk with members of their colonial legislatures. Before its temporary adjournment, the Congress appointed a committee of five to prepare a document, stating the reasons for a separation from the mother country. This document would then be ready with no time lost if the Continental Congress decided to vote for independence. On the committee were three of the leading men in the colonies: Benjamin Franklin, John Adams, and Thomas Jefferson. At thirty-three, Jefferson was already well known as a writer, and Adams insisted that he do the actual writing.

For eighteen days, tall, red-headed Tom Jefferson kept close to the upstairs room he had rented in a Philadelphia house. He worked at a small portable desk, his quill pen scratching across sheet after sheet of white paper. He wanted the document he was preparing to do more than declare the independence of a new nation; it must also state the principles on which that nation was founded. He referred to no books or pamphlets, but he remembered the work of John Locke and other great thinkers who had written about freedom. He also was influenced by George Mason's Declaration (or Bill) of Rights, recently adopted by a special Virginia Convention. The ideas presented by Jefferson in the Declaration of Independence were not new, but the words were his own—strong, beautiful words that would go ringing down the years.

When the work was finished, Jefferson showed it to the other members of the committee, who made a few minor suggestions. On July 1, the Lee resolution came up for debate. There was still considerable opposition, but John Adams argued for it so eloquently that it was adopted the following day. Then began the debate on the Jefferson document which, with a few more changes, was adopted on July 4.

Four days later a crowd gathered before the red brick building (now called

Independence Hall) where Congress had been meeting. A citizen of the city mounted a wooden platform and read aloud the Declaration which announced the birth of a new nation—the United States of America.

That night there was a grand celebration in Philadelphia and in a number of other towns and cities. Bells were rung and firecrackers were set off. People danced and sang, but John Adams was one man who did not feel like joining in the general merriment. He had written his wife a few days earlier:

I am well aware of the toil and blood, and treasure that it will cost us to maintain this Declaration and support and defend these States. Yet through all the gloom I can see . . . that the end is worth all the means, and that posterity will triumph.

History was to prove John Adams right, and not only Americans but many people in other nations, too, have looked to the Declaration of Independence for inspiration. The reason for this (in the opinion of Abraham Lincoln) was that Jefferson had introduced into what might have been just another political document "an abstract truth applicable to all men and all times."

The original Declaration of Independence, engrossed on parchment and signed by the fifty-six delegates to the Continental Congress, may now be seen in the Exhibition Hall of the National Archives building in Washington, D.C.

Declaration of Rights, Virginia. Virginia, the colony which in May, 1776, instructed its delegates to the Continental Congress to declare for independence, adopted a Virginia Declaration of Rights the following month. This document, also called the Virginia Bill of Rights, was largely the work of George Mason, a brilliant Virginia patriot. His friend Thomas Jefferson saw a copy before writing the Declaration of Independence, and a careful reading of the two documents shows how Jefferson was influenced by the Mason manuscript:

"That all men are by nature equally free and independent," George Mason wrote, "and have certain inherent rights . . . namely the enjoyment of life and liberty . . . and pursuing and obtaining happiness and safety."

Within a few years after the colonies declared their independence, several of the new states adopted Bills of Rights similar to the Mason document, which also served

Houses of Parliament

as a model for the Bill of Rights added to the U.S. Constitution as the first ten amendments.

Declaration of Rights and Grievances. This declaration, which has been called "the Magna Carta of civil liberty" in America, was among the measures adopted by the Continental Congress (Oct. 1774), and sent to the British Parliament.

One provision of the declaration read:

Resolved that the foundation of English liberty and of all free government is a right in the people to participate in their legislative council: and as the English colonists are not represented, and from their local and other circumstances cannot properly be represented in the British parliament, they are entitled to a free and exclusive power of legislation in their several provincial legislatures, where their right of representation can alone be preserved, in all cases of taxation and internal polity [policy] . . . .

In hearty agreement with the ideas expressed in the Declaration were a few liberal leaders in Parliament. Lord Chatham (William Pitt) of the House of Lords admired the patience and wisdom shown by the Continental Congress and urged that the troops sent to Boston to enforce some of the unpopular laws should be withdrawn. What right, he demanded in one speech (Jan. 20, 1775), had Parliament to take such vindictive measures against a loyal and respectable people?

"No people," the elderly statesman went on, "can ever be made to submit to a form of government they say they will not receive."

Ten days later a bill was introduced into the House of Commons that would have granted most of the demands made in the Declaration of Rights and Grievances. The fact that it was defeated by the Tory majority in Parliament undoubtedly stiffened the opposition of the colonists to British rule. The following year they decided that, only by declaring their independence, could they preserve their liberty.

See CONTINENTAL CONGRESS.

Declaration of Sentiments (antislavery). The American Antislavery Society was formed (1833) by sixty delegates representing a number of local antislavery groups in the country. Since a number of the delegates belonged to the Society of Friends and were opposed to violence, they hoped through writing and preaching to appeal to the conscience of the nation and, in that way, to bring about the abolition of slavery. At one of the meetings held in Independence Hall where the Declaration of Independence had been signed (1776), the following Declaration of Sentiments was adopted:

More than fifty-seven years have elapsed since a band of patriots convened in this place, to devise measures for the deliverance of this country from a foreign yoke. We have met together for the achievement of an enterprise, without which that of our fathers is incomplete. We believe and affirm that the slaves ought instantly to be set free and brought under the protection of law.

See ANTISLAVERY MOVEMENT.

Declaration of Sentiments (women's rights). The first women's rights convention was held in Seneca Falls, N.Y. (1848) to protest the unfair and unequal treatment accorded women in the United States. Many years would pass before American women would gain the rights for which they began working at that time, but the Seneca Falls convention marked a beginning. The Declaration of Sentiments contained some of the same phrases used in the Declaration of Independence and was strongly influenced by that document. The women's rights declaration read:

We hold these truths to be self-evident: that all men and women are created equal; that they are endowed by their Creator with certain inalienable rights; that among these are life, liberty and the pursuit of happiness . . .

The history of mankind is a history of repeated injuries . . . on the part of man toward women . . . To prove this let facts be submitted to a candid world.

He has never permitted her to exercise her inalienable right to the elective franchise.

He has compelled her to submit to laws in which she had no voice . . .

He has taken from her all rights in property, even to the wages she earns . . .

He has made her . . . an irresponsible being . . . In the covenant of marriage, she is compelled to promise obedience to her husband, he becoming, to all intents and purposes, her master—the law giving him the power to deprive her of her liberty, and to administer chastisement . . .

He has taxed her to support a government which recognizes her only when her property can be made profitable to it.

He has monopolized nearly all the profitable employments, and from those she is permitted to follow, she receives but scanty remuneration . . .

He has denied her the facilities for obtaining a thorough education, all colleges being closed against her . . .

He has endeavored, in every way he could, to destroy her confidence in her own powers, to lessen her self-respect and to make her willing to lead a dependent and abject life.

Now, in view of this entire disenfranchisement of one-half the people of this country . . . in view of the unjust laws above mentioned, and because women do feel themselves . . . deprived of their most sacred rights, we insist that they have immediate admission to all the rights and privileges which belong to them as citizens of the United States.

See WOMAN SUFFRAGE MOVEMENT.

"Democracy" is a term used to describe both a form of government and an ideal for everyday living. The word is derived from two Greek words meaning "people" and "rule," and democracy was once practiced to a limited extent as a form of government in Athens, one of the city-states of ancient Greece. Many centuries later, democracy was established as a form of government in the United States and then in other free nations in the world.

Some countries with autocratic governments have called themselves democracies, but a real democracy is one in which the people rule through their votes. When a government is truly democratic, the voters have a real choice and are free to elect the officers who make and administer the laws.

As a rule of conduct, democracy has been said to mean *not* "I'm as good as you are," *but* "You are as good as I am." It is a way of regarding and treating other people—a recognition of the dignity and worth of every human being.

"Democracy in a Republic, A." This phrase was used in "The American's Creed," by William Tyler Page, to describe the type of government we call a republic or a representative democracy. The business of government is carried on, as James Madison pointed out in one of his essays for *The Federalist* (1787), "by a small number of citizens elected by the rest." In contrast, the citizens who practice direct democracy meet together and personally decide what laws are needed, but this system is suitable for only very small communities (see TOWN MEETINGS).

In both types of democracy, officials who fail to please the public are usually defeated if they run for reelection. The voters, because they are free to choose their officials at election time, remain the source of power.

Unfortunately, the terms "republic" and "democracy" have been used—or rather misused—by several communist countries. Their governments, though, bear little resemblance to the government of a real republic or to the actual practice of democracy.

Dissent, Right of, a privilege much prized by Americans, was exercised frequently in the struggle for Negro rights and also by citizens opposed to the war in Vietnam. Though public opinion polls showed that many Americans believed the war was necessary, and support of it a patriotic duty, there were others equally sincere who disagreed.

"We are a democracy, and implicit in

a democracy is the right to dissent from governmental policies ...," said Arthur Goldberg, U.S. Ambassador to the United Nations. "The American system is a system which is a product of consensus on one hand in the form of our electoral process and dissent on the other."

Douglass, Frederick (1817?–95), the first great Negro American leader, was born a slave named Frederick Augustus Washington Bailey.

When he was a small boy in Maryland, he had a kind mistress who was teaching him his ABC's. Her husband ordered her to stop. "If you teach him how to read," the man said, "he'll want to know how to write, and this accomplished he'll be running away with himself."

So Fred had to teach himself to read and write. He picked up letters from white children he knew, found some chalk, and practiced writing the letters on walls. Somehow he got hold of a copy of a book of speeches called *Columbian Orator*. Some of the selections by great English leaders, such as Edmund Burke, were about freedom, and it was comforting to remember them when people were unkind. His master hired him out to one man who beat him so severely that he bore the scars on his back for the rest of his life. Douglass never knew his exact age, but later he recalled that he must have been about thirteen or fourteen when he made a solemn vow to gain his liberty.

The first attempt failed, and he and several other Negro youths were captured. "I was firmly tied ...," he said later. "Five young men guilty of no crime save that of preferring *liberty* to *slavery* were literally dragged behind horses a distance of fifteen miles and placed in the Easton (Md.) jail."

Not until he was about twenty-one did he have another chance to escape. Fred was working in a Baltimore shipyard when, disguised as a sailor, he took a train to New York. From there he went to New

Bedford, Mass., where he changed his name to Frederick Douglass. For several years he earned his living as a laborer, but he had not forgotten the speeches in the *Columbian Orator*. He himself began to make speeches to Negro congregations, and on one occasion a white Abolitionist happened to be present.

This chance meeting led to an invitation to address an antislavery meeting on the island of Nantucket, Mass. (1841). Fred, who had never spoken before a group of white people, had a bad case of stage fright, but his audience sat spellbound. He was tall and impressive looking, and proved to be an eloquent speaker. Later, to his surprise, he was asked to be an agent for the Massachusetts Antislavery Society, and he made speeches in a number of Northern towns and cities.

To many of his listeners it seemed incredible that a man who had spent his youth in bondage, with no advantages, could be so intelligent. To convince the doubters that his story was true, Douglass wrote his autobiography. In the *Narrative of the Life of Frederick Douglass*, first published in 1845, he told where he had been born and gave the name of his master. By revealing his identity, he increased the danger of being captured by slave catchers, and he decided to go to Great Britain. The next two years (1845–47) were spent lecturing in England and Ireland. Here, too, he was a popular speaker and earned enough money to buy his freedom on his return to the United States.

After settling in Rochester, N.Y., the ex-slave started a newspaper, which became known as *Frederick Douglass' Paper*. Under the title appeared the words: "Devoted to the Rights of All Mankind, Without Distinction of Color, Class or Clime." He hoped the slavery problem could be settled without violence, but when the Civil War broke out, he helped to recruit two Negro regiments for the Union army. President Abraham Lincoln thought highly of him and called him into consultation several times.

One result of the war was to bring freedom to the slaves, but to Frederick Douglass the right of suffrage was one of the most important benefits of liberty. The great moment of triumph came in 1870 with the ratification of the Fifteenth Amendment, providing that no citizen should be denied the right to vote because of race. At a celebration in Baltimore, the city from which he had once escaped as a slave, Douglass was the principal speaker.

"We have a future," he told the Negroes in the audience. "Everything is possible to us."

Due Process of Law. In the American Bill of Rights, the Fifth Amendment to the Constitution states that no person shall "be deprived of life, liberty or property without due process of law." Reduced to its simplest terms, the purpose of "due process" is to protect individuals against arbitrary actions by a government and to assure a fair trial to a person accused of crime. The accused is presumed to be innocent until proven guilty; he is not required to give evidence against himself; and he is entitled to ask government aid in obtaining witnesses who can testify in his behalf.

One case that reached the U.S. Supreme Court (1956) involved a defendant too poor to pay for a transcript of his trial, but who claimed that it would have shown errors in the testimony. The Court ruled that because of failure to provide the defendant with a transcript without cost, he had been denied due process.

"There can be no equal justice," said Associate Justice Hugo H. Black in the majority opinion, "where the kind of trial a man gets depends upon the amount of money he has."

The term "due process," as used in the Fifth Amendment, applied only to the federal government. Later, the Fourteenth Amendment asserted that no *state* should "deprive any person of life, liberty, or property, without due process of law." The purpose of including that provision at the time the amendment was adopted (1868) was to safeguard the rights of the newly freed Negroes of the South, but later "due process of law" came to have a wider application. A number of corporations, on occasion, have claimed the protection of this provision.

The ideas back of the American belief in due process were brought to this country from England.

Education in a Democracy. Education, Thomas Jefferson once said, is "the only sure reliance of our liberty" and no nation can expect to be both "ignorant and free." For voters to make the wise decisions necessary if they were to govern themselves successfully, he was convinced that education must be provided for all the citizens.

Shortly after the Continental Congress adopted Jefferson's Declaration of Independence, he returned to his native Virginia to work for a series of reforms in his own state. Here he was elected to the state legislature, and one of the measures he proposed was a system of education to be paid for by public taxes. Elementary schools were to be provided for all children, rich or poor; grammar (secondary) schools for bright students who wished to continue their education; and college training for those who showed unusual promise. The legislature, considering the proposals much too radical, refused to enact any of them into law; but the public school systems later adopted in the United States showed the influence of Thomas Jefferson's ideas.

America's public schools also owe a debt to some of the early New England leaders. More than a century before the American Revolution the colony of Massachusetts had tax-supported schools, and New Englanders helped to write the Northwest Ordinance (1787) which provided for a system of education in the Northwest Territory then being opened up to settlers. In each township a section of land was to be set aside, so it might be sold and the proceeds used to maintain a school.

"Knowledge being necessary to good government and the happiness of mankind," the Ordinance stated, "schools and the means of education shall be forever encouraged."

During the next century the idea gradually took hold that every child of grade-school age had an equal right to an education. Training boys and girls for citizenship was especially important in a rapidly growing country where thousands of immigrants arrived year after year. It was at school that the children of the newcomers learned American ways and, like the young native Americans, prepared to take their places as citizens when they grew older. The American ideal was that all children, whether they were native or foreign-born and whether they were rich or poor, should have an equal opportunity for an education.

The ideal, unfortunately, did not always work out in practice. Under the American system, the public schools in each state are controlled by authorities within the state, and some states are less prosperous than others. Even within a state, some rural communities, as well as districts in the poorer sections of crowded cities, have less money to spend on schools. They cannot afford to employ enough good teachers or to buy all the equipment and books that are needed. Buildings are often inadequate and overcrowded. By the 1960's a number of prominent Americans had come to the conclusion that the federal government must offer more aid to education in order to bring a greater

degree of equality to the school children of the nation.

One of the most important bills ever passed by the U.S. Congress was the Elementary and Secondary Education Act of 1965. The purpose of this law was to give aid where it was most needed. Funds were made available for improving educational facilities in communities with a concentration of poor families, but decisions concerning details about how the money was to be spent were left to local authorities. The Higher Education Bill, which President Lyndon B. Johnson signed that same year, provided for loans and scholarships for promising students who otherwise could not afford to go to college. The President was convinced that education was essential for the success of the democratic system—the greatest single factor in molding citizens of the future.

"Every child must be encouraged to get as much education as he has the ability to take," the President said. "We want this not only for his sake but for the nation's sake. Nothing matters more to the future of our country."

See also EQUAL RIGHTS IN SCHOOLS and MANN, HORACE.

Eisenhower, Dwight David (1890–   ). Before his election as the thirty-fourth President of the United States, Dwight D. Eisenhower had won fame as the leader of the allied forces that rescued western Europe from Nazi control in World War II.

After a boyhood spent in Abilene, Kan., Ike (as he was then called by his friends and later by the whole world) entered the U.S. Military Academy at West Point. Two years after he graduated (1915) and received his commission as second lieutenant, the United States entered World War I. Instead of being sent overseas as he desired, Ike was assigned to various training camps in the United States as an instructor.

Almost a quarter of a century later, during World War II, Eisenhower—by then a general—was sent to England to command all the United States forces that would be engaged in the European part of the war. A few months later he was also placed in command of a British-American invasion of North Africa (Nov., 1942), and later of the invasion of Sicily and Italy (1943). His efficiency in organizing these massive military operations, as well as his ability to get people to work together in harmony, led to his appointment (Dec., 1943) as Supreme Commander of the Allied expeditionary forces in western Europe.

The task that lay ahead of General Eisenhower was to direct "Overlord," a plan for an attack on Nazi-held France. This was a tremendous assignment, calling for the cooperation of numerous government officials and military officers from different nations. Ground, air, and naval forces all would be under Eisenhower's command. Taking part in this great combined effort to defeat the Nazis, there would be British, Canadian, and American divisions, as well as other units composed of men who had escaped to England after their homelands had been conquered by the enemy.

The invasion point chosen by the Allies was the coast of Normandy. Every detail of the sea and air invasion had to be planned with great care—and in secrecy. The Germans had placed heavy fortifications along the entire coastal area of northwestern Europe, which would make the landings difficult in any event. Success would be virtually impossible if details of the Overlord plans were learned ahead of time by the Nazis. Such knowledge would give them an opportunity to mass their troops at crucial points where Allied forces would attempt to land.

"D-Day"—the name that had been chosen for the date the invasion was to take place—finally came on June 6, 1944. Though the landings in Normandy were difficult, a beachhead was achieved, and Eisenhower was able to broadcast to the people of western Europe that the day of their liberation was approaching. "Great battles lie ahead," he said. "I call upon all who love freedom to stand with us. . . . together we will achieve victory."

Great battles did indeed lie ahead, but gradually the Germans were pushed farther and farther back toward their own country and on May 7, 1945 they surrendered.

Seven years after the end of World War II (in 1952), Eisenhower, still a national hero, was elected President of the United States. During his administration he made a number of goodwill tours to other countries, and he sincerely tried to bring about a better relationship between the United States and the Soviet Union. Though he realized the need for adequate

security and helped to increase the nation's defenses during his Presidency, he was concerned about the growing influence exerted by the military organization and the arms industry in the United States. The military and industrial combination, he warned, must not be permitted to become too powerful.

"We must never let the weight of this combination," he said in a speech (Jan., 1961) shortly before he left the White House, "endanger our liberties or our democratic processes."

After his two terms as President, General Eisenhower retired to a farm he had purchased near Gettysburg, Pa. He continued his interest in public affairs, writing and making speeches on the problems of maintaining peace and freedom. Winning freedom, he had once said, was "not to be compared to the winning of a game." No victory could be forever recorded in history.

"Freedom," he went on, "has its life in the hearts, the actions, the spirit of men, and so it must be daily earned and refreshed."

Emancipation Proclamation (1863). This historic document issued during the Civil War declared that slaves in those states or parts of states in rebellion against the U.S. government should be "thenceforward, and forever free." Abraham Lincoln, the President, had long been opposed to slavery, but it was not forbidden by the Constitution. As President he had no legal right to declare the slaves free, but as commander in chief of the armed forces he considered it his right and his obligation to do whatever was necessary to insure a Union victory. There was danger that slave labor might enable the Confederates to win the war, since slaves released their Southern masters for military duty, raised food to feed the soldiers, and were used to build Confederate fortifications.

Therefore it was as a military measure that President Lincoln issued a prelimi-

nary Emancipation Proclamation (Sept. 22, 1862). The Proclamation warned that all slaves would be set free in areas still in rebellion against the United States on January 1, 1863. The warning was not heeded. The Confederates were still fighting, perhaps more determinedly than ever, when New Year's Day dawned in 1863.

On that day the usual crowd of callers had come to the White House to pay their respects to the President. Finally he broke away and went to his study, where the members of his Cabinet were waiting. On a table was spread an engrossed copy of the Proclamation, ready for him to sign. He had shaken the hands of hundreds of visitors, and his right arm felt numb. He expressed the hope that his signature would not look shaky. Then, writing very carefully, he added the name "Abraham Lincoln" to the document that promised freedom to more than three million Negroes.

"I never in my life," he said, "felt more certain that I was doing right, than I do in signing this paper."

No one realized better than the President that the question of slavery was only partially solved by the Emancipation Proclamation. It would not free any slaves in the border states that had remained loyal to the Union, and slavery in the Confederate States would not be affected until the territory was conquered by Union forces. Nearly three years were to pass before the Thirteenth Amendment, prohibiting slavery for all Negroes, would be added to the Constitution. See FREEDOM AMENDMENTS.

The news that the Emancipation Proclamation had been signed spread rapidly, and Negroes rejoiced. White people interested in their cause joined in celebrations in a number of Northern cities. Crowds sang songs and knelt in prayer.

In Boston, the Negro leader, Frederick Douglass, read the Emancipation Proclamation aloud to a vast audience. At another celebration, another speaker, Thomas Wentworth Higginson, a well-known white clergyman and colonel of a Negro regiment, was about to begin, when the crowd burst into song:

My country 'tis of thee,
Sweet land of liberty . . .

"I never saw anything so electric," said Colonel Higginson later. "It seemed a choked voice of a race at last unloosed. . . . The life of the whole day was in those unknown people's song."

Emerson, Ralph Waldo (1803–82), American poet and essayist, has been called "the philosopher of democracy" because of his faith in the importance of every individual human being. He wrote in his *Journal* (1834):

Democracy, freedom, has its roots in the sacred truth that every man hath in him the divine reason. Though few men . . . live according to the dictates of reason, yet all are created capable of so doing. That is the equality, and the only equality, of all men.

For a few years Emerson served as minister of a Unitarian church in Boston, his birthplace. Most of his adult life was spent in the nearby town of Concord, but he traveled widely, since he was always in demand as a lecturer. "The American Scholar," a speech he delivered in Cambridge, Mass., before the Phi Beta Kappa Society of Harvard College, has been referred to as "America's Intellectual Declaration of Independence." In it, Emerson insisted that American scholars need no longer feel dependent on the learning of other lands.

> We will walk on our own feet, we will work with our own hands; we will speak with our own minds. . . . Events, actions, arise that must be sung, that will sing themselves.

Emerson made a deep impression on contemporary audiences with his lectures on the growing antislavery movement. Though usually of a serene and gentle disposition, he had only contempt for slaveholders, and became a staunch Abolitionist. "I think we must get rid of slavery," he said, "or we must get rid of freedom."

As a poet, Ralph Waldo Emerson is best remembered for his "Concord Hymn" (see separate entry).

English Heritage of Freedom. In a speech made early in 1775, Edmund Burke, a member of the British Parliament, urged his government to moderate the harsh policy it had taken against the English colonies in America. Repressive measures simply made the colonists hard to deal with, he pointed out, since they were "not only devoted to liberty, but to liberty according to English ideas and on English principles."

Burke was right; the Americans *were* devoted to liberty. Restrictions on the rights and freedoms to which they thought they were as much entitled as the people in the mother country would soon lead to the American Revolution and the demand for independence.

Many of the rights claimed by the colonists had for centuries been traditional, though not always respected, in England. But in the 1600's these rights were severely challenged by the kings of the Stuart line who ruled during most of the century. James I and the later Stuart kings considered that they ruled by "divine right" and were accountable to no one but God. It took two civil wars, the execution of one king, and the forced abdication of another to reestablish the principle that the kings of England were also accountable to the people, Parliament, and the law.

During the turbulent 1600's, the "ancient rights and liberties" of the English people were restated in specific terms in a Petition of Right (1628) and in a Bill of Rights (1689). Even the ancient Magna Carta (1215) was reinterpreted as a document that provided far more protection of rights than had been originally intended.

Thousands of people fled from England to the colonies in America during the prolonged struggles of the 1600's. They sought religious and political sanctuary in the new land, where they would be free from the persecution of arbitrary rulers.

In the next century, at the time of the American Revolution, most Americans were of English descent and had English ideas of freedom. Settlers who had come from other European countries had absorbed the same ideas of liberty. The men who led the Revolution and who founded the government of the new nation were well acquainted with the rights set forth in the English freedom documents of the previous century. They also had studied the essays of John Milton, John Locke, and other English writers of the 1600's who had supported the cause of freedom against arbitrary power. When the Americans wrote their own great documents of freedom—the Declaration of Independence, the Constitution, and the Bill of Rights—they drew upon many of the principles and ideas so ably expressed in England.

After the Revolution, the Americans also gradually adopted the English common law. This is a legal system based on precedents. In making judicial decisions, judges consider previous decisions and interpret them as they apply to current needs. For a while after the new nation was established, the Americans were not sure that they wanted to have anything to do with the legal system of their recent enemy. But finally they realized that common law was more just and reasonable than the system used in most European countries, where all the laws were written in an inflexible code that could not be adapted to changing times or to individual cases. So in the early 1800's American lawyers and law students began to study the works of Sir Edward Coke and Sir William Blackstone, the great authorities on English common law. In these works they found the examples and principles which would serve as a foundation for common law in America.

Though the United States inherited some of its ideals of liberty from several European countries, it was from England that the American people received most of the ideas and principles that Americans still consider basic to freedom.

(See INDEX for more information on documents and people mentioned above.)

Equal Rights in Schools. The unanimous decision of the U.S. Supreme Court (1954) that segregation of white and Negro students in public schools was unconstitutional probably caused more controversy than any other Supreme Court ruling of recent years. The 1954 decision overruled one made more than a half century earlier (Plessy v. Ferguson, 1896) that had set a legal stamp of approval on segregation in railroad cars, so long as "separate but equal" accommodations were provided for both races. Though it had concerned transportation, the "separate but equal" decision had been used—in a number of states—to justify segregation in education.

In actual practice, when separate public schools were provided, they were seldom equal. Not only were the elementary and high schools for Negro children usually inferior to those attended by white pupils, but many bright young Negroes had been denied admission to white schools of higher learning. In several states, Negro parents brought suit against their local Boards of Education, maintaining that the refusal to allow colored children to attend white schools was a denial of the rights guaranteed by the Fourteenth Amendment. The case of Brown v. Board of Education of Topeka (Kan.) reached the Supreme Court, and the unanimous decision was written by Chief Justice Earl Warren. The decision read, in part:

In approaching this problem . . . we must consider public education in the light of . . . its present place in American life . . . . Education is perhaps the most important function of state and local governments . . . . It is the very foundation of good citizenship. Today it is the principal instrument in awakening the child to cultural values, in preparing him for later professional training, and in helping him to adjust normally to his environment. In these days, it is doubtful that any child may reasonably be expected to succeed in life if he is denied the opportunity of an education. Such an opportunity, where the state has undertaken to provide it, is a right which must be made available to all on equal terms.

We come then to the question presented: Does segregation of children in public schools solely on the basis of race, even though the physical facilities and other "tangible" factors may be equal, deprive the children of the minority group of equal educational opportunities? We believe that it does . . . . To separate them from others of similar age and qualifications solely because of their race generates a feeling of inferiority as to their status in the community that may affect their hearts and minds in a way unlikely ever to be undone. . . .

The conclusion of the Supreme Court was that separate educational facilities were inherently unequal and that the plaintiffs, and others like them, had been denied the equal protection of the laws. In compliance with another decision of the Court (1955) that public schools be de-segregated "with all deliberate speed," a number of towns and cities reopened their schools, once segregated, on an integrated basis. In certain sections of the country, though, the decision has met with resistance, sometimes with violence. At times, progress has seemed discouragingly slow, but as each year passes, more and more colored and white children attend school together.

Equality. Perhaps no phrase in any American document has been so misunderstood as "All men are created equal" in the Declaration of Independence. Thomas Jefferson, the author, did not intend to imply that all people have the same physical and intellectual capacities, but that everyone should have the same right to "Life, liberty, and the pursuit of happiness."

Since Jefferson's time a number of later Presidents have interpreted the term, among them Abraham Lincoln. He believed the signers of the Declaration of Independence had "meant simply to declare the right [of equality]; so the enforcement of it might follow, as fast as the circumstances should permit." To President Theodore Roosevelt, equality meant that so far as humanly possible, each and every person should have an equal opportunity "to show the stuff that was in him."

Some years later, when another President, John F. Kennedy, spoke of equality, he was referring specifically to the ten percent of the American people who are Negroes. He said in an address to the nation (June 11, 1963):

> This is one country. It has become one country because all ... the people who came here had an equal chance to develop their talents. We cannot say to ten percent of the population that "you can't have that right. Your children can't have the chance to develop whatever talents they have ...." I think we owe them and we owe ourselves a better country than that.

Expression, Freedom of. Freedom of speech and of the press were among the guarantees provided by the American Bill of Rights to protect the minority of citizens against what Louis D. Brandeis once called "the occasional tyrannies of the governing majorities." That associate justice of the U.S. Supreme Court (1916–39) summed up what the men who won the nation's independence had firmly believed: "freedom

to think as you will and to speak as you think are means indispensable to the discovery of political truth."

Though freedom of expression is greatly prized by the American people, there have been times when citizens were denied this right. During the administration of John Adams, the Sedition Act (1798) imposed fines or imprisonment on anyone convicted of making false or malicious statements about the President or Congress. Because of disagreements about what was false or malicious, some outspoken editors and other Americans were sent to jail for making slighting remarks in public speeches or for writing what they considered to be the truth. The law was widely denounced as a violation of personal liberties guaranteed by the First Amendment and, in a great wave of public indignation, Adams was defeated for reelection. After Thomas Jefferson became President, the Sedition Act was never again enforced, and the men who had been jailed under its provisions were released.

A harder decision for many Americans to make concerns how much freedom of speech should be permitted in wartime. During the Civil War and again during World War I, Congress passed measures imposing heavy penalties on citizens who talked against or otherwise interfered with the war effort. One case that reached the U.S. Supreme Court (Schenck *v.* U.S., 1919) concerned a man who had written pamphlets urging Americans to resist the draft. He was convicted in the lower courts for violating the Espionage Act passed by Congress two years earlier. In the opinion of the Supreme Court, the question to be decided was whether in time of war the words used in the pamphlets were "of such a nature as to create a clear and present danger that will bring about the substantive evils that Congress has a right to prevent." The decision went against Schenck, and his conviction was upheld.

"Many things that might be said in time of peace," the Court's ruling read, were not to be endured "so long as men fight," and Schenck therefore was not entitled to the protection of the First Amendment.

Some of the provisions of the Espionage Act were much criticized, and one well-known U.S. Senator, Hiram Johnson, warned that in fighting a war for democracy abroad Americans must not forget democracy at home. Nor has war been the only national emergency that threatened liberty of speech and press. During a railroad strike in the early 1920's, William Allen White, editor of the Emporia (Kan.) *Gazette,* was severely criticized for some of the opinions expressed in his newspaper during a time of stress. It was at such a time, he replied, that "freedom of utterance" was most needed, and suppression too often led to violence.

In an editorial that was to win him the Pulitzer Prize, he said:

You can have no wise laws nor free enforcement of wise laws, unless there is a free expression of the wisdom of the people—and, alas, their folly with it. But if there is freedom, folly will die of its own poison, and the wisdom will survive.

Faneuil Hall, a Boston landmark, has long been called the "Cradle of Liberty" because of the many protest meetings held on the second floor of the building in the days preceding the American Revolution. In the 1850's it also served as a meeting place for persons who aligned themselves with the antislavery movement.

The hall was first presented to the city (1742) by a wealthy Boston merchant, Peter Faneuil, whose Huguenot ancestors had fled from religious persecution in France. The building burned, was rebuilt by the city (1763), and since then has been much enlarged. The ground floor has always been used as a public marketplace. The second floor is now a museum and is still used for public meetings.

"Federalist, The." This remarkable series of essays was published (1787–88) to defend and explain the federal Constitution which had recently been adopted by the Constitutional Convention meeting in Philadelphia. According to one of its provisions, the Constitution was to become effective only after it had been ratified by nine of the thirteen states.

There was so much opposition to the new plan of government that it was in grave danger of defeat. So Alexander Hamilton suggested to James Madison and John Jay, each of whom had taken a leading part in the convention, that they join him in writing some essays, or articles, to convince the people of the importance of ratifying the new Constitution.

Number 1 in the series (appearing first in New York newspapers) reminded the public of the inefficiency of their government under the Articles of Confederation, and stressed the fact that the existence of the Union was at stake. It had been reserved for the people of the United States, the essay continued, to decide "whether societies of men are really capable or not, of establishing good government from reflection and choice, or whether they are forever destined to depend . . . on accident and force."

The essays, more than half of them by Alexander Hamilton, are credited with swinging the vote in favor of ratification in a number of states. After newspaper publication, they were published (with eight additional essays) in book form under the title *The Federalist*. This book is still considered the most thoughtful and penetrating analysis yet written about the American government.

Four Freedoms. In his Message to Congress (Jan. 6, 1941), nearly a year before the United States was drawn into World War II, President Franklin Roosevelt summed up the war aims of the free world in these words:

In the future days, which we seek to make secure, we look forward to a world founded upon four essential human freedoms.

The first is freedom of speech and expression—everywhere in the world.

The second is freedom of every person to worship God in his own way—everywhere in the world.

The third is freedom from want—which, translated into world terms, means economic understandings which will secure to every nation a healthy peace time life for its inhabitants—everywhere in the world.

The fourth is freedom from fear—which, translated into world terms, means a world-wide reduction of armaments to such a point and in such a thorough fashion that no nation will be in a position to commit an act of physical aggression against any neighbor—anywhere in the world.

Franklin, Benjamin (1706–90). This famous citizen of Philadelphia has been called "the first American," partly because, in his own time, he was better known in Europe than any of his countrymen. When he arrived in England (1757) on business for the colony of Pennsylvania, he was welcomed as a writer and philosopher, as a scientist and inventor, and as a statesman.

Most of Franklin's time during the next eighteen years was spent in London, where he was honored for his learning and his wit. He was there during the Stamp Act controversy, and when called to give testimony (Feb., 1766) before the House of Commons, he spoke out boldly in behalf of American rights. He hoped the colonies could avoid war with the mother country, but when the American Revolution seemed inevitable, he sailed for home.

Shortly after his return to America (1775), Franklin was elected a delegate to the Second Continental Congress. The following year he served with Thomas Jefferson on the committee that was to prepare a Declaration of Independence. He was one of the signers of that historic document.

Two months later, at the request of the Continental Congress, the seventy-year-old statesman went to France, where he was immensely popular. He aroused much enthusiasm for the American cause, and the French government finally entered into a Treaty of Alliance (1778) with the struggling new nation.

Benjamin Franklin helped to draft the Treaty of Peace (1783) that brought the long War for Independence to a close. "We are now friends with England and with all mankind," he said in a letter to a friend.

It soon became apparent that the new nation needed a stronger central government to protect the liberty won at such great cost. Franklin, back home again, agreed to serve as a delegate to the Constitutional Convention which met in Philadelphia in May, 1787. Working out the details for a new plan of government proved a difficult task, and again and again—when the delegates could not agree—Benjamin Franklin suggested compromise. He himself did not fully approve of some of the features of the Constitution, yet he urged its adoption. Later he was greatly relieved when it was ratified by the states and became the supreme law of the land, for he felt confident the survival of the new nation was assured.

"If any form of government is capable of making a nation happy," he said, "ours I think bids fair for producing that effect."

During his last years Franklin served as president of the Pennsylvania Society for the Abolition of Slavery—a question that was to cause more and more concern to the American people as the years went by. Only two months before he died (1790) he signed a memorial, or petition, to the first Congress under the new Constitution, urging that slavery be abolished. To the end he was devoted to the cause of freedom for his fellowmen, not only in the United States but throughout the world. He had once said:

God grant, that not only the love of liberty but a thorough knowledge of the rights of man may pervade all the nations of the earth, so that a philosopher may set his foot anywhere on its surface and say: "This is my country."

"Free World" is a term that came into use during the Presidency of Franklin D. Roosevelt. Nearly a year before the United States was drawn into World War II, he delivered his Lend-Lease Message to Congress (Jan. 6, 1941), asking that more aid be given those countries fighting the aggressor nations. He said:

Let us say to the democracies: We Americans are vitally concerned in your defense of freedom. We are putting forth our energies, our resources, and our organizing powers to give you strength to regain . . . a *free world* . . . .

F.D.R. used the term to designate those nations opposed to the totalitarian power of the Axis (Nazi Germany, Fascist Italy, and Japan, which was then controlled by a military clique). The term today is used to differentiate non-Communist from Communist nations.

Freedmen's Bureau was a temporary agency set up by Congress (Mar., 1865) to help the recently emancipated slaves. Though the Negroes had been freed, no provision had been made for helping them to earn a living, and many former masters were not much better off than the former slaves. Farms lay in ruins, cities had been shelled, and Confederate money was worthless. Negroes, suddenly homeless, wandered through the Southern countryside.

It was to meet this situation that agents of the Freedmen's Bureau, working under Army auspices, moved into the South to establish Negro schools and set up relief stations for impoverished members of both races. In this work the Bureau was helped by thousands of volunteers from nearly a hundred freedmen aid and

relief societies organized by different religious denominations.

Another function of the Bureau was to arbitrate labor disputes. Negroes were urged to return to their former masters and work for wages, but white employers often resented what they considered the "outside interference" of agents from the North. There were some plantation owners who, having lost a fortune in slave property, did not approve of Negro education, and their antagonism was shared by many poor whites who had never owned a slave. This hostility, as well as the fact that a few of the agents may have been corrupt, as charged, hampered the work of the many fine, dedicated agents and volunteers.

In spite of the handicaps, during the seven years the Bureau was in operation, it fed and clothed thousands of Negroes and poor whites, established forty hospitals, and arranged for the treatment of nearly a million cases of illness.

It also started, or helped to start, more than 4,000 schools—the first schools most Negroes had ever had a chance to attend. The Bureau helped to support several institutions of higher learning as well (Atlanta University, Fisk University, Howard University, and Hampton Institute), which were among the first colleges especially established for Negro youth.

"Freedom," like its synonym "liberty," has often been defined, but it is unlikely that there is a better definition than that of John Stuart Mill, English philosopher, whose essay *On Liberty* (1859) is considered a classic. "The only freedom which deserves the name," said Mill, "is that of pursuing our own good in our own way, so long as we do not attempt to deprive others of theirs, or impede their efforts to obtain it."

Freedom Amendments. The purpose of several of the amendments added to the Constitution since the Bill of Rights was adopted in 1791 was the extension of the privileges of citizenship to more Americans, and the provision of safeguards for their liberties.

Amendment XIII abolished slavery in the United States. The Emancipation Proclamation issued during the Civil War had promised freedom to those slaves in "areas in rebellion against the United States." As the war drew to a close, more and more Union leaders came to feel that *all* slaves must be assured of freedom in order to fulfill the promises of freedom and justice in the Bill of Rights. The Thirteenth Amendment was adopted by Congress in January, 1865, and was ratified by the required number of states by the end of the same year. It reads: "Neither slavery nor involuntary servitude, except as a punishment for crime whereof the party shall have been duly convicted, shall exist within the United States. ...."

Amendment XIV (1868) granted citizenship to the recently freed slaves. It states that all persons born or naturalized in the United States are "citizens of the United States and of the State wherein they reside." No state, the Amendment also says, shall make or enforce any law that would abridge (lessen or interfere with) the privileges of citizens of the United States, nor shall any state "deny to any person within its jurisdiction the equal protection of the laws."

Amendment XV (1870) extended suffrage to Negro citizens. It reads: "The right of citizens of the United States to vote shall not be denied or abridged by the United States or by any State on account of race, color, or previous condition of servitude."

Amendment XIX (1920) extended suffrage to women citizens: "The right of citizens of the United States to vote shall not be denied or abridged by the United States or by any State on account of sex."

See also NEGRO RIGHTS MOVEMENT; SUFFRAGE; WOMAN SUFFRAGE MOVEMENT.

"Freedom from Want" was a phrase used by President Franklin Roosevelt in his "Four Freedoms Message" to Congress (Jan. 6, 1941). In that speech he was thinking in world terms, and freedom from want meant economic understandings which would "secure to every nation a healthy peace time life for its inhabitants."

On the domestic front, the same principles had been applied in the New Deal. "We have come to a clear realization," the President said, "that true individual liberty cannot exist without economic security and independence. Necessitous men are not free men."

Lyndon B. Johnson, then a young Congressman, remembered those words years later when he became President, and declared a war on poverty. Congress passed the Economic Opportunity Act (1964) which established the Office of Economic Opportunity (OEO). Projects initiated or planned for the relief of poverty included the Job Corps to provide training for school dropouts; the Neighborhood Youth Corps, to find useful jobs for young people in their home towns; and Project Head Start, to give special training to children from impoverished homes before they are old enough to attend regular school. Another OEO program, inspired by the success of the Peace Corps, was Vista (Volunteers in Service to America). The volunteers are usually young people, who —for a very small salary—go into the impoverished areas to help the people who live there.

Because of the magnitude of the tasks undertaken by OEO, there have been many frustrations. But R. Sargent Shriver, Jr., the first director, was confident that in a nation as affluent as the United States, the difficulties could be overcome. As a goal, he set 1976, the bicentennial of the Declaration of Independence, as the date by which poverty could be eliminated in the United States.

Freedom of Expression, *see* EXPRESSION, FREEDOM OF.

Freedom of Religion, *see* RELIGION, FREEDOM OF.

Freedom of Thought. It might be said that all the freedoms Americans prize stem from freedom of thought and opinion. This means the right of each person to think for himself and to hold the beliefs which seem to him right and proper. Oliver Wendell Holmes, Jr., an associate justice of the U.S. Supreme Court, pointed out in one of his famous dissents (U.S. *v.* Schwimmer, 1929) that if there is any principle of the Constitution more imperative than any other, it is the principle of free thought—"not free thought for those who agree with us but freedom for the thought that we hate. . . ."

Holmes believed that the theory back of the First Amendment to the U.S. Constitution is that the ultimate good is best served by free trade in ideas. In another dissent (Abrams *v.* U.S., 1919) he said, "Time has upset many fighting faiths. . . . The best test of truth is the power of the thought to get itself accepted in the competition of the market."

Freedom Pledge. A schoolroom pledge, published by the U.S. Office of Education, reads as follows:

> *I am an American. A free*
> *American.*
> *Free to speak—without fear,*
> *Free to worship God in my*
> *own way,*
> *Free to stand for what I*
> *think right,*
> *Free to oppose what I think wrong,*
> *Free to choose those who*
> *govern my country.*
> *This heritage of Freedom I*
> *pledge to uphold*
> *For myself and all mankind.*

Garrison, William Lloyd (1805–79), was a Boston newspaper editor, with little money but a great deal of courage, who devoted his life to the cause of freedom for the slaves. On New Year's Day, 1831, less than a month after his twenty-fifth birthday, he published the first issue of a four-page Abolitionist sheet he called *The Liberator*. He wrote in his first editorial:

I shall strenuously contend for the immediate enfranchisement of our slave population . . . . I *will be* as harsh as truth and as uncompromising as justice. On this subject I do not wish to think, or speak, or write with moderation. No! No! Tell a man whose house is on fire, to give a moderate alarm . . .; tell the mother to gradually extricate her babe from the fire into which it has fallen;—but urge me not to use moderation in a cause like the present. I am in earnest . . .— I will not excuse—I will not retreat a single inch—*and I will be heard.*

In spite of many difficulties, Garrison did manage to make himself heard. He had to earn enough in other ways to live frugally and to rent a dingy garret which he used as an office, but nearly every week, during the next thirty-five years, he brought out an issue of *The Liberator*. In 1833 he was one of the founders of the American Antislavery Society in Philadelphia, and the movement spread rapidly to other Northern cities. Within ten years these societies had enrolled a quarter of a million members. Many of them, more moderate in their views than the editor of *The Liberator*, believed that emancipation should come gradually, but Garrison hammered away at one idea: abolish slavery and do it at once.

Though he was a mild enough looking man, persecution only made William Lloyd Garrison more determined. People either liked him or detested him, and that was the way he wanted it. In the fight he was waging, he had no use for neutrals, and he felt it was his mission "to give the slaveholders and their apologists as much uneasiness as possible." This "uneasiness" generated by him and other Abolitionists undoubtedly helped to bring on the Civil War. It was a day of triumph for William Lloyd Garrison when he published the text of the Emancipation Proclamation in his newspaper. From then on he supported President Lincoln, whom he had once opposed as being too moderate.

After the war ended (1865) in a Union victory, Garrison visited the South. There had been a time, he told one audience of Negroes, when the government had offered them no protection. "Now all is changed!" he said. "Thank God you are free."

After the Thirteenth Amendment was passed, prohibiting slavery in the United States, Garrison decided *The Liberator* was no longer needed. The final issue was published December 29, 1865, and its founder then turned his attention to other reforms, including that of woman suffrage.

Gettysburg Address. This speech, made by President Lincoln at Gettysburg, Pa., summed up in less than 300 words what he thought democracy meant. The occasion was the dedication (Nov. 19, 1863) of a national cemetery on the battlefield where so many brave men had died the summer before during the three-day battle of Get-

tysburg. The principal address at the dedication ceremonies was delivered by a well-
known New England orator, Edward
Everett, and he spoke so eloquently that
Lincoln feared his own brief remarks were
a failure. Everett knew better.

"I should be glad," he wrote the
President the next day, "if I could flatter
myself that I came as near the central
idea of the occasion in two hours as you
did in two minutes."

Edward Everett's verdict has been
confirmed by time. Of the Gettysburg
Address and Lincoln's Second Inaugural,
it has been said, "They are among the
glories and beauties of mankind."

The Gettysburg Address follows:

Fourscore and seven years ago our fathers
brought forth on this continent a new nation,
conceived in liberty, and dedicated to the prop-
osition that all men are created equal.

Now we are engaged in a great civil war,
testing whether that nation, or any nation so
conceived and so dedicated, can long endure.
We are met on a great battlefield of that war.

We have come to dedicate a portion of that
field as a final resting place for those who here
gave their lives that that nation might live. It
is altogether fitting and proper that we should
do this.

But in a larger sense, we cannot dedicate
—we cannot consecrate—we cannot hallow—
this ground. The brave men, living and dead,
who struggled here, have consecrated it, far
above our poor power to add or detract. The
world will little note, nor long remember, what
we say here, but it can never forget what they
did here. It is for us the living, rather, to be
dedicated here to the unfinished work which
they who fought here have thus far so nobly
advanced. It is rather for us to be here dedicated to the great task remaining before us,
that from these honored dead we take increased
devotion to that cause for which they gave the
last full measure of devotion—that we here
highly resolve that these dead shall not have
died in vain—that this nation, under God,
shall have a new birth of freedom—and that
government of the people, by the people, for
the people, shall not perish from the earth.

At the request of friends, President
Lincoln made several copies of his famous
speech. One is now in the Lincoln Room

at the White House, one is in the Cornell University library, one in the Illinois State Historical Library, and two are in the Library of Congress.

Glorious Revolution, The. In the spring of 1689 the English colonists in America received the news that despotic King James II was no longer their ruler. During the previous winter a bloodless revolution had taken place in England. As a result, James was an exile in France; and Mary, his daughter, and her husband, William, were ruling England as joint sovereigns.

Because of the slow transportation of the time, information had been late in reaching the colonies concerning this change in government, known as the "Glorious Revolution."

Incensed at James's increasing tyranny, seven prominent Englishmen had sent a message to the king's son-in-law, the Dutch Prince William of Orange, asking him to come to England to restore the country's liberty. When William arrived in England with an army, James was deserted by his own troops and soon fled to France (Dec., 1688).

Early the following year, representatives from the different towns and counties in England held a convention. They announced that by fleeing the country the king had abdicated. An invitation was then extended to William and Mary to become king and queen of England.

But there was a condition attached to the invitation. The English people had had their fill of despotism. If William and Mary accepted the throne, they would also have to accept the provisions in a Declaration of Rights, which placed limitations on their power. William and Mary agreed (Feb., 1689), and later that year Parliament enacted the Declaration as a permanent law, known as the English Bill of Rights.

The Bill proclaimed that no king had the right to levy money, suspend the laws, or maintain a standing army without Parliament's consent. Furthermore, freedom of speech and debate must be allowed in Parliament. The Bill also asserted that various rights of the people, such as the right to petition the king and to be tried by impartial juries, must no longer be violated.

The colonists in America particularly liked the parts of the English Bill of Rights that emphasized the rights of the people. They felt that they also were entitled to those rights, and insistence on having them became part of the colonial tradition.

Probably even more important in the minds of the colonists than the guarantees made in the English Bill of Rights were the events that had led to its acceptance. The Glorious Revolution had made it very clear that tyranny was not acceptable to the English people. That example was not forgotten in the colonies in later years. The leaders of the American Revolution realized full well that royal tyranny— whether of a James II or of a George III— need not and should not be endured.

Gompers, Samuel (1850–1924), the first president of the American Federation of Labor, realized that workers must be protected in their economic, as well as in their political rights, if they were to be truly free. He had come to this conclusion even as a child in London. Many years later, in his autobiography, *Seventy Years of Life and Labor*, he told of an incident that had influenced his entire career.

Due to the invention of some new machinery, many English silk weavers had lost their jobs and no longer had a trade. Samuel Gompers recalled:

Burned into my mind was the cry of these men, "I've no work to do." That cry, ringing through the street day after day, never failed to draw me to the window of my little home to watch these men struggling against despair. We could not but share their suffering and their feeling of injustice.

When Samuel was thirteen, his father, a cigarmaker, brought the family to America, and the boy found a job in a cigar factory in New York City. For his schooling he had to depend on night classes, but he was getting an education of a different kind as a member of the local cigarmakers' union. At the age of twenty-four he became its president and was deeply concerned about labor problems. There were too many small unions, he decided, none of them very effective in helping the members. What was needed, Gompers was convinced, was one strong union made up of smaller unions, so that many types of workers could unite in an effort to improve conditions for all.

The American Federation of Labor (A. F. of L.), which Samuel Gompers helped to found (1886), was made up of a number of separate trade unions. Except for one year, he served as president from the time it was formed until the end of his life. During his presidency, the A. F. of L. worked for increased wages, safer working conditions, and shorter working hours. The trade unions, by combining their efforts, were able to realize many of their aims. Speaking of trade unions, in a speech (1898) Samuel Gompers said:

> They were born of the necessity to protect and defend themselves [the workers] from encroachment, injustice and wrong . . .; to protect them not only as equals before the law, but also their rights to the product of their labor; to protect their lives, their limbs, their health, their homes, their firesides, their liberties. . . .

Because Samuel Gompers was the first outstanding leader to help the workers of the nation to attain these aims, he has been called "the grand old man of labor."

See LABOR MOVEMENT.

Government by Consent. Governments, stated the Declaration of Independence, derive "their just powers from the consent of the governed." The U.S. Constitution, which is the supreme law of the land, begins with the words, "We the people." Its purpose was to provide a plan of government that would enable the people to govern themselves through their elected representatives and officials.

"It has been said," President Thomas Jefferson told his listeners in his first Inaugural Address (1801), "that man cannot be trusted with the government of himself. Can he then be trusted with the government of others? . . . Let history answer that question."

Jefferson believed that history would prove him right. Though he realized that under a democratic government the people might make mistakes, he had confidence that the system and their own good sense would enable them to correct the mistakes. The first great test of this theory came during the Civil War (1861–65). It was being fought, said President Abraham Lincoln in his Gettysburg Address, to decide if a nation "conceived in liberty"—one in which the people ruled themselves—could "long endure."

The nation survived that crisis and has survived other crises since then. Near the beginning of the depression, when Franklin D. Roosevelt was still Governor of New York State, he presented a theory that to some people seemed new, but was really a restatement of old principles. He believed it was the duty of government to extend emergency aid to those unfortunate citizens who, through no fault of their own, were unable to obtain the necessities for a bare existence. To critics who maintained that this was not the function of government, he replied that the people *were* the government. This theory was summed up in a speech (Aug. 28, 1931) to the New York State Legislature:

> What is the State? It is the duly constituted representative of an organized society of human beings, created by them for their mutual

protection and well-being. "The State" or "The Government" is but the machinery through which such mutual aid and protection are achieved . . . . The people have created it; the people, by common consent, permit its continual existence. . . .

Government by Consent v. Dictatorship. In the United States and other countries of the free world the government of a state (nation) exists for the benefit of the people who live there. The citizens have freedom of choice, inasmuch as they control their government through their votes. In free countries, there are at least two major political parties, each with a slate of candidates, and the voters have an opportunity to choose. Their government is an instrument for carrying out the will of the majority, and the fact that the government may be changed, if the majority so wishes, is a protection against tyranny.

In countries with a totalitarian form of government—one ruled by dictators—it is quite different. Instead of having a government that exists to serve the people, the chief function of the people—so they are told—is to serve the state. Though they may go through the motions of voting, there is usually only one political party and one list of candidates selected by the leaders of that party. The voters themselves have little choice.

"Government of the People, by the People, for the People," the words made famous by the Gettysburg Address, did not originate with Abraham Lincoln. Theodore Parker, well-known Unitarian minister of Boston, had expressed much the same thought in a speech (1854) and again in a sermon delivered four years later. A democracy, he said, "is a government of all the people, by all the people, for all the people. . . . For shortness' sake I will call it the idea of freedom."

It is a matter of record that Lincoln read and marked this passage in a collec-

tion of Parker's sermons. He may also have been familiar with two earlier statements by famous Americans. Daniel Webster had defined democracy (1830) as "the people's government, made for the people, made by the people, and answerable to the people." A similar idea had been expressed (1819) in a Supreme Court decision written by Chief Justice John Marshall:

The government of the Union . . . is emphatically and truly a government of the people. In form and substance it emanates from them. Its powers are granted by them, and for their benefit.

The idea was not new even then. Nearly five centuries earlier, John Wycliffe, English priest and religious reformer, believing that the people themselves should be permitted to read the Scriptures, had been principally responsible for the first English translation (1384) of the Bible. In the Preface, Wycliffe said, "This Bible is for the government of the people, by the people and for the people."

Greek and Roman Heritage of Freedom. In colonial times many leading Americans were well acquainted with the writings of the ancient Greeks and Romans. They read this classic literature—sometimes in translation, sometimes in the original Greek or Latin—because they wanted to know what great thinkers of the past had said about freedom, government, and law—subjects in which American scholars and leaders were deeply interested.

They found the ideals of Greek democracy summed up in words attributed to Pericles, the famed leader of Athens during that city's "golden age." In a funeral oration delivered (431 B.C.) in honor of the Athenian war dead, Pericles is said to have declared that the form of government in Athens "favors the many instead of the few; that is why it is called a democracy."

In this same oration, Pericles said:

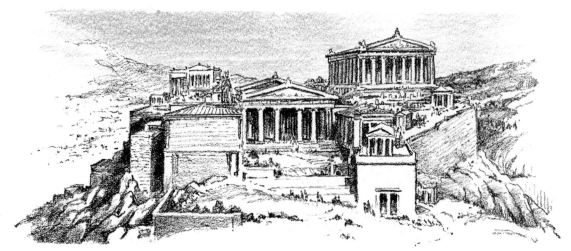

Ancient Athens

If we look to the laws, they afford equal justice to all . . . ; advancement in public life falls to reputation for capacity, class consideration not being allowed to interfere with merit; nor again does poverty bar the way. . . .

From reading of the life of Socrates, the colonists learned that this greatest of Greek philosophers insisted that virtue is knowledge and that nothing must be allowed to stop men from searching for knowledge. They studied the writings of the idealistic Plato and of the more practical and scientific Aristotle. The colonists doubtless agreed with both these Greek philosophers that governments must be founded on right and justice. But since the Americans were ardent believers in the rights of the individual, many of them must have been skeptical about Plato's and Aristotle's conviction that a man was important only as part of his city-state.

The colonists seemed to prefer the teachings of the Epicurean and Stoic schools of philosophy that came later. These teachings had spread throughout the Roman world, and many Americans admired the writings that came from both

of these schools of thought in the great days of Rome. They emphasized man's importance as an individual rather than as a member of the community. The Stoics became especially famous for their belief that there exists a universal law, based on reason, that applies to all human beings (see NATURAL LAW).

In pre-Revolutionary times, the American leaders often drew upon their knowledge of Greek and Roman literature when they denounced the restrictive measures placed on the colonies by the English government. They quoted Thucydides, for example, to prove that the people in the Greek colonies had the same rights and freedoms as those in the homeland. And when all appeals for their rights failed the colonists, they turned to the theory of natural law to justify their Declaration of Independence.

Though the greatest part of the political philosophy of the men who founded the United States was based on the ideas of their English ancestors, their belief in man's right to freedom certainly was also shaped by their study of the ancient classics.

"Habeas Corpus," Writ of, is a court order directing that a person who has been detained or imprisoned be brought before a judge who will decide if the detention is legally justified. The prisoner, or a friend or lawyer acting in his behalf, may apply to a judge for such a writ. The judge then directs the jailer or the sheriff or some other person who may be holding the prisoner in custody to bring him before the court at a specified time. Should the judge decide the prisoner has been detained without sufficient reason, he is released at once.

The writ usually is issued on behalf of a prisoner in jail. On occasion the right of *habeas corpus* has been invoked to bring before a judge a person being held in a mental hospital.

Literally, the Latin words *habeas corpus* mean, "You have the body." From the time this "great writ of personal liberty" became a part of the English law in the 1600's, its purpose has been to protect individuals from unlawful imprisonment. More than two centuries later, what Americans consider one of their basic freedoms was guaranteed to them in Article I, Section 9, of the Constitution:

"The privilege of the writ of *habeas corpus* shall not be suspended, unless when in cases of rebellion or invasion the public safety may require it."

How speedily a prisoner may benefit from a writ of *habeas corpus* depends on individual and local circumstances. In spite of occasional delays, it remains—as Winston Churchill, great English statesman and honorary American citizen, once said—the crucial distinction between civilization and tyranny.

Hamilton, Alexander (1755?–1804), one of the most brilliant of Americans, was also one of the most contradictory. In contrast to Thomas Jefferson, the Virginia aristocrat with whom he disagreed on theories of government, Hamilton had been a poor boy, born in the West Indies. Yet it was Jefferson who believed in the ability of average men to govern themselves, whereas Hamilton once called the people "the great beast." Though he had no faith in democracy, he helped to give us a government strong enough to make it possible for Americans to enjoy the benefits of democracy today.

Even as a youth, Hamilton had shown unusual ability, and friends helped him to come to the colonies, where he attended King's College (now Columbia University). During the American Revolution, he acted as General Washington's secretary, with the rank of lieutenant colonel. After the war he studied law and became a successful lawyer in New York City. In 1786 he represented his state at the Annapolis (Md.) Convention which had been called to discuss certain interstate commercial problems. The meetings accomplished little except for Hamilton's suggestion that another convention be held to consider ways of making the federal government more efficient. This suggestion was endorsed by the Continental Congress, which issued a call to the thirteen states to send delegates to a federal convention in Philadelphia the following May (1787).

Twelve of the thirteen states responded to the call and sent delegates. Their instructions from the Continental Congress were to revise the Articles of Confederation which had served as the central government since 1781. Alexander Hamilton, one of the three men representing New York, was among those who realized that the new nation was in difficulty because the central government was too weak. He brushed aside the objections of the more timid delegates, who felt that to do more than amend the old Articles of Confederation would be exceeding their authority.

"The great question is," he said, "what provision shall we make for the happiness of our country?"

After more than three months of discussion, the convention adopted an entirely new Constitution. It did not provide for the strong central government, controlled by men of wealth and aristocratic background, that Alexander Hamilton had advocated, but he feared there might be anarchy in the country if the Constitution were rejected. It still had to be ratified by nine states, and no one worked harder to bring this about. As coauthor of *The Federalist*, a series of remarkable newspaper essays, later published in book form, he helped to win support for the new plan.

As the first Secretary of the Treasury, after the Constitution went into effect, Hamilton worked out a system of taxation that enabled the nation to pay its debts and meet the expenses of government, thus restoring confidence in the government, both at home and abroad. Though he and Jefferson were political enemies, Hamilton supported Jefferson in the disputed election of 1800, when both Jefferson and Aaron Burr were candidates for the Presidency. Several years later, Burr, whom Hamilton distrusted and suspected of treachery, challenged his adversary to a duel in which Hamilton was killed.

See CONSTITUTIONAL CONVENTION.

Hancock, John (1737–93), as president of the Second Continental Congress, was the first member to sign the Declaration of Independence (1776). "There, King George can read that without his spectacles," he said, after writing his name in letters twice the usual size. Since that time the words "John Hancock" have come to mean a signature, especially one that is large and legible. In the events leading to the American Revolution, Hancock, a wealthy young Boston businessman, and his friend Sam Adams, had been among the leading

U.S. Treasury

agitators in Massachusetts opposing British policies.

Henry, Patrick (1736–99), who was called "the Voice of the American Revolution," is best remembered for two speeches. The first was an eloquent appeal to the Virginia House of Burgesses, shortly after he had been elected as a delegate, urging the other members to oppose the Stamp Act (1765). He suggested that a series of resolutions be sent to Parliament, asserting the right of the colonies to make their own laws. Some of the older Burgesses, still loyal to the English king, were shocked, but Patrick Henry shouted them down.

"Caesar had his Brutus, Charles the First his Cromwell, and George the Third—"

At this point, Henry was interrupted by cries of "Treason!" After a brief pause he continued.

"George the Third," he said, "may profit by their example. If this be treason, make the most of it."

The second speech most often quoted was delivered in Richmond, Va., ten years later. Failure to resolve the difficulties with the government of the mother country had convinced Henry that war was inevitable, and he pleaded with his fellow Virginians to arm themselves for the coming struggle:

If we wish to be free . . . we must fight! . . . Is life so dear or peace so sweet, as to be purchased at the price of chains and slavery? Forbid it, Almighty God! I know not what course others may take, but as for me give me liberty or give me death.

From that day forward, Henry was influential in persuading, not only Virginians, but many other Americans that they must take drastic steps to protect their liberty. He was a member of the Continental Congress (1774–76) and of the Virginia Convention that adopted a new state constitution (1776). He was elected governor several different times, serving his state, and serving it well, during a trying period of its history.

After the United States won its independence, Patrick Henry disagreed with some of his old friends about the merits of the new Constitution adopted in 1787. When it was presented to the various states for approval, he called forth all his old eloquence to argue against its ratification by the Virginia Convention. He feared that the rights of the states had not been sufficiently protected; but when the new plan of government became the supreme law of the land he agreed to support it.

Then began a vigorous campaign to have the Constitution amended, "so as to be compatible," Patrick Henry said, "with the safety, liberty, and happiness of the people." On behalf of Virginia, he wrote a series of resolutions addressed to the first Congress elected under the new government, urging the passage of the Amendments we now call the Bill of Rights.

Holmes, Oliver Wendell, Jr. (1841–1935), son of the celebrated New England poet of the same name, has been called the greatest Supreme Court Justice since John Marshall. After his appointment (1902) as an associate justice, he became known as "the Great Dissenter." The decisions of the Supreme Court are based on the opinions of the majority of the justices, but the minority—the justices who disagree—have the privilege of writing a dissent, setting forth their reasons. Holmes's dissents were so logical and eloquently stated that they helped to shape history. Time proved him right so often that future lawmakers remembered his decisions in the making of future laws.

Oliver Wendell Holmes served his country for more than seventy years. As a young man he joined the Union Army during the Civil War, was wounded three times, and rose to the rank of captain. After he was mustered out, he studied law at the Harvard Law School and later returned there to teach. By the time Holmes was forty, he had written a book, *The Common Law*, that was to become a legal classic. The law, Holmes maintained, reflected man's experiences through the centuries and must continue to meet "the felt necessities of the time." As an associate justice of the U.S. Supreme Court (1902–32) he gave further expression to this theory by approving social legislation that to some of his contemporaries seemed rather far advanced.

In one case (Lochner *v.* New York, 1905), Joseph Lochner, owner of a Utica, N.Y. bakery, had broken a New York State law which forbade bakery employees to work more than ten hours a day. The law had been passed as a health protection measure. But when Lochner's appeal reached the Supreme Court, his attorney argued that the bakery owner had been denied "equal protection of the laws," guaranteed by the Fourteenth Amendment. The majority of the Court decided the law was a "meddlesome interference" with the right of contract, or the right of an employer to make whatever kind of contract he wished with the persons who worked for him. Justice Holmes dissented. He agreed with the lawmakers who had felt the health of the bakers must be protected. Though a law might seem "novel and even shocking" [to some people], he said, that did not mean it was unconstitutional. His minority opinion read:

This case is decided upon an economic theory which a large part of the country does not entertain . . . . But a constitution is not intended to embody a particular economic theory . . . . It is made for people of fundamentally differing views.

A good law, thought Holmes, was one that would help the people, and he held to this view throughout his long years of

Supreme Court Building about 1910

service on the Supreme Court bench. When he retired at the age of ninety, the nation was in the midst of the depression.

The following year (1933) a new President, Franklin D. Roosevelt, called on him to pay his respects. "Justice Holmes," he said, according to the witnesses who were present, "you have lived through half of our country's history; you have seen its great men. This is a dark hour. What is your advice to me?"

In that moment the older man's thoughts must have gone back sixty-eight years to his experiences as a soldier. "You are in a war, Mr. President. I was in a war, too," he said. "And in a war there is only one rule: *Form your battalions and fight.*"

When Justice Holmes died two years later, he left his entire estate to the U.S. government. "Clearly he sought with a generous emphasis," said President Roosevelt, "to mark the full measure of his faith in those principles of freedom which the country was founded to preserve."

Hooker, Thomas (1586?–1647), was an early New England clergyman, some of whose beliefs were far in advance of his time. After his arrival from England to preach in Newtown (now Cambridge), Mass., he did not hesitate to condemn the Puritan practice of allowing only church members to vote. His congregation was impressed by his democratic ideas, and most of the members joined him in a mass migration (1636) into the fertile Connecticut valley, where they founded the town of Hartford.

Soon other settlements were started in the Connecticut valley by people who had been dissatisfied in England or in Massachusetts. Representatives from three of the towns worked out a joint plan of government called the Fundamental Orders, based on principles advocated in a sermon by the Reverend Mr. Hooker. Under this constitution—believed to have been the first written one in history—the people of Connecticut enjoyed a greater degree of freedom than did many of the other colonists. Though the governor was required to be a member "of an accepted congregation," there was no religious qualification for voting, as there had been in Puritan Massachusetts. The Fundamental Orders established the principle, important to the development of American democracy, that a government should be responsible to the people it governs.

"The foundation of authority," said Thomas Hooker, "is laid, firstly, in the free consent of the people."

Hughes, Charles Evans (1862–1948), served first as an associate justice of the Supreme Court (1910–16), resigned to be the Republican candidate for President, was defeated, and fourteen years later was appointed Chief Justice of the United States. In spite of his earlier record as a reform governor of New York State (1906–10), many Americans believed him to be more interested in property rights than in human rights. During his term as Chief Justice (1930–41), he surprised these people with decisions that consistently supported measures insuring civil liberties.

Hughes was especially alert to any evidence of racial discrimination in the courts. The Scottsboro Case, which reached the Supreme Court in 1932, concerned nine Negro youths—one only thirteen—who under torture had confessed to a crime of which they later declared they were innocent. To use such confessions as a basis for conviction and sentencing, in the opinion of the Chief Justice, was clearly a denial of due process of law.

"The rack and torture chamber may not be substituted for the witness stand . . .," he said angrily. "It would be difficult to conceive of methods more revolting to the sense of justice."

At a ceremony (Feb. 1, 1940), observing the 150th anniversary of the first session of the Supreme Court, Charles Evans Hughes was the principal speaker. There must be justice, he said, not only between man and man, but between government and citizens, in order to realize democracy's "promise of liberty and human betterment."

Huguenots. Perhaps no followers of any religious faith were ever more cruelly persecuted than were the French Protestants known as Huguenots. Consequently, thousands of them fled from France during the 1600's. Many settled in America where their descendants—including Paul Revere and General Francis Marion, who fought the enemy in the Carolina swamps —played an important part in winning freedom for the colonies. Today, in a number of the states, societies have been formed, made up of men and women who proudly claim a Huguenot among their ancestors.

"Unlike many others who were persecuted," said the president of one of these societies, "the Huguenots believed in freedom of religion for everyone, not just themselves. The Huguenots gave us the true spirit of democracy."

Hutchinson, Anne Marbury (1591–1643), a fearless and brilliant resident of the Massachusetts Bay Colony, dared to speak out against the Puritan leaders who demanded strict obedience in both religious and civil matters. It was Mrs. Hutchinson's custom to hold weekly prayer meetings for women, at which she preached against some of the prevailing teachings of the established clergy. The specific points on which they disagreed seem less important today than her insistence on every person's right to his own faith. Because she challenged the right of those in authority to regulate religious matters, she may be considered one of the early pioneers in establishing the American principle of separation of church and state.

As a result of her activities, Anne Hutchinson was brought to trial before the Massachusetts General Court which branded her "a leper" and ordered her to leave Massachusetts. With her family and several friends, she found refuge for a while on an island near Providence, the town recently founded by Roger Williams in the present state of Rhode Island. Today a statue of her with one of her children stands outside the State House in Boston, the capital of Massachusetts—the same Massachusetts from which she had been banished while it was still a colony. On the base of the statue is an inscription that reads: *A courageous exponent of civil liberty and religious toleration.*

tendent of finance. He did more than any other one person to raise the money needed to keep an army in the field.

Toward the end of the war, Morris had the help of Haym Salomon, a patriotic Polish Jew. Salomon, having failed to find liberty in Poland, was eager to show his gratitude to his adopted country. After becoming a successful broker in Philadelphia, he used his personal credit to negotiate loans for the rather shaky government of the new United States. He lent money, without interest, to members of the Continental Congress and army officers who otherwise could not have afforded to serve. Before he died, his fortune had been spent on behalf of "the cause," as he always referred to the American struggle.

After the United States gained its independence, many people in Europe began to realize the significance of what had happened. The new republic, founded on the principles that "all men are created equal" and that governments "derive their powers from the consent of the governed" offered the victims of political persecution fresh hope. Others, like some of the earlier settlers, came to America in search of religious liberty; still others came to find release from the poverty that had been their lot in their old homelands. The desire for freedom and the opportunity to better their economic condition brought more than forty-two million immigrants to the United States during the first century and a quarter after it took its place among the nations of the world.

In the beginning, the majority of newcomers were from western and northern Europe. They were a part of what has been called the "old immigration." The "new immigration" took place in the latter years of the 1800's, when the majority of those who came were from southern and eastern Europe, as well as from the Orient. They helped to man the factories, mine the coal, build the railroads, and settle the vast empty spaces in the West.

Immigration. Most of the early settlers in what is now the United States were English, but a variety of nationalities have had a part in the making of America. Even in Jamestown, Va., the first permanent settlement, there were Polish and German workmen. When the Dutch colony of New Amsterdam surrendered to the English (1664) there were, in addition to the Dutch, seventeen other nationalities living there. Swedes and Finns had settled in Delaware, and dissatisfied people from Scotland and Ireland, Germany and France, soon began crossing the Atlantic in increasing numbers. Their descendants, and also many recent arrivals, fought side by side with soldiers of English descent in the American Revolution. Together they won independence for the new nation called the United States.

It has been estimated that just one country—Ireland—furnished one third of the men who served under General George Washington. Scots and Germans, also, were among his sturdiest fighters. Eight signers of the Declaration of Independence were not native born. One of the signers— Robert Morris, a wealthy Philadelphia businessman who had emigrated from England as a youth—was appointed superin-

Among the immigrants who sought freedom in America, and then worked to give it to others, were Carl Schurz and Samuel Gompers (see separate entries). The English-born Anna Howard Shaw, a leading suffragette, helped to gain equal rights for women. Edward Corsi from Italy, who was appointed Commissioner of Immigration (1931), helped many immigrants adjust to conditions in what to them seemed a strange new world. Another Italian-born immigrant, Constantino Brumidi, spent the last thirty years of his life covering the walls of the Capitol in Washington, D.C., with paintings that depicted American scenes.

"My one ambition and my daily prayer," he said, "is that I may live long enough to make beautiful the Capitol of the one Country in the World in which there is liberty."

Not all immigrants were as fortunate as Brumidi. Many of them, especially those who belonged to the "new immigration," did not find the liberty they craved or the opportunities for which they had hoped. By the end of the century there were fewer empty spaces in the West to be developed, and industry could no longer absorb so many new workers. Organized labor resented them, because they were satisfied with smaller wages than labor unions demanded for their members.

Also, some well-intentioned Americans feared it would be impossible for so many thousands of foreign-born people to learn American ways. Language was a great barrier. Many of the more recent immigrants did not understand English; some could neither read nor write in any language. As a result of the general feeling of concern, during the 1920's Congress passed several laws limiting immigration.

The National Origins quota system (1929) specified that the number of people to be admitted from any one nation in any one year was to be decided on a percentage basis, according to the number of people of their nationality who had been living in the United States in 1920. This law favored the countries of western and northern Europe, which seldom used up their quotas. It discriminated against the peoples of southern and eastern Europe, the Middle East, Asia, and Africa. For that reason many Americans insisted that the quota system violated the fundamental principles of democracy. Several Presidents favored the repeal of this law, not only because it was unjust but also because it was not efficient.

After World War II, thousands of victims of Nazi, Fascist, and Communist tyranny were left homeless. Some of the displaced persons, or "D.P.'s," were children whose parents had been killed, or men and women anxious to be reunited

with relatives in America. A number of well-known scientists and other persons of special talent also applied for admission. In order to prevent injustice, and to bring to America men and women who would have much to offer their adopted country, Congress frequently found it necessary to pass special laws applying to specific cases. In a message to Congress (Jan., 1965) President Lyndon B. Johnson urged that the nation return to an immigration policy that would both serve the national interest and continue traditional ideals.

"No move," he said, "could more effectively reaffirm our fundamental belief that a man is to be judged—and judged exclusively—on his worth as a human being."

The immigration bill that Congress enacted the following June did not change the overall number of immigrants who could be admitted to the United States. But it abolished the quota system, which had been the cause of much injustice and hardship, and the President signed the bill (Oct. 3, 1965) in a ceremony in New York City at the foot of the Statue of Liberty. He pointed out that those who had come in the past "to make a home for freedom" had come from many places, and the nation had been nourished by many cultures brought here by many peoples. The new law, he said, would make it possible for those who wished to emigrate to America to be admitted on the basis of their skills and their close relationship to those already here.

"This is a simple test," he went on. "It is a fair test. Those who can contribute most to this country—to its growth and strength and spirit—will be the first to be admitted to our land."

See also GOMPERS, SAMUEL; SCHURZ, CARL.

Independence Day (July 4) is celebrated as the birthday of the United States in commemoration of that day in 1776 when

the Declaration of Independence was adopted by the Continental Congress. The first anniversary (1777) was observed throughout the new nation with parades, the ringing of bells, fireworks, the firing of guns, and illuminations.

"Thus may the Fourth of July, that glorious and ever memorable day," wrote one Philadelphia editor, "be celebrated throughout America by the sons of freedom from age to age, till time shall be no more."

The name, "the glorious Fourth," appealed to the public, as did the custom of celebrating with fireworks. These caused so many accidents that thoughtful citizens finally began to promote the idea of a "safe and sane Fourth," and the sale of fireworks is now forbidden in many places. Instead, many towns have large community celebrations with elaborate displays of fireworks set off under careful supervision.

It is one of the coincidences of history

that Thomas Jefferson, author of the Declaration of Independence, and John Adams, the champion who was probably most responsible for its adoption, should both have died on July 4, 1826, the fiftieth anniversary of the nation's birth. The two former Presidents, one eighty-three years old, the other ninety, had been invited to attend a jubilee celebration in Washington, D.C., but both declined because of failing health. Jefferson's letter of regret, composed ten days before his death, affirmed again his faith in the triumph of liberty.

"All eyes are opened or opening to the rights of man ...," he wrote. "Let the annual return of this day forever refresh our recollection of these rights and an undiminished devotion to them."

Independence Hall. This famous red brick building, now a museum and part of the Independence National Historical Park in Philadelphia, was the State House for the colony of Pennsylvania when the Second Continental Congress met there in 1775. It also was the meeting place for the Constitutional Convention that adopted the U.S. Constitution (1787). Though the Assembly Room where the Declaration of Independence had been signed was often referred to as the Hall of Independence, it was not until 1852 that the building was officially renamed Independence Hall.

See LIBERTY BELL.

Indians, American. The discovery of America and the westward movement across the continent meant increased opportunities for the white newcomers, but loss of freedom for many Indians.

Though some of the early settlers took what land they wanted from the red men living near the Atlantic seaboard, there were others like Roger Williams and William Penn who paid the Indians a fair price and won their friendship. After the United States became independent, and

more and more settlers wanted to go farther west to live, the new government entered into treaties with a number of Indian tribes. According to these treaties, the red men agreed to give up certain areas and move elsewhere.

Sometimes the treaties were fair, sometimes not; sometimes they were kept, but sometimes they weren't. The chief underlying cause, though, of the disastrous wars that took place between the native Americans and those whose ancestors had come from Europe was that the two races held entirely different views about property. No individual Indian owned land. To the red men, the land was a gift from the Great Spirit, to be shared by all their people. Sometimes the Indians who agreed to a treaty did not realize they were giving up permanent possession of their hunting grounds. If they did realize and refused to make a treaty, the land might be taken from them by force.

This was what happened in the southeastern part of the United States, which had long been the home of the Five Civilized Tribes (so-called because of the high degree of civilization they enjoyed). By the 1830's most of these Indians had been subdued by the U.S. Army.

Most distressing of all, perhaps, was the plight of the Cherokees, one of the Five Tribes. When they learned they were to be moved to a land called "Indian country," west of the Mississippi River, they knew it was hopeless to resist, but the leaders of the tribe addressed a protest to the U.S. Senate. Their petition stated that all "were children of the same Great Parent ... bound to be kind to each other."

But their plea not to be driven from their homes was ignored. More than 15,000 Cherokees, most of them on foot, were escorted by U.S. troops (1838) over the "Trail of Tears" to the "Land of the Red Man" (Oklahoma). The tribe was promised that this land should be theirs "as long as grass shall grow and rivers run,"

but in time Oklahoma was also opened (1889) to white settlers.

To the native red men it seemed that the white men's desire for land would never be satisfied. As the settlers continued their relentless march westward across the continent, some of the tribes put up a fierce resistance. They were often cruel, but so were some of the U.S. soldiers sent to subdue them. The Indians of the Great Plains depended on the herds of buffalo to provide them with food and clothing. With the coming of so many white hunters and settlers, the buffalo were being killed off. The future looked dark and, when a band of red men swooped down on a lonely farmhouse and massacred the victims, they hoped, by doing this, to frighten other settlers into leaving. The Indians reasoned that if they did not kill the white invaders, the invaders would kill them, their women, and their children—something that happened too often.

After years of warfare, the tribes that had continued to hold out against the white men were defeated and sent to live on reservations. In the beginning they were not permitted to leave these large tracts of land which the government had set aside for their use—a ruling that a people accustomed to wander over large areas to fish and hunt found hard to obey. They had an eloquent spokesman in Chief Joseph, a great warrior of the Nez Percé tribe, who was granted permission to make the long trip across the continent to the nation's capital. In Washington, D.C., where he talked with the President, he made a plea for justice for his people, and President Rutherford B. Hayes was deeply moved.

"Many, if not all of our Indian wars," he admitted, "have had their origin in broken promises . . . on our part."

Later Chief Joseph wrote a magazine article in which he summed up his ideas of equality and brotherhood. All men were brothers, he said. The earth was the mother of all people, and therefore all people should have equal rights upon it. Many white Americans agreed and wanted to atone for past wrongs. Teachers, missionaries, doctors, and other private citizens went among the Indian tribes trying to help them. Government officials also became more interested in solving the problems of the first Americans.

In 1924 citizenship was extended to all Indians born in the United States. An Indian Claims Commission was established (1946) to review cases of tribes whose members felt their ancestors had been underpaid and unjustly treated when they turned their land over to the federal government. Efforts to improve the health of the Indian people have brought encouraging results, and a race that once seemed in danger of dying out has increased.

Some Indians have been more fortunate than others. Many of the descendants of the Cherokees who once walked the "Trail of Tears" to Oklahoma discovered oil on their reservations, making it possible for their children to enjoy advantages most Indian boys and girls have never known. In other states where Indians live, many are still quite poor. When President Lyndon B. Johnson announced his antipoverty program (1964) he said he wanted Indians to be given special consideration, "because they had suffered more from poverty than any other group."

Among the first to benefit have been Indian children of preschool age whose advantages had been so limited that they needed special training to be ready for the first grade. Like thousands of other children throughout the nation, many Indian boys and girls have been enrolled in Project Head Start centers. Here special teachers help to give them "a head start" in preparation for more useful years ahead. By the time these youngsters are grown, it is hoped they will be able to share equally with other Americans in the benefits of freedom.

Freedom is part of the Indians' heritage, and within their own tribes they have usually been very democratic. The meaning of equality was summed up years ago by Hiamovi, a wise Cheyenne chief, in these words:

There are birds of many colors—red, blue, green, yellow—yet all one bird. There are horses of many colors—brown, black, yellow, white—yet all one horse. So cattle; so all living things—animals, flowers, trees. So men in this land where once were only Indians are now men of every color—white, black, yellow, red—yet all one people.

Jackson, Andrew (1767–1845), the seventh President, was the first chief executive from the part of the country then called "the West." This successful Tennessee lawyer and military hero, unlike the earlier Presidents who had grown up in comfortable homes near the Atlantic seaboard, had spent his youth in a log cabin on the frontier. The fact that he had overcome poverty and hardship and now lived in a fine house was the kind of success story many Americans admired. His courage in fighting the Indians and his defense of New Orleans in the final battle of the War of 1812 only added to his popularity.

General Jackson was extravagantly admired, not only by Westerners but by the plain people of the East, including many shopkeepers, mechanics, and owners of small farms. They called him "a man of the people," and they believed he understood their problems.

His first inauguration as President (Mar., 1829) was not like that of any of his predecessors. At a reception held in the White House, frontiersmen wearing ill-fitting homespun clothes and coonskin caps mingled with fashionable ladies and gentlemen. There were probably many raised eyebrows that day, but the tall, gaunt President, a man of courtly manners in spite of his reputation as a backwoods fighter, made everyone feel welcome.

The next few years were a stormy period in American history. Always a fighter, Andrew Jackson never hesitated to oppose anything he considered wrong. Large sums of government money were on deposit in the U.S. Bank, an institution privately owned, which some years earlier had received a charter from Congress permitting it to carry on business. In 1836 the Congress voted to renew the charter, but when the bill was sent to the President for his signature he refused to sign. The directors of the bank had been charged with using the money collected from the people's taxes to further their own interests. In making loans and extending credit, they often ignored the applications of men of moderate means and gave preference to men of wealth. When the President vetoed the bill, he returned it to Congress with the explanation that he was opposed "to the advancement of the few at the expense of the many."

It was to be regretted, he went on, when the rich and powerful tried to make themselves even richer by an act of Congress. The humble members of society, who had neither the time nor the means of securing like favors for themselves, had a right to complain. "It is time to pause . . .," the President said, "to review our principles and, if possible, revive that devoted patriotism which distinguished . . . the fathers of our Union."

The voters of the nation went to the polls that November and in overwhelming numbers registered their approval of the President's policies. During his second term he continued to try to help the people —at least, the white people. The Indians did not fare so well. Many of those who lived in the southeastern part of the United States were forcibly removed from their old homes and settled in a new location west of the Mississippi River. The land left vacant by their removal was then sold by the government at a fair price to white settlers.

Andrew Jackson was a man of contradictions. He could be both gruff and kind, strongwilled and gentle. Because of his imperious ways, his enemies called him "King Andrew." His admirers, who far outnumbered his detractors, preferred the nickname "Old Hickory." To the frontiersmen who lived in log cabins and to the eastern factory workers who knew how it felt to be poor, Andrew Jackson became a symbol of what they, too, hoped to accomplish.

"Let the people rule!" was the slogan of the men who had rallied around him at election time, and for some of them the slogan came true. President Jackson gave positions in the federal government to many plain and humble men who had never had such opportunities before.

Andrew Jackson was responsible for a new spirit in American politics, which has been called "Jacksonian democracy."

Jefferson, Thomas (1743–1826). *I have sworn upon the altar of God, eternal hostility against every form of tyranny over the mind of man,* one of the Virginia patriot's best-known sayings, is carved on the marble walls of the handsome Jefferson Memorial in Washington, D.C. The words first appeared in a letter dated 1800, but the man who wrote them had dedicated himself to the cause of liberty a third of a century earlier.

As a student at William and Mary College in Williamsburg, Va., young Tom Jefferson read the works of the great English and French philosophers who advocated more freedom for the individual. Later, while studying law in Williamsburg, he often attended the sessions of the House of Burgesses and was present (1765) when Patrick Henry made his impassioned plea to resist the Stamp Act. After Jefferson's own election to the House of Burgesses (1769) he consistently opposed what he considered other oppressive measures passed by the British Parliament. In a pamphlet published in 1774, Jefferson claimed that Parliament had no legal right to interfere with the internal affairs of the colonies.

"Let no act be passed by any one legislature," he wrote, "which may infringe on the rights and liberties of another. ... The God who gave us life gave us liberty at the same time."

This pamphlet, *A Summary View of the Rights of British America,* established

Jefferson Memorial

Jefferson's reputation as a writer. After his election to the Second Continental Congress, he was appointed to a committee to draft a Declaration of Independence, the great document that was to bring him even greater fame. A few weeks later he resigned from the Congress to reenter the Virginia legislature, in the hope of making his own state more democratic. Here he worked—sometimes successfully, sometimes not—for the passage of new laws more consistent with the ideals he had expressed so eloquently.

After the United States won its independence, Jefferson again served in the Continental Congress (1783–1785), and then as U.S. ambassador to France (1785–1789). Here he saw how much misery a corrupt government could cause, and he had a close-up view of the conditions that were to lead to the French Revolution. "How little do my countrymen know what precious blessings they are in possession of," he wrote to a friend in America, "and which no other people on earth enjoy."

Jefferson was dismayed, though, when he returned to the United States (Oct., 1789) and saw the changes that had taken place in his absence. Some of the most influential citizens had come to feel that only aristocrats should have a voice in the government, but Jefferson condemned what he called "an artificial aristocracy founded on wealth or birth." He preferred "a natural aristocracy," based on "virtue and talent."

However one chose to define the term, Jefferson himself was an aristocrat. He was the owner of a large plantation, one of the most learned men of his time, and the descendant of a prominent Virginia family. He had little personal contact with the masses of people in the country, yet he was both their hero and their champion. He was confident that with education they would be capable of self-government. As Secretary of State (1790–1793), as Vice President (1797–1801), and as President (1801–1809), he was concerned for the welfare of all Americans. The sole object of government, he maintained, was "the freedom and happiness of man."

At the end of his second term as President, Jefferson retired to Monticello, his beautiful home on a Virginia mountaintop near Charlottesville. Here the Sage of Monticello, as he was called, lived for another seventeen years. Much of his time was spent planning a new college, to be based, he said, "on the illimitable freedom of the human mind." The University of Virginia, which he founded, was the accomplishment of which he was most proud during his later years.

Those same years were troubled, though, by new threats to freedom in the increasing bitterness between North and South over the question of slavery. But Jefferson never lost faith in the ideals set forth in the Declaration of Independence.

"I shall not die," he wrote in a letter to his old friend John Adams, "without the hope that light and liberty are on a steady advance."

Johnson, Lyndon Baines (1908–   ), the thirty-sixth President, succeeded to his high office (Nov. 22, 1963) following the sudden and tragic death of John F. Kennedy. A native Texan, Lyndon Johnson had served in both houses of Congress, and proved himself a competent and astute politician, first as the minority leader (1953–55), and then the majority leader (1955–61) of the Senate, before his election to the Vice Presidency.

In his first address to Congress after he became President, he pledged himself to work for the passage of several bills which had been proposed by his predecessor—bills to bring a greater measure of freedom and opportunity to more Americans.

"This is our challenge," said the new President, "not to hesitate, not to pause, not to linger over this evil moment, but to

icans, regardless of race (see NEGRO RIGHTS MOVEMENT).

But Lyndon Johnson was a man with ideas of his own; and he summed up his hopes for the nation in three words, "the Great Society,"—the kind of society that could bring an end to poverty and injustice. In his State of the Union Message to Congress (Jan., 1964), he said:

For a century we labored to settle and subdue a continent. For half a century we called upon unbounded invention and untiring industry to create an order of plenty for all of our people. The challenge of the next half century is whether we have the wisdom to use that wealth to enrich and elevate our national life, and to advance the quality of our American civilization . . . . We have the opportunity to move, not only toward the rich society and the powerful society, but upward to the Great Society. The Great Society rests on abundance and liberty for all.

On the President's recommendation, Congress passed the Economic Opportunity Act, more often referred to as the Antipoverty Act. It established an Office of Economic Opportunity (OEO) which initiated programs to provide needy Americans with jobs or train them for work that would enable them to earn a decent living. The President had high hopes for this project, among others, as did the majority of the American people. When he ran for election in his own right, he was given the largest majority vote any President had ever received.

In spite of this overwhelming vote of confidence, the President's second term was marked by increasing difficulties. Chief among these were the deep concern and the divided opinions of the American people about the war in Vietnam. While Dwight D. Eisenhower was President, the American government had committed itself to help this small nation in southeast Asia resist Communist efforts to take over the country. In this endeavor the South Vietnamese Communists—the Viet Cong

continue on our course, so that we may fulfill the destiny that history has set for us."

The American people had been grateful for the calm and efficient manner in which Lyndon Johnson had assumed his new responsibilities in a time of crisis, and during the next few months they were amazed by his success with Congress. Several important bills, for which there had seemed small chance of success, were enacted into law.

The new measures included a Higher Education Facilities Act to give "all our youth the education they deserve," to quote President Johnson, and the Civil Rights Act of 1964, the purpose of which was to bring equal justice to all Amer-

—had the aid of North Vietnam, the Communist neighbor to the north. President Kennedy had honored this commitment of the U.S. government, and under President Johnson the efforts to help Vietnam maintain its freedom and independence were greatly expanded.

This war was not of President Johnson's making, but many Americans blamed him and his advisers for its escalation. Many others approved of the decisions that had sent thousands of members of the armed forces into Vietnam.

The President said:

To defend freedom, to permit its roots to deepen and grow without fear of external suppression—is our purpose in Vietnam. Unchecked aggression against free and helpless people would be a grave threat to our own freedom— and an offense to our own conscience . . . . Peace for the people of Vietnam is the purpose of our presence there, our only purpose.

The military struggle did not tell the whole story. According to the Declaration of Honolulu, signed by President Johnson and the president of South Vietnam (Feb., 1966), the United States agreed to continue to aid the Vietnamese by efforts to improve the health of the people, to increase food production, and provide educational opportunities—in short, to aid "the people of that country even while they fight."

The expense of the escalation of the war threatened the antipoverty program at home, but Lyndon Johnson insisted that the United States was affluent enough to afford both. It was his conviction, as he had said in his Inaugural Address (1965), that in a nation conceived in justice, all its citizens must "share in the fruits of the land." In a land of wealth, families must not live in hopeless poverty or children go hungry. Neighbors must not suffer and die unattended for lack of medical help; children must be taught to read and write. The nation would succeed, "not because of

what we have but what we are; not because of what we own but what we believe. . . ."

"We believe," he said, "that every man must someday be free."

Jury Trial. The right to trial by jury is an important part of "due process of law" guaranteed by the U.S. Constitution. Article III applies to criminal cases, as does Amendment 6 which states: "The accused shall enjoy the right to a speedy and public trial by an impartial jury. . . ." Amendment 7 provides that the right of a jury trial shall be preserved in "suits at common law where the value in controversy shall exceed twenty dollars." This amendment makes it possible for one person who is suing another for more than twenty dollars to ask that a jury decide the case.

In a criminal case, where the crime is of a capital or infamous nature, the accused person may not be brought to trial unless he is first indicted by a grand jury (Amendment 5). A grand jury in closed session must decide, on the basis of facts presented, if there is sufficient evidence against the accused (who is not necessarily present) to warrant bringing him to trial. If a grand jury finds enough evidence of guilt, it brings in an indictment, a formal, written charge.

A person indicted is tried in open court by a *petit* jury, which listens to evidence presented by witnesses and to arguments by the lawyers for the prosecution and for the defense. On the basis of facts presented, the jurors try to render a fair verdict of "Guilty" or "Not guilty." Every effort is made to protect the rights of the accused by choosing jurors who are not prejudiced and who have not formed an opinion before hearing all the evidence presented in the courtroom.

An accused person is presumed innocent until proven guilty. One who pleads

"Guilty," instead of having a jury trial, may ask the presiding judge in the trial to decide if he is to be sentenced and what the sentence is to be. But because of the safeguards provided the accused by the jury system, it remains one of the most prized of American rights. It is an attempt to provide a fair trial, so that no citizen may be deprived of freedom without just cause. For that reason, trial by jury has been called the palladium, or safeguard, of American liberty.

For the right of trial by jury, Americans are indebted to England. This system was substituted long ago for the barbaric and superstitious methods once used to determine the innocence or guilt of a person accused of a crime.

Kennedy, John Fitzgerald (1917–63). Few people who witnessed the inauguration of John F. Kennedy (Jan. 20, 1961), the youngest man ever to be elected President, will forget the speech he made that day. There had been a blizzard in Washington the night before, but the President seemed oblivious of the cold wind that whipped across the Capitol plaza. His voice was confident, as he spoke of his ideals for the nation he had been chosen to lead:

In the long history of the world, only a few generations have been granted the role of defending freedom in its hour of maximum danger. I do not shrink from this responsibility —I welcome it. I do not believe that any of us would exchange places with any other people, or any other generation. The energy, the faith, the devotion which we bring to this endeavor will light our country and all who serve it—and the glow from the fire can truly light the world.

Not all that needed to be done, the President pointed out, could be accomplished in a hundred days—nor even in a thousand days—but a beginning could be made. As it turned out, his beginning was his triumph. The thousand days John Kennedy had mentioned—and a few additional ones—were all that he had left before his life was brought to an abrupt close by assassination. That was not enough time to realize his plans for bringing a fuller measure of freedom and opportunity to many of his fellow Americans, but a number of his ideas—including a Civil Rights bill and bills to fight poverty and give aid to education—were carried out by his successor, President Lyndon B. Johnson.

Kennedy's most urgent problems during his short term as the thirty-fifth President of the United States concerned foreign affairs. To him peace and freedom were indivisible; without one, the other could not survive and to maintain them required firmness and courage. It was this conviction that prompted his determined and immediate action in the Cuban missile crisis (Oct., 1962).

Aerial photographs taken from American planes had revealed a massive build-up of Soviet military equipment on the Communist island of Cuba just ninety miles off the coast of Florida. Missile bases were under construction, supervised by Russian technicians. Jet bombers capable of carrying nuclear weapons that might bring destruction to a number of American cities were being assembled. The President ordered a naval blockade of Cuba, with instructions that any ship bound for the island with a cargo of offensive weapons was to be stopped. At the risk of nuclear war, he demanded that the Soviet Union withdraw its missiles and dismantle its bases—and the Soviet government complied.

The following year John F. Kennedy completed negotiations for a test-ban treaty between the two nations. According to this treaty, signed by American and Soviet officials (Aug., 1963), they agreed to a partial ban on the testing of nuclear weapons in the atmosphere. Such testing had imposed health hazards on millions of people, and the President also hoped that the treaty marked a first step toward permanent peace. He was proud that the

United States had been the nation to take that first step, and the test-ban treaty is usually considered the outstanding accomplishment of his administration.

Perhaps as great an achievement was his legacy of words, which many believe will continue for years to come to inspire Americans and others throughout the world who love liberty and justice. To John F. Kennedy freedom was not an abstract theory but "the most effective instrument for advancing the welfare of man." He had faith that "however serious the outlook, however harsh the task, the one great irreversible trend in the history of the world is on the side of liberty." The American goal, he declared, was "not the victory of might, but the vindication of right—not peace at the expense of freedom, but both peace and freedom ... around the world."

That was his ideal. That was his great hope.

In one speech (June, 1963), he said:

We are called to a great new mission, not a mission of self-defense alone—for that is a means, not an end. It is not a mission of arbitrary power—for we reject the idea of one nation dominating another. The mission is to create a new social order, founded on liberty and justice, in which men are the masters of their fate, in which states are the servants of their citizens, and in which all men and women can share a better life for themselves and their children.

King, Martin Luther, Jr. (1929–1968) was the youngest man ever to be awarded the Nobel Prize for peace.

The award was made in recognition of his peaceful leadership in the U.S. Negro Rights Movement. When he went to Oslo, Norway (Dec., 1964), to accept the prize, he said he considered it not a tribute to himself but to the many Negroes and white people who had supported him in his methods of passive resistance. It was Dr. King's belief that nonviolence was "the answer to the crucial political and moral question of our time—the need for man to overcome oppression and violence without resorting to violence and oppression."

Martin Luther King, Jr., following the example of his father, had decided to enter the ministry, and after attending college had received his Ph. D. degree from Boston University. He was serving as pastor in a Montgomery, Ala., Baptist church in 1955 when he was called on to lead the Montgomery bus strike. His success made him a national figure almost overnight and the unofficial leader of the Negro Rights Movement (see separate entry). To refuse to cooperate with injustice was in the American tradition, he said, and during the next ten years he led a number of marches and demonstrations in several Southern cities. He wanted to dramatize for the public the fact that many Negroes were being denied their constitutional rights.

In that same period Dr. King went to jail fifteen times, saw his church reduced to ashes, had his home rocked by a bomb, and lived constantly with the threat of death. Yet he never lost faith in his policy of passive resistance. He said:

> As a race, Negroes must work . . . unrelentingly for first-class citizenship . . . but they must never use second-class methods to get it. They must never succumb to the temptation to use violence in the struggle . . . . A piece of freedom is no longer enough for human beings nor for the nation of which Negroes are a part. They have been given pieces—but, unlike bread, a slice of liberty does not finish hunger. Freedom is like life. It cannot be had in installments. Freedom is indivisible—we have it all, or we are not free.

In the middle 1960's Dr. King turned his attention to the distress of Negroes living in the filthy ghettos of Northern cities. In the summer of 1966 he led a number of demonstrations in Chicago to arouse enthusiasm for an open-housing bill under consideration by the U.S. Congress. It was Dr. King's contention that white neighborhoods should be open to Negroes who could afford to buy or rent a home there. "Negroes hold only one key to the double lock of peaceful change," he said. "The other is in the hands of the white community."

Because of his stand on open housing, Dr. King was praised by some people and bitterly criticized by others. Public opinion also was divided when he denounced (1967) American participation in the war in Vietnam. Even many of his admirers, who themselves disapproved of the war, believed he was hurting the Negro cause.

On April 4, 1968, in Memphis, Tenn., Dr. King was killed by an assassin's bullet. In a speech the night before, referring to threats on his life, he said: "It really doesn't matter what happens now. I have been to the mountaintop. . . .'Mine eyes have seen the glory of the coming of the Lord.' "

Labor Movement. In the early days of the American republic, freedom, to the majority of Americans, meant political freedom, or the right to have a voice in their government. With the passing of time many of them came to feel that they could not benefit from political freedom unless they also had economic freedom. They demanded a certain degree of security, and it was this demand that strengthened what we call the labor movement.

Life was often hard when the nation was young, but it was simple and uncomplicated. Almost any ambitious and industrious family could own a farm. If there was no good, cheap land left in the settled part of the country, they could go farther west and start a farm in the wilderness. Except for Negro slaves, most men worked for themselves. Those who stayed in towns and cities usually made a living as owners or employees in small factories and shops. If the owner of a business found it necessary to hire others, he had personal knowledge of the men he employed. Employers and employees often worked side by side.

The situation changed after the invention of labor-saving machinery. By the time the United States celebrated the Centennial of the Declaration of Independence (1876), a number of new machines had been invented to do many tasks once done by hand. Machines, though more efficient, were expensive, and it was usually necessary for several employers to band together and form companies.

Sometimes the companies combined in even larger organizations called corporations, and shares were sold to people who had money to invest. The shareholders seldom saw the places where their money was invested and, like the directors and the manager who ran a business, they wanted to make a profit. The managers tried to keep the production costs as low as possible. Too often they accomplished this by paying starvation wages and demanding long working hours.

So it was the workers who suffered. Conditions in many industries were indescribably bad. Men, women, and even small children worked sixteen or eighteen hours a day in dirty, ill-ventilated, poorly lighted factories and mines. The money they earned was hardly enough to keep them and their families alive, but they seldom complained. Jobs were scarce and there were always other workers to take their places. More and more, working men and women came to realize that only by uniting could they bring about any improvements.

During the early 1800's a few trade unions had been formed by workers and craftsmen in the same or related lines of work. They established the principle of collective bargaining and, by standing together, hoped to be in a better position to secure decent wages, reasonable working hours, and improved working conditions. Though the unions met with some success, it was not until Samuel Gompers (see separate entry) organized the American Federation of Labor that the labor movement became really effective in the United States.

The A.F. of L., formed in 1886, was

not an organization of individual members, but a combination of craft unions, such as the electricians' union, the machinists' union, and other unions made up of workers in some special trade. This form of organization meant that employees in the same plant or factory might belong to a number of different unions, and unskilled laborers were usually not organized at all.

In order to extend the benefits of union membership to more workers, a committee of A.F. of L. members started the Congress of Industrial Organizations. It was open to all employees in the same industry, including unskilled workers. The two mammoth organizations finally combined to form the AFL-CIO, with a total membership in the millions. Several powerful independent unions have added several other millions to the ranks of organized labor. It has been estimated that one out of every four business and industrial workers in the United States today is a union member.

Unfortunately, there have been some dishonest labor leaders, just as there have been dishonest leaders in business. The unions within their own ranks have not always practiced the democracy they preached. From time to time laws have been needed to protect union members, as well as the general public, from the acts of corrupt union officials. One Congressional investigation (1959) revealed that some of these officials had been virtual dictators and that the rank and file of union membership had very little to say about the management of their organizations. It became clear to the members of the investigating committee that in some of the unions the majority of members were being denied the rights to which, as American citizens, they were entitled.

The Landrum-Griffin Act, passed in 1959, sometimes referred to as "labor's bill of rights," guaranteed union members the right to attend union meetings and to express themselves freely. The law also required unions to hold regular elections at which officers would be chosen by secret ballot. Union officials were to report to the government on the use of union dues, and dues were not to be raised, or special assessments demanded without the consent of the majority of the membership.

In spite of many as yet unsolved problems, the labor unions have benefitted employees and employers alike. It is taken for granted today that satisfied workers make better workers, and their increased purchasing power has brought increased prosperity to the nation. Most American workers are among the most prosperous in the world.

They have achieved not only political freedom but economic freedom—what Samuel Gompers once called "a fair share of the abundance that their labor has made possible."

Lafayette, Marquis de (1757–1834). "Liberty has to be won over and over again," said the Marquis de Lafayette in one of his last speeches—a statement that had been borne out by his own life. At the age of nineteen, this wealthy French nobleman had learned of the gallant fight the American colonies were waging for their independence. He crossed the Atlantic to offer his services as a soldier, and in spite of his youth the Continental Congress voted to give him a commission as a major general.

He soon proved himself worthy of this confidence, and General Washington came to regard him almost as a son. Lafayette shared the hardships of the soldiers at Valley Forge and later distinguished himself in several battles. He used his own money to buy uniforms and equipment for the troops under his command. By the time independence was won, the dashing French officer was one of the most popular men in America.

He was equally popular when he returned to France (Dec., 1781). After fighting for freedom abroad, he realized much better than before that there was great injustice in his native land. The masses were kept poor paying heavy taxes so that their king and his extravagant nobles might live in luxury. On a wall of Lafayette's home in Paris, he hung a copy of the Declaration of Independence. Beside it he left a vacant space, reserved—he said—for a similar declaration of French rights.

During the next few years the Marquis de Lafayette worked for reforms in the French government. As a member of the National Assembly, meeting in Versailles, he helped to compose a Declaration of the Rights of Man and Citizen, which he read aloud to the Assembly (July 11, 1789). Unrest was growing in Paris, and a few days later (July 14) a hysterical mob stormed the Bastille where political prisoners were kept. The guards were quickly overpowered, the governor of the prison killed, the prisoners released, and

Storming the Bastille

the work of destroying the grim gray fortress was begun. Louis XVI, the well-meaning but stupid king, feared further violence and agreed to respect the people's rights. Lafayette, hastening to Paris to tell the people there of the king's decision, was wildly cheered. In the days that followed, he might easily have made himself dictator, but such a course was not for him.

"I want to see the law respected," he said in one speech. "Without the law there is no liberty."

At the time Lafayette thought the worst of France's troubles were over, but people were still hungry. They still rioted in the streets, and the fall of the Bastille marked the beginning of the French Revolution. Radical, cruel leaders came into control of the Assembly, and men and women who opposed them were ruthlessly murdered. Because Lafayette protested against such violent methods, he was branded a traitor. As he attempted to flee his native land, he was captured by Austrian soldiers, whose government was at war with France, and his next five years were spent in German and Austrian prisons. When Napoleon Bonaparte came to power in France, he obtained Lafayette's release, then offered him a choice of several important positions in the new French government. But the French patriot who had already suffered so much for the cause of liberty refused to serve under a man he considered a dictator.

After Napoleon's abdication, France passed through other troubled times, during which Lafayette always remained true to his liberal principles. His fortune was gone, but when he returned to the United States for a final visit (1824–25), Congress voted him a township of land and a cash gift of $200,000 in appreciation of his services. On a tour of the young republic, Lafayette realized that he had laid by a fortune of another kind—a fortune in the gratitude of the American people whose freedom he had helped to win. He saw again many of the soldiers who had served under him during the American Revolution, and there were reunions with other old friends.

"He made our cause his own," said Thomas Jefferson. "In truth it was the cause of his native country also."

Law, Liberty under. Men are helped to live together in civilized society by laws, or rules, that control individual conduct for the benefit of the community as a whole. Such rules, of course, limit the liberty of the individual to some extent, but how much freedom would anyone have if there were no laws at all?

John Locke, an English philosopher whose writings were greatly admired in the American colonies, gave a common-sense answer to that question, an answer that is as sound today as it was in colonial times. In writing about law, he said:

> The end of law is not to abolish or restrain, but to preserve and enlarge freedom .... Where there is not law there is no freedom. For freedom is to be free from restraint and violence from others, which cannot be when there is not law. ... For who could be free, when every other man's humour [whim] might domineer over him?

League of Nations. On the insistence of President Woodrow Wilson, provision for a League of Nations was made a part of the treaty drawn up by the Peace Conference at Versailles, France, after World War I. The Covenant, or constitution, accepted by the Conference (Feb., 1919) was the work of a special commission headed by the American President. Though he believed some of the terms imposed by the treaty too harsh, he was convinced that any mistakes could be corrected by the League and, therefore, that the compromises he had been obliged to make were justified.

To Woodrow Wilson, the idealist, the

League of Nations was a blueprint for a better world. By doing away with war, he hoped it would enable all nations, large and small, to share in the benefits of freedom. This had been "the dream," he said, "of the friends of humanity through all the ages."

The purpose of the League, as stated in the preamble to the Covenant, was "to promote international cooperation and to achieve international peace and security by the acceptance of obligations not to resort to war" in settling disputes. Membership was open to all nations, but the U.S. Senate, which must approve all treaties, would not permit the United States to join. Nonetheless, the League, with an initial membership of forty-one countries, established headquarters in Geneva, Switzerland. During the twenty-six years it remained in existence (1920–46), American observers attended a number of important conferences held under League auspices.

Among the many useful activities of the new organization were relief projects for war refugees, and the work of commissions appointed to study means of controlling epidemic diseases and the distribution of harmful drugs. The League settled several disputes between smaller nations, but had no way of enforcing its decisions unless a nation wanted to obey. It was not able to prevent World War II, and some historians believe this war might have been averted had a strong nation like the United States been willing to participate as an active member.

By 1945 the attitude of the American people had changed. As a result of World War II, the majority of them were convinced that a stronger international organization was needed and that this time the United States must do its part. When another President, Franklin D. Roosevelt, presented a plan for the United Nations, there was practically no opposition.

Three months after the first U.N. General Assembly met in London, the League held its final meeting in Geneva (Apr., 1946), having voted to turn all of its physical assets over to the United Nations. In this latter organization, what someone had once called Woodrow Wilson's "unconquerable idea" had a dramatic rebirth.

Lee was the name of a Virginia family, well known since colonial days, that furnished notable leaders during several crises in the American freedom story. Among these were:

LEE, RICHARD HENRY (1732–94), a staunch defender of colonial rights during the ten years that led up to the American Revolution. He represented Virginia in the Continental Congress (1774–79), and is best remembered for the resolution he offered (June 7, 1776) which was to change the course of American history.

"Mr. Chairman," he said, "as instructed by my colony, I submit the following motion: Resolved that these united colonies are, and of right ought to be, free and independent states."

Both he and a younger brother, FRANCIS LIGHTFOOT LEE, were signers of the Declaration of Independence which was adopted a few weeks later (July 4).

A cousin, HENRY LEE, was a cavalry commander during the American Revolution, better known as "Light-Horse Harry" because of his daring raid on an enemy outpost. His fame as a soldier paved the way for his election as Governor of Virginia in 1791, but he was as reckless in civilian life as in time of war. Unwise investments brought his family close to poverty, and his last years were harassed by debts and ill health.

It was "Light-Horse Harry," always charming, always gallant, who suggested the famous words of the eulogy on George Washington, adopted by Congress shortly after his death: "To the memory of the Man, first in war, first in peace, and first in the hearts of his countrymen."

Henry Lee was the father of ROBERT E. LEE.

Lee, Robert E. (1807–70), the son of "Light-Horse Harry," had a difficult decision to make when secession threatened to break up the Union. He was a colonel in the U.S. Army, with a fine military record behind him, when he was called to Washington, D.C. (Apr., 1861). On orders from President Lincoln, Lee was urged to take command of the Union Army being raised to put down what most Northerners called the rebellion in the South.

It was a tempting offer for a professional army man. Lee did not approve of secession, and the few slaves he had inherited had been set free. He loved the Union, but he had grown up feeling that his first allegiance was to his own state. When Virginia seceded and joined the newly organized Confederate States of America, he regretfully resigned his commission in the U.S. Army. Instead of leading a Union invasion of the South, he became a general in the Confederate forces to try to repel that invasion.

As commander of the Army of Northern Virginia, Lee soon proved himself a brilliant and well-loved leader. He agreed with most Southerners that the South was fighting for the cause of freedom, and one of his first orders to his troops read:

The safety of your home and the lives of all you hold dear depend upon your courage and effort. Let each man . . . swear that the right of self-government, liberty, and speech shall find in him a defender.

During the first part of the war, the Confederates won most of the victories, due in part to the military strategy of General Lee and other able Confederate officers. Another important factor in Lee's success was his ability to inspire his men to deeds of courage, but in the end courage was not enough to defeat the superior resources of the North. By the time Lee was appointed commander in chief of all the Confederate armies, he realized the cause was hopeless. The Confederates were outnumbered three to one, and in the spring of 1865 the Army of Northern Virginia was surrounded by the enemy. The Southern soldiers were without food; their uniforms were ragged; many were barefooted. To avoid needless suffering, Lee wrote General Ulysses S. Grant, the Union commander, asking for terms of surrender.

The meeting between the two men, who had served together in the Mexican War, took place (Apr. 9, 1865) in the Virginia village of Appomattox Court House. General Grant later described that meeting in his memoirs:

What General Lee's feelings were I do not know . . . . But my own feelings, which had been quite jubilant on the receipt of his letter, were sad and depressed. I felt like anything rather than rejoicing at the downfall of a foe who had fought so long and so valiantly.

Grant's terms of surrender were generous, and Lee proved himself as great in defeat as he had been in victory. He never regretted the choice he had made in 1861. "I did only what my duty demanded," he said, but once the war was over he believed his duty was to set an example of loyalty to the U.S. government. His estate at Arlington, Va., had been occupied by Union forces since the beginning of the war, and he had forfeited most of his fortune when he chose the Confederate side. Yet he showed no bitterness, and he rejected more lucrative offers from abroad to become president of Washington College in Lexington, Va., at a modest salary. By helping young Southerners adjust to the new conditions, he believed he could be of the greatest service to the South and to the nation.

Lee estate at Arlington

"There must be peace in this country and there must be better understanding," he said. "I believe the duty of every one is to unite in the restoring of the country."

The school in Lexington which Lee served as president (1865–70) has been renamed Washington and Lee College in his honor. The estate at Arlington across the river from Washington, D.C., for many years now has been the site of the Arlington Memorial Cemetery where thousands of American war dead lie buried. From the east portico of the mansion, which for thirty years was the home of the great Confederate general, there is a spectacular view of the nation's capital. Standing between the tall white pillars one may look across the river to the marble Lincoln Memorial with the tall shaft of the Washington Monument just beyond. The Memorial Bridge that connects the two shores of the Potomac has become a symbol of a reunited United States.

Levellers, The. This political group arose in England in the 1640's during the struggle for power between the stubborn King Charles I and Parliament. The Levellers maintained that supreme authority lay not with the king or with Parliament, but with the people. They also believed that all men are born equal and that they have natural rights to political and legal equality.

One Leveller expressed the basic principles of the group when he said:

Really, I think that the poorest he that is in England hath a life to live, as the greatest he; . . . and I do think that the poorest man in England is not at all bound in a strict sense to that government that he hath not had a voice to put himself under.

Most of the Levellers were soldiers and minor officers in Oliver Cromwell's army that fought on the side of Parliament against the king in the first English Civil War (1642–46). After Charles was defeated, the Levellers feared, with reason, that Parliament itself was becoming tyrannical, and they drew up a document known as the "Agreement of the People," which outlined the type of government they thought the country should have. They wanted the Agreement to serve as a written constitution—so that the people's liberties would always be protected.

According to the Agreement, representation in Parliament should be based on the number of people in a voting district. By this, the Levellers meant that every man should have the right to vote, not just men of property, as in the past. Certain powers, such as the right to enact laws and to make war and peace, were to be delegated to Parliament. But the Levellers wanted to be very sure that the authority of Parliament, as well as that of the king, was limited. They listed rights that were to be retained by the people, including freedom of worship and equal treatment under the laws.

The Agreement was presented (1647) to Cromwell and other important army officers in the hope of gaining their support. But some of the Levellers' ideas were considered too radical and, though the officers agreed that government reform was needed, they refused to endorse the Agreement.

The Leveller movement, never large at any time, soon faded into history. But Leveller ideals were not to disappear entirely. They were carried to America by some of the colonists and were absorbed into the thinking that later led to the American system of government, with its written Constitution established by "We the People," and its Bill of Rights.

Lexington and Concord. The first battles of the American Revolution took place in the little town of Lexington, Mass., and the neighboring town of Concord (Apr. 19, 1775). Here, "by the rude bridge that arched the flood," was fired "the shot heard round the world," as Ralph Waldo Emerson described it in his popular poem (see CONCORD HYMN).

For some time tensions had been increasing between Massachusetts patriots and British forces occupying Boston. Companies of Minutemen, so called because

they had agreed to be ready to fight at a minute's notice, were organized in several towns. When the British commander learned that patriots had hidden a store of guns and ammunition in Concord, he ordered 700 of his regular troops to march out of Boston and seize the supplies. The plan was discovered by the Sons of Liberty, and two of their members, Paul Revere and William Dawes, set out on horseback to warn the countryside.

The result was that when the Regulars passed through Lexington at dawn, a company of Minutemen was drawn up on the village green, and in the skirmish that followed several of them were killed or wounded. In Concord more Minutemen were waiting, and this time the British were defeated. After a sharp battle at the North Bridge, they were forced to beat a hasty retreat back to Boston.

Though the battles at Lexington and Concord are considered the beginning of the American Revolution, in the words of John Adams the Revolution was already "in the hearts and minds of the people."

"Liberals" and "Conservatives." Each term has been used to convey different meanings at different times. Many enlightened Americans have considered themselves both liberal and conservative, and have had a part in establishing and maintaining freedom in America. Franklin D. Roosevelt, though he has been called one of the most liberal of American Presidents, once characterized himself as "a true conservative." He continued:

Wise and prudent men—intelligent conservatives—have long known that in a changing world worthy institutions can be conserved only by adjusting them to the changing time . . . . I am that kind of conservative because I am that kind of liberal.

Today the word "liberal" is sometimes used—or misused—to indicate a man or woman who is really a radical—one who wants to bring about change more rapidly than may be wise. The word "conservative" is sometimes used to indicate a person who is closer to being a reactionary—one who is likely to react against any change at all.

Liberty, as it has been defined in decisions handed down by several State Supreme Courts, embraces the right of a citizen to use his faculties in all lawful ways; to earn his livelihood in any lawful way; and to pursue any lawful trade or avocation.

The difficulty in defining liberty, as President Abraham Lincoln once pointed out during the Civil War, was that people who used the word did not always mean the same thing. In a speech delivered in Baltimore (Apr. 18, 1864), he said the world had never had a good definition and that the American people were in need of one. Then to emphasize his point, he used one of his homespun analogies for which he was well known:

> The shepherd drives the wolf from the sheep's throat, for which the sheep thanks the shepherd as a *liberator*, while the wolf denounces him for the same act, as the destroyer of liberty. Plainly the wolf and the sheep are not agreed upon a definition of the word liberty; and precisely the same difference prevails today among us human creatures . . . all professing to love liberty.

The word is still open to varying interpretations, both in our own country and abroad. On the world scene, leaders in Communist nations that have forced or tried to force their form of government on neighboring countries invariably call their aggressions "wars of liberation"—a term with which the majority of individuals in the weaker countries would hardly agree. In the United States, Negroes struggling for the liberties guaranteed by the Bill of Rights are often opposed by white people who complain that *their* rights and liberties are being threatened.

What liberty is may best be summed up perhaps, in a quaint old folk saying: "The freedom [or liberty] of my fist stops where the other man's nose begins."

Liberty, Limitations on. "Individuals entering into society, must give up a share of liberty to preserve the rest," wrote George Washington (Sept. 17, 1787) in a letter to the Continental Congress.

The Constitutional Convention, of which he was president, had framed a new Constitution to be submitted to the Congress, which in turn would send it to the thirteen original states for approval. Washington realized that the problem of each state was similar to that of an individual who wishes to live under a government strong and efficient enough to preserve freedom for all.

Many of the delegates to the state conventions, called to decide whether or not to ratify the new Constitution, had their doubts. They feared that a strong central government, as provided for in the new plan, might endanger the freedom for which they had fought in the American Revolution. Edward Pendleton, well-known jurist and president of the Virginia Convention, argued that this was not true. He believed it necessary that society lay down rules in order to preserve liberty; otherwise there would be only lawlessness and turbulence.

"There is no quarrel between government and liberty," he insisted. "The former is the protector and shield of the latter."

Enough delegates to the different state conventions shared Pendleton's point of view to make possible the ratification of the Constitution. One question still to be decided was whether a state in the Union could do exactly what its legislature wished, in a matter affecting the entire nation, without regard for the wishes expressed by the majority of the voters in the United States. That matter was settled by the Civil War (1861–65), but what about the individual who wants to do exactly as he pleases? Unless people consider the rights of others, there is no liberty for anyone, which is why rules and laws are necessary.

An associate justice of the Supreme Court, Oliver Wendell Holmes, Jr., summed up the problem in a single sentence when he handed down an opinion in an important Court decision (Schenck *v.* U.S., 1919). This decision concerned free speech, but his words apply equally to all aspects of liberty. "The most stringent protection of free speech," said Justice Holmes, "would not protect a man in falsely shouting fire in a theatre and causing a panic."

Liberty Bell. This great bell, weighing more than two thousand pounds, now on exhibit in Independence Hall, Philadelphia, was brought there (1752) from England while Pennsylvania was still a colony. By order of the Pennsylvania Provincial Assembly, the bell had been inscribed with a quotation from the Bible: *Proclaim lib-*

erty throughout all the land unto all the inhabitants thereof (Leviticus 25:10).

As it turned out, the inscription was even more appropriate than anyone realized at the time. Twenty-four years later the bell was rung (July 8, 1776) to summon the people of Philadelphia to a public reading of the Declaration of Independence.

During the British occupation of the city (1777–1778) the bell was moved to Allentown, Pa., and hidden under the floor of a church for safety. After its return to Philadelphia, it was rung each Independence Day and on other special occasions until it was badly cracked while tolling for the funeral of Chief Justice John Marshall (1835). On D-Day (June 6, 1944) during World War II, the bell was tapped by the mayor and the tone broadcast throughout the nation by radio.

See INDEPENDENCE HALL.

"Liberty of the Community." The term was first used by Franklin D. Roosevelt as a member of the New York State Senate (1912). He was vitally interested in conservation and much concerned about the waste of natural resources, including the forest lands of his state. In one speech he pointed out how a few rich lumbermen, anxious to make a quick profit, had cut down far too many trees. No new seedlings had been planted to replace them and, unless some action were taken, future generations would be deprived of timberland. Also, without trees, the topsoil was washed away, filling up streams and causing floods.

"They [the lumbermen] do not care what happens after they are gone and even do not care what happens to their neighbors," said twenty-four-year-old Franklin Roosevelt. The liberty to do whatever suited them must be checked, he went on, for the sake of what he called "the liberty of the community."

A few years earlier, President Theodore Roosevelt had called such men "land grabbers." One of T. R. 's great contributions to his country had been his efforts to conserve the natural riches of the nation for the benefit of the people, and he had emphasized the need for "collective action" to protect the public. The younger Roosevelt was making the same point when he spoke of "the liberty of the community."

"Liberty Song," by John Dickinson (1732–1808). Several lines from this song—"In freedom we're born, and in freedom we'll live" and "By uniting we stand, by dividing we fall"—were popular catchwords in the days preceding the American Revolution. The author, a Philadelphia lawyer, later served in both the Continental Congress and the Constitutional Convention.

Lincoln, Abraham (1809–65), the 16th President, once said he "never had a feeling politically that did not spring from the Declaration of Independence." What gave it significance, he went on,

> . . . was not the mere matter of the separation of the colonies from the motherland, but something in that declaration giving liberty, not alone to the people of this country, but hope for the world for all future time.

That Lincoln should become President when a man of his firmness and integrity was most needed was one of the fortunate events of history. A self-made lawyer, tall and gaunt, homely but popular, he had served briefly in the House of Representatives (1847–49), then returned to his law practice in Springfield, Ill. He seemed to lose interest in politics until his indignation was aroused by the passage of the Kansas-Nebraska Act (1854). This new law made it possible to open up the vast western lands to slavery, and no one was more vigorous in his opposition than Lawyer Lincoln.

"If slavery is not wrong, then nothing is wrong," he once said, but since the U.S. Constitution did not forbid slavery he did not see what could be done about it in states where it already existed. What could be done, he hoped and believed, was to prevent its spread into regions that were still free.

In 1856 he joined the new Republican party which had been organized to prevent the extension of slavery. Two years later the Illinois Republicans nominated him for the U.S. Senate. His opponent was Senator Stephen A. Douglas, who was running for reelection on the Democratic ticket.

It was Douglas, often referred to as "the Little Giant," both because of his short stature and his brilliant mind, who had introduced the Kansas-Nebraska Bill into Congress. In one of the most interesting and bitterly contested campaigns in American politics, the two men held a series of joint debates in seven towns in different parts of Illinois. These Lincoln-Douglas Debates (Aug. 21–Oct. 15, 1858) were reported in newspapers throughout the nation and brought to public attention the opposing views of the candidates on a controversial subject.

Abraham Lincoln insisted that the arguments over slavery were only the continuation of the eternal struggle between two principles. He said:

> The one is the common right of humanity and the other the divine right of kings. It is the same spirit that says, "You work and toil and earn bread, and I'll eat it." No matter in what shape it comes, whether from the mouth of a king who seeks to bestride the people of his own nation and live by the fruit of their labor, or from one race of men as an apology for enslaving another race, it is the same tyrannical principle.

In the race for the Senate, Lincoln lost to Douglas, but the debates had made him a national figure. He was invited to speak in a number of towns and cities, and throughout the North people began to think of him as the man best able to solve the grave problems facing the nation. At the Republican Convention (May, 1860) he was nominated for the Presidency, and a split in the Democratic party over slavery threw the election to the Republicans. The following February Abraham Lincoln left for Washington, D.C. to be inaugurated as President—President, though, of a divided country.

By that time seven states (to be joined later by four others) had seceded from the United States and formed a new nation, the Confederate States of America. This action was taken because many Southerners were convinced that their rights—specifically the right to own slaves —would not be protected under a Chief Executive so opposed to slavery. It was Lincoln's conviction that no state had a legal right to secede. In his Inaugural Address (Mar. 4, 1861) he reminded his audience that he derived his power from the people, and no power had been conferred on him "to fix terms for the separation of the states."

In the same speech the new President tried to make it clear that Southerners stood in no danger from his administration. It was not his intention to interfere with the institution of slavery in their states; he had no lawful right to do so.

As Abraham Lincoln read his speech, his steel spectacles slipping down his nose, the 10,000 people gathered before the east portico of the Capitol listened intently. A report had leaked out of an attempt to assassinate him on his way to Washington. A glance at many of the windows of the Capitol building showed the protruding rifle barrels. The rifles were trained on the platform where the inauguration ceremonies were taking place, to protect the President, and the knowledge that such protection was considered necessary added to the crowd's uneasiness.

Abraham Lincoln showed no sign of fear. There were deep lines in his face, but they were lines of sadness. It would be his duty, he said, to see that the federal laws

were obeyed, but he assured his countrymen in the South that there would be no civil war unless they themselves were the aggressors.

"I am loath to close," he said. "We are not enemies but friends. We must not be enemies. Though passion may have strained, it must not break our bonds of affection."

In spite of the hope that an armed conflict could be prevented between North and South, the Civil War began (Apr. 12, 1861) when Confederate troops fired on a U.S. fort in the harbor at Charleston, S.C. From the beginning of hostilities, pressure was brought to bear on Lincoln to declare that all the slaves were free, but he felt the Constitution would not ordinarily give him that right. At first he also feared the effect of such a declaration on several border states that had remained loyal to the Union. If they should join the Confederacy, the result might be disastrous for the Union cause. In answer to a critical editorial (Aug. 20, 1862) by Horace Greeley, influential editor of the *New York Daily Tribune*, Lincoln wrote an open letter:

My paramount object in this struggle is to save the Union . . . . What I do about slavery and the colored race I do because I believe it will help save the Union; and if I forbear, I forbear because I do not believe it would help to save the Union . . . . I have here stated my purpose according to my view of *official* duty; and I intend no modification of my oft-expressed *personal* wish that all men everywhere could be free.

The plan for Negro freedom Lincoln had advocated was gradual emancipation of the slaves, with the slaveholders to be compensated with funds from the federal treasury, but nothing had come of the proposal. Not until it was obvious that slave labor might enable the Confederates to win the war, did the President issue the Emancipation Proclamation as a military measure. Saving the Union was

still his main objective, and the following November he summed up the fundamental purpose of the war in his brief and moving address at Gettysburg, Pa. (see EMANCIPATION PROCLAMATION and GETTYSBURG ADDRESS).

By the time President Lincoln began his second term (Mar. 4, 1865), the war was drawing to a close. With Union victory in sight, his chief concern was to make it easy for the seceding states to resume their old places in the nation. The next task, he said, in his memorable Second Inaugural Address, was "to bind up the nation's wounds."

Less than six weeks later Abraham Lincoln was assassinated (April 14, 1865) by a fanatic, but though he died before he could carry out his policies, his ideals have lived on. In Washington, D.C., thousands of Americans, as well as visitors from foreign countries, have climbed the marble steps of the Lincoln Memorial with its superb statue by Daniel Chester French. Thousands have shared in the same rush of emotion as they look up at the seated figure of the Great Emancipator, his rugged face lighted as he gazes thoughtfully over the Mall.

On the marble wall back of the statue are engraved the words:

In this temple,
as in the hearts of the people
for whom he saved the Union
the memory of Abraham Lincoln
is enshrined forever.

On another wall of the Memorial may be read the words of the Gettysburg Address—words that speak of a "new birth of freedom" for the nation he preserved.

Locke, John (1632–1704) was an English philosopher whose political writings were widely read and admired in the American colonies. Especially influential was the second of his *Two Treatises on Civil Government* (1690).

It was Locke's belief that all men have natural rights to life, liberty, and property, and that to preserve these rights governments are established by mutual consent. If a government, Locke asserted, betrays the trust placed in it by failing to protect the rights of the people, then the people are entitled to change the government.

The political treatises, or essays, by John Locke were written to justify the Glorious Revolution (1688–89), which had freed the English people from the tyrannical rule of King James II. By the time the essays were published, the revolution in England was over. It was, therefore, in America and in France, where revolutions were still to occur, that Locke's ideas had their greatest impact. His influence is especially apparent in the Declaration of Independence, which heralded the final break of the colonies with Great Britain.

Lovejoy, Elijah (1802–37), a clergyman and Abolitionist originally from Maine, edited a religious journal *The Observer* in St. Louis, Mo. during the early days of the antislavery struggle. Slaveholders in the town were furious when he condemned (1835) a mob that had burned a Negro to death. The young editor replied in a stinging editorial reminding his readers of the right of free discussion guaranteed by the U.S. Constitution:

I do, therefore, as an American citizen and a Christian patriot, and in the name of liberty and law and religion, solemnly protest against all these attempts to frown down the liberty of the press.

Fearing for the safety of his family, Lovejoy moved to Alton, Ill., a town farther up the Mississippi River. His printing press was destroyed by a mob. A second press was purchased, and it too was destroyed. But there were antislavery as well as proslavery citizens in Alton. A convention meeting to form a State Antislavery Society passed a resolution, demanding in the interest of human rights and of liberty of speech and of the press, that the Alton *Observer* be reestablished. A third printing press was then ordered, and when it arrived (Nov. 7, 1837) was placed in a warehouse for safekeeping.

That night the Reverend Lovejoy and a group of loyal companions were standing guard, when an armed mob gathered before the building and threatened to set it on fire. When Lovejoy stepped outside to protest, there was a blast of gunfire. He died a few minutes later, but the thirty-five-year-old martyr was to wield a greater influence in death than in life.

His murder, wrote John Quincy Adams, then Secretary of State, sent "a shock as of an earthquake throughout the continent." Though there were those who condoned the action of the mob, there were many others who were outraged. They protested the violation of two of the most prized rights guaranteed by the First Amendment—freedom of speech and freedom of the press. Many Americans, who until then had given little thought to slavery, were converted to the antislavery cause.

OWEN LOVEJOY, a younger brother, was present when Elijah was killed, and vowed to continue the fight against slavery. He, too, was a clergyman, but later entered politics and served in the U.S. House of Representatives (1856–64). He supported Abraham Lincoln's policies and had been among the first to urge him to accept leadership in the new Republican party.

MacArthur, Douglas (1880–1964), a distinguished American soldier and strategist, served in both world wars. He was in command of American and Filipino forces in the Philippines when the Japanese invaded the islands early in World War II. His forces were greatly outnumbered, and he felt obliged to order a retreat to the peninsula of Bataan. After receiving secret orders from the President to proceed to Australia and assume supreme command of all the Allied forces in the southwest Pacific, General MacArthur made a dramatic escape by motor torpedo boat (Mar. 11, 1942) under cover of darkness.

"I shall return," he promised the Filipinos, and the promise was kept some two and a half years later. After victories won against great odds in the southwest Pacific, U.S. Army and Navy forces under the general command of Douglas MacArthur launched an attack on the Japanese occupying the Philippines. Several more months of hard fighting were required before the Philippine Islands were finally liberated (July 5, 1945).

Following the surrender of Japan the following month, General MacArthur was placed in command of the Allied military forces that occupied the Japanese islands for several years. The aloof attitude and exaggerated sense of dignity that had made him unpopular with many Americans won him the respect, almost the veneration, of many Japanese. Hirohito, the emperor, was allowed to keep his throne, and gave his full cooperation. In the past the emperor had been little more than a tool for the military clique that had brought on the war, and he appeared to be as relieved as most of his subjects to be free of military domination.

The Japanese people had had enough of war, and with American economic aid

made a rapid recovery. The commander of the occupation forces brought about many reforms. Liberal Japanese, who once had had little to say about public affairs, were encouraged to adopt a new constitution providing for a representative form of government. Though difficulties remained, the average Japanese enjoyed a greater degree of democracy than he had ever known.

The main credit for this went to General MacArthur. He had been a brilliant soldier, but he was convinced—and most of his countrymen agreed—that his greatest contribution was what he called "the advance of peace" in Japan.

See WORLD WAR II.

Madison, James (1751–1836), the fourth President, is honored today chiefly as "the father of the Constitution."

Madison's interest in government began as a student (1769–72) at the College of New Jersey (now Princeton). After his return to Montpelier, his Virginia home, he was elected as a delegate to the Virginia Convention. This convention instructed its delegates to the Continental Congress to present a resolution declaring all of the colonies independent. It also voted to adopt a constitution for Virginia, and young Madison was on the committee appointed to draft a new plan of government that would meet the needs of an independent state.

Later Madison served in the Continental Congress (1780–83), then returned to Virginia and was elected to the Virginia legislature. He was one of its most liberal leaders, and worked wholeheartedly for measures first proposed by his friend Thomas Jefferson to make the state more democratic. It was due in large part to Madison's efforts that the Virginia Statute for Religious Freedom was finally passed (1785).

These years of experience were to prove invaluable in preparing him for the influential part he was to play in the Constitutional Convention. As one of the delegates from Virginia, "the great little Madison," as he was called because of his small stature and brilliant mind, was responsible for some of the basic ideas that went into the framing of the U.S. Constitution. After its adoption by the convention, he was coauthor of *The Federalist*, a series of essays that convinced many of the leaders in the new nation that their states should ratify the proposed plan of government. He was elected to the first House of Representatives that convened after the Constitution went into effect and introduced into the House the amendments later to become known as the Bill of Rights.

James Madison's service as Secretary of State (1801–09) and his administration as President (1809–17) were less successful than his earlier career. He was a thinker rather than a man of action, and his important contributions to the cause of freedom had been made when he was comparatively young. His philosophy of freedom was summed up in his definition of property, which to Madison meant not only material possessions, but "everything to which a man may attach a value and a right." He continued:

A man has property in his opinions and in the free communication of them. He has a property of peculiar value in his religious opinions. . . . He has property very dear to him in the safety and liberty of his person . . . . In a word, as a man is said to have a right to his property, he may be equally said to have a property in his rights.

Magna Carta was one of the basic documents of English liberty. One day more than 750 years ago (June 15, 1215) a group of rebellious barons confronted their ruler, tyrannical King John of England, in a meadow known as Runnymede. Runnymede was a few miles from Windsor Castle from which the king had ridden to meet the barons.

The barons were united in their defiance of the ruthless king. They were determined that he must cease trespassing on their traditional rights and ignoring the laws and customs of the land.

This was not the first time the barons had insisted that the king mend his ways. But John had shunted aside their earlier demands and then had tried to stir up support for himself among the rest of the population. His efforts had been in vain, for he was disliked and distrusted throughout all England. When he finally realized how little help he could count on in a conflict with the armed and angry nobles, he arranged to meet them at Runnymede.

The barons were ready for him, having already prepared a list of their demands. John, though doubtless seething with suppressed fury, quickly agreed to the barons' terms. He placed his seal upon the list, which was then drawn up into the formal document known as Magna Carta, or the Great Charter.

Magna Carta was not a democratic document, nor was it meant to be. It was written in medieval times and most of its provisions dealt with the relationship between the barons and their feudal lord, the king. The barons, mainly concerned with their own rights and privileges, had little interest in protecting the rights of the thousands of half-free serfs who worked the land.

But there were a few provisions in the charter intended to protect all free Englishmen, even those who were not nobles, from the injustice of an arbitrary king. In the most famous of these provisions the king promised that:

No freeman shall be seized or imprisoned, or dispossessed, or outlawed, or in any way brought to ruin . . . save by legal judgment of his peers or by the law of the land.

This did not mean that a trial must be by jury. At the time the charter was drawn up, trial by jury was a procedure seldom used except in cases involving real estate. It would be a hundred years before jury trials were commonly used in all kinds of cases. What the provision in the charter did mean was that a man had the right to be judged by his peers, or equals, according to customary laws. No longer could he be seized by the king's agents and deprived of life, liberty, or property for some trumped-up reason or simply by royal command. He was entitled to what was later known as "due process of law."

Several of King John's successors reissued the charter, thus acknowledging the basic principle it had established: that no one, not even a king, is above the law. Then as medieval customs gradually disappeared in England, many sections of the document no longer applied to new conditions, and interest in it lessened. But some four hundred years after the events at Runnymede, the charter gained a new importance.

During the early 1600's English kings were again trampling on the rights of Englishmen. This time, they were flagrantly ignoring the right to trial by jury, the right of *habeas corpus,* and the right of "no taxation without representation." During the long struggle of the 1600's against the royal tyranny, prominent lawyers read new meanings into Magna Carta. They reinterpreted it as a guarantee of the very rights the monarchy was abusing.

It was this new interpretation of Magna Carta that English colonists carried to America. In the troubled years preceding the Revolution, Magna Carta was one of the documents the colonists often spoke of when insisting on their rights as Englishmen.

Though the Revolution brought separation from Great Britain, the English belief in the importance of individual rights remained rooted in the hearts and minds of the former colonists. The ideals of legal justice written into the American

Constitution and the Bill of Rights reach back to principles expressed in the charter. Today in the United States as well as in England, Magna Carta is regarded as a cornerstone of freedom.

Mann, Horace (1796–1859). "In a republic ignorance is a crime," said Horace Mann, who gave up a promising law practice to serve as the first secretary of the newly established Massachusetts State Board of Education (1837–48). Though Massachusetts had been the first colony to foster free, tax-supported schools, after the American Revolution some schools simply ceased to exist. Many children, in Massachusetts and elsewhere, grew up illiterate, and even those who were lucky enough to attend a one-room schoolhouse were often taught by a teacher who did not know much more than his pupils. Convinced that education was essential if young people were to grow up to govern themselves successfully, Mann made speech after speech in towns throughout the state.

"To get people interested in the schools," he said, "is like trying to break down a mountain with one's fist."

The mountain he spoke of—the mountain of indifference—was broken down

One-room schoolhouse

through his persistent efforts. Laws passed by the Massachusetts state legislature made it possible for him to organize a system of public schools that was to serve as a model for the rest of the nation. He also helped to establish the first normal school (1839) where teachers could be trained, and in 1852 he became the president of Antioch College, a new institution of higher learning in Ohio. But he is most gratefully remembered as "the father of the American public school," because of his success in improving elementary education.

Marshall, George C. (1880–1959), one of America's greatest generals, served with distinction in both world wars; but it was during his term as Secretary of State that he made his greatest contribution to the cause of freedom. As a result of World War II, most of Europe was poverty-stricken. Cities had been bombed, factories had been destroyed, farms lay idle, and many people were so desperate that they were tempted to turn to Communism as a way out of their troubles. In a speech delivered at the Harvard University Commencement exercises (June 5, 1947), General Marshall outlined a plan whereby the United States could help Europe recover. The purpose, he said, would be to create the conditions "in which free institutions can survive."

The European Recovery Program, more often called the Marshall Plan, met with an immediate and enthusiastic response in western Europe. Representatives from sixteen nations met in Paris to discuss their most pressing needs and decide on a program of mutual cooperation. Large sums of money, appropriated by the U.S. Congress early the following year, were used to rebuild factories; construct roads and docks; furnish raw materials, machinery, and farm equipment; and provide food needed to keep thousands of people alive until they could find work.

The result of the Marshall Plan was a surprisingly rapid recovery. The nations of western Europe began to produce products to sell to other countries and, with revival of their trade, the United States benefitted, too.

Joseph Stalin, then the Soviet dictator, refused to permit the Soviet Union or any of Russia's satellite nations to cooperate in the plan. It may have been Stalin's hope that, if conditions in western Europe became desperate enough, more people would be willing to submit to Communist domination. By 1947, when General Marshall attended a meeting for foreign ministers in Moscow, "the cold war" was in its third year. This was a conflict fought without guns—a war of ideas—which brought into sharp focus the contrasting concepts of government held by the United States and the Soviet Union.

In a speech summing up the American ideal General Marshall said:

We believe that human beings have rights that may not be given or taken away. They include the right of every individual to develop his mind and his soul in the ways of his own choice, free of fear and coercion—provided only that he does not interfere with the rights of others . . . . To us a society is not free if law-abiding citizens live in fear of being denied the right to work or of being deprived of life, liberty, and the pursuit of happiness.

Marshall, John (1755–1835), who is still spoken of as "the great chief," presided over the Supreme Court for thirty-four years during the early days of the Republic.

As a youth on the Virginia frontier, he had been largely self-educated, but studied law for a few months at William and Mary College. After enlisting in the Continental Army during the American Revolution, he soon rose to the rank of captain, and his genial disposition helped to keep up the morale of his men during the privations suffered at Valley Forge. The Continental Congress was so weak and ineffectual that it could do little to help the soldiers, and the young captain came to realize the importance of having a strong government.

After leaving the army, Marshall practiced law and served in the Virginia Convention called to ratify the new Constitution recently adopted (1787) in Philadelphia. In answer to objections raised by some of the delegates that the Constitution would be a threat to freedom, Marshall insisted that the opposite was true:

We prefer this system [that provided by the Constitution] . . . because we are convinced that it has a greater tendency to secure our liberty and promote our happiness. We admire it, because we think it is a well regulated democracy.

During the long period when Marshall served as Chief Justice of the United States (1801–35), he became known as the expounder, or interpreter, of the Constitution. When he took office, the justices were meeting in a small room in the still unfinished Capitol. The Court was without prestige, but by the time he died he had transformed it into a powerful arm of the national government, thereby making the government much stronger. He had no precedents to guide him, but his opinions have provided precedents for other justices and judges down through the years. He said:

We must never forget that it is a *constitution* we are expounding . . . a constitution intended to endure for ages to come, and consequently, to be adapted to the various *crises* of human affairs.

As John Marshall grew older, he became more conservative. Though he heartily approved of manhood suffrage, he did not share Thomas Jefferson's confidence in the wisdom of the people. Marshall feared that, without safeguards, the rule of the majority might become unjust and intolerant. He and Jefferson were distant cousins, yet neither approved of the other.

They were an example of how two men, both patriots but with widely different views, could both contribute to "the general welfare" mentioned in the Preamble to the Constitution. Jefferson inspired the people with his ideals of freedom. Marshall helped to make the government strong enough to enable the ideals to survive.

When John Marshall died at the age of seventy-nine, the Liberty Bell in Independence Hall rang out the sad news. It was said that not since the passing of George Washington had any American leader been so greatly mourned.

"Such men are found only when our need is greatest," said Associate Justice Joseph Story who had served with "the great chief" on the Supreme Court bench. "His proudest epitaph may be written in a line—Here lies the expounder of the Constitution."

Mason, George (1725–92), brilliant Virginia aristocrat and planter, was less well known than his friends George Washington, Thomas Jefferson, and Patrick Henry, but he exerted a powerful influence on American liberal thought. He was the author of the Virginia Declaration of Rights, and later when he represented Virginia at the Constitutional Convention, he advocated a form of government that would "attend to the rights of every class of people."

A bitter opponent of slavery, Mason made an eloquent plea for a provision in the new U.S. Constitution that would prohibit the slave trade. Finally the delegates agreed to insert a statement that Congress should not prohibit the importation of slaves "prior to the year 1808" (Article I, Section 9). George Mason was indignant about this provision, and it was one reason

**Importation
of slaves**

why he refused to sign the Constitution.

Yet he was responsible for one of its most important features. His earlier Declaration of Rights for Virginia had aroused public opinion, and several states agreed to ratify the proposed new form of federal or national government only on condition that a similar Bill of Rights be added, guaranteeing that certain liberties of the people would always be protected.

Gunston Hall, the beautiful home on the Potomac River where Mason lived, has been restored and opened to the public.

Mayflower Compact. The people now called Pilgrims, who sailed from England in September, 1620 on their crowded little ship, the *Mayflower,* were better known as

who had joined the expedition, a patent, or permission, to settle in Virginia. On the voyage across the Atlantic, the *Mayflower* was blown off its course by storms, and it was the latter part of November before the vessel anchored off the coast—not of Virginia, as planned—but of New England several hundred miles farther north.

The London Company had no authority in New England, and there were a few discontented passengers on board who were pleased at the prospect of having no laws to obey. They boasted they "would use their own liberty" to do whatever they pleased, failing to take into account the dangers that might confront the colony in a strange wild region.

Responsible leaders of the expedition

Separatists in their own time. After separating from the Church of England, they had been persecuted for their religious beliefs, and so sought freedom of worship in the New World. The London Company, a trading company in charge of the Virginia colony, granted the Pilgrim families, their servants, and a number of others

realized the peril of such an attitude. Before going ashore, a meeting was called in the cabin of the *Mayflower,* and a document called the "Mayflower Compact" was presented to the passengers. Most of the men on board were persuaded to sign, agreeing to enact and obey such "just and equal laws" from time to time as would be thought "most meet and convenient for the general good of the colony."

After the colonists, 102 in all, founded the town of Plymouth in what is now Massachusetts, the Mayflower Compact served as the basis for government for many years. The Mayflower Compact was an emergency measure that applied to only one little colony. Yet the Pilgrim fathers established an important precedent by organizing a government with the consent of those who were to be governed—a principle now considered indispensable to a government like that of the United States.

Milton, John (1608–74). "Give me the liberty to know, to utter, and to argue freely according to conscience, above all liberties." Thus wrote the great English poet John Milton (1644) who, during his middle years, used his mighty pen to write numerous pamphlets on the problems of the times.

England was in the midst of a political and religious civil war when Milton wrote the words quoted above. They are from *Areopagitica* (see separate entry), a pamphlet in which he protested against a law that restricted freedom of the press. No idea, whether false or true, should be suppressed, he insisted, for "who ever knew truth put to the worse in a free and open encounter?"

Milton's sympathies were with Oliver Cromwell's Puritan army in its struggle against political and religious oppression. Soon after the success of the Puritans and the execution of the tragic King Charles I (1649), Milton published a pamphlet defending the people's right to depose unjust rulers. This pamphlet, *The Tenure of Kings and Magistrates*, resulted in his appointment as foreign secretary in the government of the new Commonwealth that was established (1649) in England. In this position he carried on a wide cor-

respondence with the leaders of other nations and wrote pamphlets to try to justify the Commonwealth in the eyes of the world.

The intensity of his work was harmful to his failing eyesight, and within three years he was completely blind. In one of the few poems written during his years of public service, Milton said his blindness was endurable because it had resulted from overwork "in liberty's defense."

With the help of an assistant, he continued with his official duties until the restoration of royal rule (1660). He then returned to his career as a poet.

Milton's prose works as well as his poetry were widely read and greatly admired in the American colonies. Among the many who were impressed by his writings in defense of liberty were John Adams and Thomas Jefferson. In the Virginia Statute for Religious Freedom (1785) Jefferson wrote that "truth is great and will prevail if left to herself"— words that distinctly echo Milton's *Areopagitica*.

Areopagitica is still considered one of the greatest defenses ever written for liberty of speech and press.

Minority Rights. The United States is a nation ruled by the majority of the voters, but America's early patriots believed that the purpose of government was to provide justice for all. In his first Inaugural Address (1801), Thomas Jefferson pointed out that, though the will of the majority was to prevail, the minority possessed equal rights. The rights of the minority must also be protected by law.

It had been to prevent what has been called "the tyranny of the majority" that the Bill of Rights had been added (1791) to the U.S. Constitution. These first ten amendments listed the rights that the government can never take away from the individual; and when lived up to they continue to serve as a shield against despotism for all citizens alike. "If liberty is ever lost in America," said Alexis de Tocqueville in his remarkable book *Democracy in America,* "it will be the fault of the omnipotence of the majority, which will have brought the minorities to despair and will have forced them to appeal to physical force."

Such a possibility doubtless exists in any minority group that has been denied the rights and liberties guaranteed under the U.S. form of government. Fortunately, most Americans have realized the wisdom of the words of Wendell Willkie, Republican candidate for President in 1940. "Freedom is an indivisible word," he said. "If we want to enjoy it, we must be prepared to extend it to everyone."

Monroe Doctrine was a statement made by President James Monroe in his annual message to Congress (Dec. 2, 1823). Several Spanish colonies in South America had recently declared their independence, and an alliance of European monarchies was planning to subdue the new republics. The people of the United States, having won their own independence only forty years earlier, were naturally concerned, and they were fearful of what might happen if European armies should invade the Western Hemisphere. There also was some anxiety that Russia, then owner of Alaska, might extend its claims farther south to the Oregon country and California.

The time had come, Secretary of State John Quincy Adams suggested, to make clear to Europe what American policy was to be. When President Monroe turned to the former President, Thomas Jefferson, for advice, he was urged to support the new Latin American nations.

"Our endeavor," said Jefferson, "should surely be to make our hemisphere that of freedom."

In the message that Monroe sent to Congress a short time later, he pointed out the differences between the political system of the allied European powers and that of the United States. Americans, he said, preferred their own system, won at the cost of "so much blood and treasure," and any attempt to impose another political system on any part of the Western Hemisphere would be considered a threat to the peace and safety of the United States. The document also served notice that the American continents were "henceforth not to be considered as subjects for future colonization by any European powers."

The warning issued by President Monroe, mostly as a doctrine of self-defense, helped the Latin American countries to keep their independence. Though the Monroe Doctrine was never enacted into law, for some years it remained an important part of the foreign policy of the United States.

It has not always been a popular policy. The fact that a nation has gained independence does not mean necessarily that the majority of its people support the government in power. From time to time disorders and revolutions have broken out in parts of Latin America, and European governments were tempted to send troops to collect just debts or to protect their own citizens or subjects who were living there. After Theodore Roosevelt became President of the United States (1901), he maintained that he did not want any European nation to have an excuse to interfere on the American continents. Therefore, at times he sent troops into Latin America to keep order.

Many Latin Americans, though, resented having their countries policed by troops from *any* outside nation. They came to distrust the United States; but in recent years the United States government has made a determined effort to live on friendlier terms with the neighbor nations to the south.

Herbert Hoover, after his election to the Presidency, made a goodwill tour of South America before he took office (1929). Four years later President Franklin Roosevelt announced his "Good Neighbor" policy and urged that all American nations have a share in enforcing the Monroe Doctrine. During John F. Kennedy's short term as President (1961–63), he stressed the same idea. If the nations of the Western Hemisphere would unite in support of the Monroe Doctrine, John Kennedy believed they would be better able to meet the threats to freedom arising from subversion or aggression. His hope was to make the American continents "an example to all the world that liberty and progress walk hand in hand."

Montesquieu, Charles Louis de Secondat, Baron de Montesquieu (1689–1755), was a French political philosopher whose theories on the separation of governmental powers influenced the framers of the American Constitution.

Montesquieu's abhorrence of his own despotic French government led him to study at firsthand the laws and customs of other countries. He later reported and analyzed his observations in his book, *The Spirit of the Laws* (1748). Of particular interest to his many readers in America was his discussion of political liberty:

When the legislative and executive powers are united in the same person, or in the same body of magistrates, there can be no liberty. . . . Again, there is no liberty if the judicial power be not separated from the legislative and executive powers.

After the American Revolution, Montesquieu's warning was not forgotten by the delegates to the Constitutional Convention (1787). His forceful words played an important part in the decision to distribute among three branches—legislative, executive, and judicial—the powers of the United States government.

National Archives is the official name of the United States Bureau that serves as a depository for documents, records, and exhibits connected with the nation's history. The three great charters of American freedom—the Declaration of Independence, the Constitution, and the Bill of Rights—are on display in the Exhibition Hall of the National Archives Building in Washington, D.C., where they are viewed every year by thousands of Americans and visitors from other lands.

The documents, protected from further fading by filtered glass, are encased in airtight bronze cases that may be lowered at night or, in an emergency, into a large safe of steel and reinforced concrete under the floor of the hall. Though time has dimmed the writing inscribed on the parchment, the viewer who looks closely may still make out some of the words that have safeguarded our liberty down through the years.

The National Archives, a part of the government General Services Administration, also provides a reference service for researchers, and administers the following Presidential libraries: the Herbert Hoover Library, West Branch, Iowa; the Franklin D. Roosevelt Library, Hyde Park, N.Y.; the Harry S. Truman Library, Independence, Mo.; and the Dwight D. Eisenhower Library, Abilene, Kans.

National Association for the Advancement of Colored People (NAACP). This organization was formed to meet the threat to the Constitutional rights and even to the lives of American Negroes at a time when they were frequently lynched and otherwise cruelly treated by white terrorists. The founders of the new group—prominent men and women of both races—included such educators as John Dewey of Columbia University and Mary E. Woolley, president of Mt. Holyoke College;

National Archives

Rabbi Stephen S. Wise; Lincoln Steffens, journalist; two pioneer social workers, Jane Addams of Hull House in Chicago and Lillian D. Wald of the Henry Street Settlement in New York City; and W. E. B. Du Bois, Negro scholar and author of *The Souls of Black Folk.* Dr. Du Bois was editor of *Crisis,* official magazine of the organization from the time it began active work (1910) until 1932.

Through the years the NAACP has worked through legal means to end segregation and racial discrimination, providing legal advice for many Negroes whose civil rights had been violated. It has sought to bring about better understanding between the races and to obtain improved job and educational opportunities for Negroes. Partly due to NAACP's consistent efforts, segregation in public schools was finally outlawed by a U.S. Supreme Court decision in 1954.

Among the distinguished Negroes who have served as officials of the organization are:

JAMES WELDON JOHNSON, the executive secretary (1916–30), was well known as a lawyer, a consul in the U.S. diplomatic service, a poet, and author of *The Autobiography of an Ex-Colored Man.* It was his belief that one of the great contributions the Negro made to America was "the fortitude with which he has borne himself and steadily forced his way forward." Johnson was voicing the hope and faith of many Negroes when he wrote:

> *Sing a song full of faith*
> *That the dark past has taught us . . .*
> *Facing the rising sun*
> *Of our new day begun . . .*

WALTER FRANCIS WHITE, sociologist and author of *A Man Called White,* was assistant (1916–31), then executive secretary (1931–55). He had only a small percentage of Negro blood, and with his blue eyes and blond complexion could easily have passed for a white man. This he refused to do, because he believed that as a Negro he could accomplish more for members of the race.

During the days before the United States entered World War II, White urged that Negroes be given the same opportunity as other Americans to work in war plants and to "fight for democracy." He was the author of an Executive Order issued by President Franklin D. Roosevelt in 1941, banning discrimination because of race in the U.S. Army and in job training for defense. What is usually considered an even greater accomplishment was the passage by the U.S. Congress, in 1949, of an anti-lynching bill. This was a law for which White had lobbied for more than thirty years. In *How Far the Promised Land,* a book published after his death in 1955, White said:

> The job of curing and preventing man's mistreatment of man because of his race or color in the United States or, for that matter anywhere in the world, is not done. But we are on our way. . . .

ROY WILKINS was a well-known newspaperman before he became executive secretary of the NAACP in 1955. In answer to the criticism on the part of some Negroes that he and some of his fellow officers were too moderate in their methods of solving Negro problems, Wilkins insisted that no group had been more radical in opposing all forms of segregation. He said, at the 1967 convention:

> The NAACP remains committed to its primary goal of eliminating all forms of racial discrimination and achieving equal rights and equal opportunities for all Americans.

Natural Law. The words "the laws of nature" appear in the first sentence of the Declaration of Independence. When Thomas Jefferson wrote them, he was referring to a belief that had long been an ideal of Western civilization.

The idea originated in ancient Greece that above man-made law there exists an unwritten moral law which is the standard of right and justice. This belief was later spread through the Roman world by students of Greek Stoic philosophy, and it had a profound influence on Roman law.

The principle of moral, or "natural," law has probably never been better expressed than it was more than 2,000 years ago by the great Roman orator and lawyer, Cicero. In an essay, *The Republic* (52 B.C.), he wrote:

There is a true law, right reason, which conforms to nature, is universal, unchangeable, and eternal. Its commands urge us to duty, and its prohibitions restrain us from evil.

During the Middle Ages, after the fall of the Roman Empire, the Christian Church carried the same ideal to all parts of western Europe as a "law of God." Later, in the 1600's and 1700's, English and other European philosophers claimed that the laws of nature give all men certain basic rights (see NATURAL RIGHTS).

Many leading American colonists of the Revolutionary era, such as Thomas Jefferson, John Adams, and James Madison, were scholarly and well-read men. They were thoroughly familiar with both the ancient writings on natural law and more recent works on the subject. The references made to the laws of nature in American speeches and documents, before and after the War of Independence, show that the founding fathers considered natural law an essential basis for justice and good government.

Political scientists have maintained for many years that the theory of natural law cannot be proved by logic. But most Americans and other free men have continued to believe that such a law does exist, even if unseen and unproved. In a message to Congress on civil rights in 1963, President John F. Kennedy said:

Justice requires us to insure the blessings of liberty for all Americans and their posterity —not merely for reasons of economic efficiency, world diplomacy and domestic tranquility—but above all, because it is right.

"Because it is right"! Surely those words echo the age-old belief in an unchanging law, a standard for men and governments.

Natural Rights. When the British government tightened its control of the American colonies in the 1760's, the colonists protested vigorously. In speeches, pamphlets, and petitions they insisted that the new and stricter measures violated their rights as Englishmen. When George III and Parliament continued to ignore their protests, the colonists began to stress their claim to "natural rights." They were referring to those basic rights which they considered to be the inborn possession of every man.

Finally, in the great documents of 1776, they declared that any government destructive of such rights should be altered or abolished. The phrase "inherent rights" was used in the Virginia Declaration of Rights in June, 1776; "unalienable rights" was used the next month in the Declaration of Independence. To the colonists, "inherent," "unalienable" (as "inalienable" was spelled), and "natural" rights were essentially the same thing.

American Revolutionary leaders had acquired their ideas about natural rights largely from an essay written in the previous century by John Locke, an English philosopher (see separate entry). Locke believed that governments were formed mainly to protect men's natural rights, which he thought of as rights to life, liberty, and property.

Locke's theories were received with much enthusiasm in colonial America, and in most political writing and discussion "natural rights" were interpreted as meaning "life, liberty, and property." But in the Declaration of Independence Thomas Jefferson departed from the usual tradition. He wrote that all men have "certain unalienable rights, that among these are life, liberty, and the pursuit of happiness." The right of property was so taken for granted by then that Jefferson must have felt no specific mention of it was needed. Therefore, the phrase "the pursuit of happiness" was substituted, thus placing the search for well-being and peace of mind among mankind's essential rights.

The logic of the theory of natural rights and of a natural law, upon which such rights are supposedly based, has been questioned by many political scientists (see NATURAL LAW). But the belief that man does possess fundamental rights has served, and still serves, the cause of freedom. For example, the Preamble of the Universal Declaration of Human Rights (United Nations, 1948) calls for the recognition of the "inalienable rights of all members of the human family." The international committee that wrote those words evidently believed that, as the Declaration of Independence had stated, the existence of such rights is "self-evident."

Negro Rights Movement. "The Emancipation Proclamation," said Wendell Phillips, well-known antislavery leader (1863), "frees the slave but ignores the Negro."

During the century that followed the Civil War, many Negroes would have agreed. Even after the Fourteenth Amendment (1868) conferred citizenship on members of the race and the Fifteenth Amendment (1870) gave them the right to vote, comparatively few of them enjoyed any real freedom as most white people would define the word. This was especially true in the South where—except for a brief period known as "The Reconstruction"—few Negroes had the franchise. Colored citizens were automatically excluded from the polling booths by the requirement in several states that voters must take a literacy test and pay a poll tax which few Negroes could afford.

Other humiliating restrictions were known as "Jim Crow laws," after a popular ditty, "Jump, Jim Crow," about a little colored boy. These laws required Negroes to ride in separate railroad cars, to attend separate schools, and to eat at separate lunchrooms; and most other public facilities were segregated according to race. Many privileges enjoyed by their poorest white neighbors were denied the Negroes.

Some of these same neighbors formed organizations, such as the Ku Klux Klan, to make sure that the Negro "kept his place," an expression often employed by poor whites. Colored people in many communities lived in terror of beatings and torture and even of lynchings. It was to meet these threats to the Negro's safety that the National Association for the Advancement of Colored People, usually referred to as the NAACP, established headquarters in New York City in 1910 (see separate entry).

The purpose of the National Urban League, founded the same year, was to improve social and economic conditions for Negroes in Northern cities.

Other organizations formed since that time include the Congress of Racial Equality, or CORE; the Southern Christian Leadership Council (SCLC), founded by the well-known Negro clergyman, Dr. Martin Luther King, Jr., (see separate entry) ; and the Student Non-violent Coordinating Committee, or SNCC. These organizations all have the same general goal —equality and increased opportunities for American Negroes—though they differ in the methods they advocate to attain that goal.

What many considered the greatest triumph since the abolition of slavery came in 1954 when segregation in public schools was declared unconstitutional by the U.S. Supreme Court. This decision was obeyed reluctantly in many communities, and sometimes not at all. But it marked a great step forward in the Negro Rights Movement. (See EQUAL RIGHTS IN SCHOOLS.)

By then, in spite of all handicaps, many Negroes had risen to positions of influence in the nation. Some of them had become well known as musicians and entertainers, educators, scientists, and statesmen. Thousands had served in two world wars, many with distinction, and after fighting for freedom abroad they were no longer satisfied with anything less than freedom at home. They wanted to have the right to vote, and to send their sons and daughters to good schools so the children would be qualified to fill better jobs when they grew up.

The smaller indignities to which Negroes were subjected also rankled. They found it embarrassing not to be permitted to eat at a lunch counter in stores where they spent their money in other departments. In some states Negroes were discriminated against on public buses, though they paid the same fare as the white passengers did.

It was because of an incident on a city bus in Montgomery, Ala. (Dec., 1955) that the Negro Rights Movement, as we think of it today, began almost by accident. When Rosa Parks, a seamstress, boarded a crowded bus, there were no vacant seats in the colored section; however, she did find a seat in the section reserved for white passengers. A local ordinance forbade Negroes and whites to sit together on buses, but when the bus driver ordered Mrs. Parks to give up her seat to a white man, she refused. As a result, she was arrested.

"I don't know why I wouldn't move," she said later. "I was just tired. My feet hurt."

Probably no one was more surprised than Mrs. Parks when her arrest ignited a long-smouldering spark. The Montgomery Improvement Association was organized and the Negroes of the city were urged to boycott the city bus lines. Most of them responded, and for more than a year they either walked to work or used car pools. Several Negro women brought suit against the bus company, and Alabama courts were asked to pass on the legality of the law that had made it possible for Mrs. Parks to be arrested. In 1956 the Supreme Court upheld the decision of a lower court that segregated seating on public buses was illegal. From then on Negro and white passengers of Montgomery rode the public buses on a first come, first served basis.

The president of the Montgomery Improvement Association, the man who led the boycott, was twenty-seven-year-old Martin Luther King, Jr., pastor of a local church. A dynamic speaker, he soon emerged as leader of the Negro Rights Movement in the South, and during the months after the Montgomery bus boycott his policy of passive resistance met with amazing success.

The struggle against segregation was waged on a number of fronts. Negro young people, often joined by white sympathizers, staged "sit-ins" at lunch counters. Though they refused to leave, their behavior was quiet and dignified. Negroes, together with white friends, also took "freedom rides" on interstate buses, demanding that the two races be accorded equal rights on buses and in bus waiting rooms.

Such demonstrations were legal, inasmuch as the First Amendment guaranteed the rights of all Americans "peaceably to assemble." Yet the demonstrators were often beaten up by white toughs or sent to jail by some local authorities on flimsy pretexts.

The followers of Dr. King were not permitted to carry guns or knives, even to defend themselves, and they refused to resort to violence. Their courage and patience aroused the sympathy and admiration of many white citizens of good will who became increasingly aware of the injustice to which Negroes had been subjected.

In 1963—the Centennial of the Emancipation Proclamation—President John F. Kennedy recommended a Civil Rights Bill to Congress. Its purpose was to protect the Negro's right to vote and also to do away with various forms of discrimination. Hoping to speed the passage of this bill, about 200,000 people, most of them colored, but including many white sym-

pathizers, staged a mammoth march on Washington. On August 28 they gathered on the Mall that stretches between the Washington Monument and the Lincoln Memorial in the nation's capital. During the course of the day most of the Negroes signed a pledge that read:

Standing before the Lincoln Memorial in the Centennial year of emancipation, I affirm my complete personal commitment for the struggle for jobs and freedom for all Americans. . . . I will pledge my heart and my mind and my body . . . without regard to personal sacrifice, to the achievement of social peace through social justice.

It was an orderly but enthusiastic crowd that waited before the Lincoln Memorial for the program to begin. Again and again the crowd burst into song. Again and again could be heard three lines from their favorite "Freedom Song"—

> We shall overcome,
> Black and white together,
> We shall overcome someday.

The Civil Rights Bill for which President Kennedy had worked was not passed during his lifetime. But it was signed into law (July, 1964) by his successor, President Lyndon B. Johnson. But it soon became apparent that a stronger law was needed—one that would do away with the barriers imposed by some of the states to prevent Negroes from registering so they could vote in elections. Congress passed the Voting Rights Bill in 1965, and President Johnson signed it on August 6 in a special ceremony in the Capitol.

The vote, he said, was "the most powerful instrument ever devised by man for breaking down injustice," but the Negroes must learn to use the vote wisely so their choices would advance their own interests and the interests of the nation. For Roy Wilkins, the executive secretary of the NAACP, the ceremony marked "a moment at the summit of our nation." He said, later:

I never doubted that the day would come. But I also never dreamed that in my lifetime a President of the United States would stand up before the world and speak as Mr. Johnson did. . . . The completeness and warmth of his commitment! He stood there before the world and put his role in history on the line.

Unfortunately, neither the Voting Rights Bill nor any succeeding bill passed by Congress could solve all of the problems of the Negroes. Some of those in the North found their situation even more difficult than those in the South. Many of them had migrated from Southern communities to Northern cities, hoping to find work, only to learn that they did not have the necessary training for the jobs that were open. They lived, crowded together, with members of other minority groups, in filthy ghettos.

Frustrated, often desperate, some of them had little use for the doctrine of passive resistance preached by Dr. King. On the West Coast there were riots in Watts, a part of Los Angeles. On the East Coast there were riots in New York City, and violence erupted in many other places across the country.

Responsible Negro leaders, though they realized the riots were often caused by inability to find work or a decent place to live, warned the rioters that they were hurting the Negro Rights Movement. In the opinion of Whitney Young, Jr., director of the National Urban League, the violent activities of a small minority were deplored by 95 per cent of the Negro population. The slogan, "Black Power," was a cause of concern to many people, both colored and white. Negroes who repeated the phrase did not always agree about the meaning. Some insisted it was merely a rallying cry to influence them to use their voting and purchasing power to bring them better economic opportunities, but Roy Wilkins warned against it. However one tried to explain "black power," he said, it gave the impression of one race against another—a sort of Ku Klux Klan in reverse.

Many Negro leaders agreed, among them Dorothy I. Height, president of the National Council of Negro Women. She believed that a more constructive rallying call was needed. She said (Dec. 19, 1966):

We do not want Black Power for the American Negroes. We don't want white power for American whites. The kind of power we seek is the power of freedom in a colorless society—the power to help build a constructive nation and a constructive world together with our fellow Americans.

New Deal. The phrase was used by Franklin D. Roosevelt when he stood before the Democratic Convention in Chicago (July 2, 1932) to accept its nomination for the Presidency. The country was in the depths of the depression and he wanted to assure his audience that, if elected, he would take affirmative and immediate action. The phrase was intended to imply that the government under his administration would try to help, not just important leaders in business, but all Americans alike.

"I pledge you—I pledge myself," he said, "to a new deal for the American people."

After F.D.R. was elected and inaugurated, the words came to mean the body of legislation passed by Congress on the recommendation of the new President and his advisers. The program had a threefold purpose: relief, recovery, and reform.

In the beginning, emergency legislation provided relief for Americans in want. Among other measures, public works were started that would give jobs to the unemployed, increase their pur-

Jobs for the unemployed

chasing power and—by getting more money into circulation—help private business to recover.

Reform legislation, passed in the hope of preventing depressions in the future, included laws to protect investors and to insure bank accounts. Later (1935) the first Social Security Act provided for monthly payments to retired workers over a certain age (from a fund to which they and their employers would both contribute). Provision also was made for payments to widows and dependent children and to persons who had lost their jobs. The purpose of social security, as well as of other New Deal measures, had been summed up in an earlier Message to Congress.

"Among our objectives," the President said, "I place the security of the men, women and children of the nation first."

Not all of the new laws were successful, and some of them were declared unconstitutional by the Supreme Court. But many of the New Deal measures have been retained by succeeding Presidents, both Democratic and Republican. The New Deal, which was the outgrowth of the Square Deal and the New Freedom, in turn laid the groundwork for later reform programs that would be known as the Fair Deal, the New Frontier, and the Great Society.

Northwest Ordinance. This Act, passed by the Continental Congress (1787), provided a system of government for the vast tract of land known as the Northwest Territory, north of the Ohio River and extending as far west as the Mississippi.

According to the treaty (1783) which had ended the American Revolution, Great Britain recognized the claim of the new

United States to this entire region. Times were hard along the Atlantic seaboard, especially for the families of the men who had served in the Revolutionary Army, and many Americans wanted to look for new homes farther west where there was plenty of good, cheap land. The Continental Congress, meeting in New York, finally arranged for the sale of land to settlers on terms they could afford, and worked out a plan of government known as the Northwest Ordinance or the Ordinance of 1787.

This Ordinance was a remarkable document that made it possible for the thousands of settlers, soon to pour into the Northwest Territory, to live under a democratic form of government. Even before there was an American Bill of Rights, the settlers in the new region had been guaranteed freedom of speech and worship. Slavery was forbidden. Education was to be encouraged, "knowledge being necessary [in the words of the Ordinance] to good government and the happiness of mankind."

Though the Northwest Territory was to be governed temporarily by officials appointed by Congress, the Ordinance provided for self-government in the future. As soon as there were 5,000 free males (at that time only white men were allowed to vote), they were to elect their own legislature to make their local laws. Ultimately the Territory was to be divided into several sections, and when the population in any section reached 60,000, the people could apply for statehood. By 1848, five new states (Ohio, Indiana, Illinois, Michigan, and Wisconsin) had been admitted to the Union on an equal basis and with the same privileges as the original thirteen states.

The policies established by the U.S. government in the Northwest Territory have been followed in dealing with other territories acquired later, out of which new states were to be carved.

Oglethorpe, James Edward (1696–1785), British philanthropist, founded the colony of Georgia so that many unfortunate debtors in English prisons might be "restored to light and freedom." As a member of Parliament, he had been appointed to a commission to investigate prisons and was appalled by the conditions he found. He saw many men, and sometimes entire families, living in jail, because they owed small debts they were too poor to pay. Oglethorpe was evidently a persuasive speaker, for he convinced Parliament that whenever possible such prisoners should be freed and given a fresh start in America. He was named one of a group of trustees to establish and govern a colony to be named Georgia in honor of King George II.

In January, 1733, Oglethorpe arrived in the New World with a shipload of settlers. His sympathies embraced not only men who had been imprisoned through no fault of their own, but many other people who had been unfairly treated. Because of his policy of religious toleration toward most faiths, the new colony soon began to attract Protestants from the Scottish highlands and the continent of Europe, and Jews also were made welcome.

**Families
living
in jail**

Yet in most respects James Oglethorpe was a wise and benevolent leader. As long as he was in control, slavery was not permitted in his colony, and by dealing fairly with his Indian neighbors he won their friendship. Unfortunately, much of his time had to be spent fighting the Spaniards who were then in possession of the region called Florida, to the south of Georgia. Oglethorpe's colony did not thrive, as he had hoped, and financial difficulties forced his final return to England (1743). He always kept up his interest in Georgia, and it was a source of grief to him that slavery was permitted there after his departure.

He also was distressed by the disagreements that were to lead to the American Revolution, and he repeatedly spoke out in defense of the colonies. After the British government recognized the independence of the United States, John Adams arrived in London (1785) as the first U.S. Minister to Great Britain. The founder of Georgia, who had brought freedom to many unfortunate individuals, and the diplomat, who had helped to bring freedom to a new nation, exchanged calls. James Oglethorpe, then eighty-eight and with only three more weeks to live, expressed his deep satisfaction that the two countries had come to an understanding and were at peace.

Otis, James (1725–83). Fifteen years before the Declaration of Independence was adopted, James Otis, Boston lawyer and patriot, made an impassioned speech in which he stated that God had "given to all men a natural right to be free."

Some of the laws passed earlier by Parliament to restrict the trade of the colonies had been mostly ignored, until British revenue agents received orders to enforce the laws more rigidly. In their efforts to discover smuggled goods, the agents used Writs of Assistance—general

Religious toleration, however, was not complete, for Papists, as Catholics were sometimes called, were not permitted to settle in Georgia. In excluding them, Oglethorpe was a victim of some of the prejudices of his time. It was an age when Protestants, if they were dominant, often persecuted Catholics; and Catholics, when they had the opportunity, often persecuted Protestants.

search warrants—that made it possible for them to enter any man's house without permission.

Indignant merchants of Boston decided to fight the measure, and Otis resigned his position as a royal officer so that he might act as their lawyer. When the case came to trial before the Superior Court of Massachusetts, he argued that it was a fundamental principle of English law for a man to be secure in his own house. John Adams, who was present, made a note: "Otis was a tongue of fire."

Some years later Adams expanded his notes. "Every man of an immense crowded audience," he said, "appeared to me to go away as I did, ready to take up arms against the Writs of Assistance. Then and there the child independence was born."

Though the court decided against the merchants, the use of Writs of Assistance was discontinued after a few years. Later Otis took part in a number of events that in time would lead to the separation of the colonies from the mother country, and he warned that this might happen unless Great Britain changed its policies. A brilliant man, he was often bitter and extreme in his statements, and one day an infuriated British agent attacked him. A severe blow on the head resulted in a loss of sanity, and James Otis was a broken man long before the American Revolution began. It was said, though, that he "fired the opening gun."

A phrase attributed to Otis by Adams was: *Taxation without representation is tyranny.* Whether or not he was the first to use the words, they became a popular slogan in the struggle of the colonists to maintain their rights.

Paine, Thomas (1737–1809). "The sun never shined on a cause of greater worth ...." said Tom Paine, writing of the American Revolution in his pamphlet *Common Sense*, urging separation from Great Britain. He then went on:

O! ye that love mankind! Ye that dare oppose not only the tyranny but the tyrant, stand forth! Every spot of the Old World is overrun with oppression .... O! receive the fugitive, and prepare in time an asylum for mankind.

This pamphlet, published in January, 1776, was the work of an Englishman recently arrived in America. His sympathies were entirely with the Americans, and he argued that there was no possible advantage to them in a continued association with Great Britain. *"Common Sense* ran like wild fire through the colonies," Thomas Jefferson recalled later. "The lingering doubts of many peaceable folk reluctant to break with Britain were dispelled."

Within three months Paine's pamphlet sold 120,000 copies, and helped to bring about a great change in public opinion. Several colonial assemblies instructed their delegates to the Second Continental Congress to vote for separation from Great Britain, and the Declaration of Independence was adopted (July 4, 1776). Several years of hard fighting still lay ahead, and Tom Paine served for a time in the Continental Army. But it was as a writer who bolstered the morale of soldiers and civilians alike that he made his greatest contribution.

"These are the times that try men's souls," he said in the first of a series of articles called *The Crisis*. The first article, written in December, 1776, when the American cause seemed doomed, was read aloud to George Washington's discouraged little army shivering on the banks of the Delaware River. Paine's ringing reminder that the soldiers were fighting "to set a country free" inspired them to greater efforts, and a few days later they won a brilliant victory at Trenton, N.J. Many civilians were encouraged to join General Washington's forces, marking a turning point in the war.

Several years after the United States won the War of Independence, Tom Paine was in London, trying to raise funds to build an iron bridge he had designed. While there he wrote *The Rights of Man*, a popular two-volume work in defense of the French Revolution. The book angered the leaders then in control of the British government, and Paine, learning that he was to be arrested for treason, fled to France.

In France he was made an honorary citizen, but later he became disillusioned and sickened by the violent turn the Revolution had taken. During the Reign of Terror, the radical leaders sent him to prison, where he worked on another book, *The Age of Reason*. It was a protest against the atheism he saw on every side in France, yet he himself was wrongly accused of being an atheist. He believed in one God and said that "to do good was his religion," but many of his ideas challenged accepted church teachings.

Several years after his release from prison he returned (1802) to the United

States to find himself very unpopular. His religious views were misunderstood, and because of his support of the French Revolution in its early stages many Americans considered him a political radical as well. Almost forgotten, for a while, were his services to his adopted country during the dark days of the American Revolution.

Though Tom Paine's books had earned large sums, most of the money had been given to friends in need, or to organizations dedicated to the ideals of liberty, and he died in poverty. During his last years he spent part of the time on a farm that had been given him by New York State after the War of Independence. Later the location of this farm, in what is now New Rochelle, was marked by a monument in memory of a man who had dedicated most of his life to the cause of freedom. The Thomas Paine Cottage where he lived, lonely and neglected, has been preserved as a museum.

Parker, Theodore (1810–60), well-known reformer and clergyman in Boston,

reached an even wider audience through his lectures and printed sermons. A fervent Abolitionist, he aided many runaway slaves, and his home was always open to them. After the Fugitive Slave Law of 1850 made such activities illegal, he was arrested.

"All right, let them bring me to trial," he declared, and set to work to prepare a 300-page defense. His arguments were so logical and eloquent and his following so great that the case against him was dropped.

Another high point in Parker's career was the speech he made at a mass meeting (1854) in Faneuil Hall to protest the arrest of Anthony Burns, a runaway slave who had been captured in Boston. The clergyman made a moving plea, but his eloquence did not help the unfortunate Negro. At Burns's trial, it was decreed that, under the provisions of the Fugitive Slave Law, he must be returned to his master in the South.

This decision caused such indignation in Boston that it was necessary to call out

Thomas Paine cottage

several military units, as well as the local police, to escort Burns to the dock where he was to board a ship for his master's home. Crowds lined the streets, weeping and shouting, "Shame!" At the dock many people knelt in prayer. The incident may well have influenced Theodore Parker's decision to join a secret committee to furnish financial aid to John Brown (see separate entry) who had some rather vague plans—not thoroughly understood by many of his supporters—to free the slaves.

Penn, William (1644–1718), the founder of the colony of Pennsylvania, put into practice some of the same principles that were to motivate the founding fathers of the American nation a century later. He proved, as had Roger Williams in the earlier colony of Rhode Island, that democracy could be a practical form of government. Penn's problems were more complicated, since Pennsylvania was much larger than Rhode Island and soon had a population made up of several nationalities. Yet he never veered from his fundamental purpose—to "found a free colony for all mankind" in America.

During his youth in England, William Penn had enjoyed many privileges as the son of an influential English admiral, but angered his father when he joined the Society of Friends. The Quakers, as members of this then-despised sect were called, were cruelly persecuted; and because young Penn had insisted on preaching and writing tracts in their behalf, he was sent to prison several times. Even before that, as a student at Oxford, he had begun to dream of founding a colony where Quakers and other persecuted people could find a refuge.

When the elder Penn died, King Charles II, who had owed him a large sum of money, settled the debt by granting the son a vast tract of land in America. At last he could carry out his plans for a colony. He wanted to call it "Sylvania,"

meaning "woods." But the king insisted it be named Pennsylvania in honor of the late admiral.

After William Penn's arrival in America (1682) he called together an assembly, made up of representatives from different parts of his domain. They were assured that the colonists would be governed by laws of their own making, and Penn then presented "a frame of government"—a constitution—which he had prepared while still in England. This constitution could be amended or altered as the Assembly wished.

"I am ready to settle such foundations as may be for your happiness," said William Penn.

It was his habit to respect the rights of everyone, including Indians. Though Penn had come into possession of Pennsylvania through the payment of a debt, he reasoned that the red-skinned neighbors of the region were the rightful owners. He entered into several treaties with them for the purchase of the land in his colony, and because he always kept his promises they loved and respected him. During the next fifty years, the people of Pennsylvania, unlike many other colonists, were able to live in peace with the Indians.

This peace, and the fact that people of all creeds were made welcome, were largely responsible for the colony's rapid growth and prosperity. Though non-Christians could not hold office, no one was molested because of his religious beliefs.

"We must give the liberty we ask," said William Penn, and he wrote a pamphlet assuring all who wished to come to Pennsylvania that they would have complete freedom of conscience and also be able to purchase land on easy terms. This pamphlet was widely read in Europe, and soon many people who had been persecuted for their religious beliefs began to arrive in Pennsylvania. They came not only from England, but from Holland and Germany,

Ireland and Wales. All wanted to share in the benefits of what Penn called his "holy experiment."

It was an experiment that presented many problems. Men and women from different countries, speaking different languages, used to different customs, and holding a variety of beliefs, could not be expected always to agree. In time, though, they learned to live together on terms of equality, just as the people of a new nation, the United States, would have to learn to live together in the days to come.

In a number of ways, the example set by William Penn was to influence a nation that did not exist during his lifetime. When, due to the growth of the colony, the original Frame of Government was no longer sufficient to meet the needs of the people, the Pennsylvania Charter of Privileges was issued (1701). This Charter reaffirmed Penn's ideas that government should be based on the consent of the governed and that men, to be happy, must have religious freedom.

William Penn's last years were saddened by financial worries and ill health. Nothing, though, could ever erase the satisfaction he had felt when he first learned that he was to be granted Pennsylvania.

"My God that has given it me through many difficulties," he had said, "will, I believe, bless and make it the seed of a nation."

Petition, The Right to, is one of the fundamental rights that the United States inherited from England. Inasmuch as Englishmen had long been in the habit of petitioning their king or Parliament for a redress of grievances, the English colonists felt they should have this same privilege. Among the measures adopted by the First Continental Congress was a respectful Petition to the King, stating their grievances. The fact that it was ignored helped to bring on the American Revolution. After the Americans became independent

and adopted a new Constitution, they wanted to make sure that the "right to petition" could never be taken away. It was for this reason that specific mention of the right was included in the First Amendment added to the U.S. Constitution.

"Congress shall make no law . . .," the Amendment states, "abridging the right of the people . . . to petition the government for a redress of grievances."

The right was never seriously contested during the early days of the republic. But by 1836 many Americans had become deeply concerned about Negro slavery and so many petitions poured into Congress, urging that slavery be abolished, that the House of Representatives passed a resolution known as the "Gag Rule" (1836). This resolution forbade the reading of any more petitions on the subject. After repeated attempts by Congressman John Quincy Adams, the gag rule was repealed (1844).

Since then the right of the people to petition Congress, as guaranteed to them in the First Amendment, has not been questioned, but the right is now exercised in a different manner. One of the modern substitutes is the vast amount of mail and telegrams received by Congressmen (and sometimes by state legislators) from individual citizens, stating their views. Civic-minded groups, such as the League of Women Voters, bring pressure to bear on lawmaking bodies to enact legislation they consider necessary for the welfare of the people.

Other pressure groups, called lobbyists, seek to influence lawmakers to pass or repeal certain laws for the benefit of special businesses. For the protection of the public, Congressional lobbyists are required to register (since 1946) and state the purpose of their activities. They often perform a valuable service by providing their representatives in Congress with information needed to form an opinion regarding the need for certain laws.

Petition of Right (1628) was an important document in the long struggle of Parliament to limit the power of the English monarchs. King Charles I, who had come to the throne three years earlier, believed that his authority was supreme and that he had the right to run the kingdom as he saw fit. When Parliament refused to grant him funds to carry on foreign wars, he ordered his subjects to lend him the money. There was a great deal of resistance to the forced loans, and some of the men who refused to pay were thrown into prison and held without being charged.

When even the use of such arbitrary methods failed to raise the money the king needed, he was obliged to turn once more to Parliament for funds. Again the members of Parliament refused. They had no intention of granting money to a king whose recent actions had trampled on the rights and liberties of the English people. Instead they drew up the Petition of Right. The first part of the Petition called attention to the ancient laws and statutes that the king had violated.

"No man hereafter," the Petition continued, should "be compelled to make or yield any gift, loan, benevolence, tax, or such like charge, without common consent by Act of Parliament."

The Petition also said that there must be no more imprisonments unless a definite reason was stated. In addition, it noted two other illegal practices that must be stopped: the billeting of soldiers in private homes and the use of martial law in peacetime.

Only after Charles reluctantly agreed to accept the provisions of the Petition did Parliament vote him a grant of money. It was not long, though, before the king began to evade his promises and to rule in the despotic manner that led to civil war (1642) and to his execution seven years later.

Even before the English Civil War broke out, while Charles was still in power, thousands of Englishmen had migrated to America to escape religious and political persecution. These Englishmen were well acquainted with the Petition of Right, which became part of the political heritage of the colonies.

More than a century later, what the people in America considered a violation of the rights listed in the Petition and other great English documents led to widespread discontent—a discontent that was a contributing cause of the American Revolution.

Phillips, Wendell (1811–84), a member of a prominent New England family, was one of the more extreme Abolitionists. He sacrificed a promising law career in Boston to lecture against slavery, and believed that only through "uninterrupted agitation" could the people be made to realize the dangers that threatened liberty. He considered Abraham Lincoln too moderate in his views, and even after Lincoln became President and issued the Emancipation Proclamation, the fiery and handsome Boston orator was not satisfied. (See NEGRO RIGHTS MOVEMENT.)

During the final year of the Civil War (1865), Phillips became president of the American Antislavery Society, remaining in that post until the passage of the 15th Amendment guaranteed that no citizen's right to vote should be denied "on account of race, color, or previous condition of servitude." He then turned his attention to other reforms, including fair treatment for Indians and woman suffrage.

Pilgrims, as the band of Separatists that founded Plymouth Colony in Massachusetts are usually called today, settled first in Holland (1608) and later in America (1620) in their search for religious freedom. Because they had wandered so far, they took comfort from a passage in the Bible (Hebrews 11, 13–16) which referred to "strangers and pilgrims on the earth" that "seek a better country."

"Plimoth Plantation," as the settlement was first called, was named for the English town from which the Pilgrims had set sail. A replica of the *Mayflower,* the tiny vessel in which the Pilgrims made their long voyage across the Atlantic, and the village they built during their first hard years in the new land, may be seen in Plymouth today.

Forge. She was among a number of wives who washed and cooked for the soldiers, and later she accompanied her husband's regiment when it left to take part in the battle of Monmouth (June 28, 1778). In spite of the sweltering heat, Molly filled her pitcher again and again at some nearby springs and carried water to the fighting, sweating troops. It was then that they began to call her Molly Pitcher.

On the monument that now marks her grave in Carlyle, Pa., is told the other story for which she is remembered. Her husband fell, wounded and overcome by heat, while manning one of the cannons, but Molly took his place and continued to fire until the battle was over.

After Private Hayes's death (1789), Molly married another Revolutionary soldier, George McCauley, but due to his indolent ways she had to work as a laundress. In 1822 the Pennsylvania leg-

Pitcher, Molly (1754?–1832), is the name by which this Pennsylvania heroine is known to history. She was born Mary Ludwig, married John Casper Hayes and, after he joined the Continental Army, shared with him the hardships of Valley

islature finally voted her a small but welcome pension in recognition of her heroism.

Pitt, William, Earl of Chatham (1708–78). This great English statesman proved

himself a staunch friend to the American patriots in the troubled days before the American Revolution. At the time of the Stamp Act, he reminded his fellow members in the House of Commons that the Americans were sons of England and had the same love for freedom; and it was largely through his influence that the Stamp Act was repealed.

After Pitt was created Earl of Chatham and was entitled to a seat in the House of Lords, he continued to befriend the Americans. He condemned other harsh measures passed by Parliament, and praised the wisdom and patience of the Continental Congress.

"You cannot but respect their cause," he said, "and wish to make it your own."

Lord Chatham continued to support the stand taken by the Congress until it adopted the Declaration of Independence. When France entered the war on the side of the Americans, fear of England's ancient enemy caused some of the members of Parliament to favor recognizing the independence of the new United States. But not Lord Chatham! He advocated giving

the Americans complete control of their internal government, but his last speech, made shortly before his death, was an eloquent plea that every possible effort should be made to keep the colonies in the British Empire.

By then it was too late, for the Americans were determined to have a separate nation. Had Pitt's advice been followed earlier by the British Parliament, there might never have been a Declaration of Independence.

Pledge of Allegiance: *I pledge allegiance to the flag of the United States of America and to the republic for which it stands, one nation under God, indivisible, with liberty and justice for all.* These words are repeated by thousands of children at the start of each school day and also by patriotic groups on numerous other occasions. Each person stands, holding his right hand over his heart (see Frontispiece).

The special occasion for which the pledge was composed was Columbus Day, Oct. 12, 1892, the 400th anniversary of the discovery of America by Christopher Columbus. On that day ground was broken in Chicago for the World's Columbian Exposition, which would be held the following year.

The suggestion that a Pledge of Allegiance was needed had come from the publisher of the *Youth's Companion*, a popular family magazine, and one of the editors, Francis Bellamy, was principally responsible for the version read in Chicago. The pledge became popular immediately, but it was not until Dec. 28, 1945, that the U.S. Congress officially designated it the "Pledge of Allegiance to the Flag."

The phrase "under God" was added by Act of Congress (1954), and the bill specifying this addition was signed into law on Flag Day (June 14) by President Dwight D. Eisenhower.

See also AMERICAN'S CREED.

Political Parties, operating within the framework of the U.S. Constitution, have enabled American citizens to maintain control over their government. Though the Constitution made no provision for political parties, their influence has grown stronger through the years. Not since the Civil War has a minority refused to abide by the expressed wishes of the majority in an election.

In spite of the disadvantages of the party system, such as the expenditure of huge sums and the rise of tempers during the heat of election campaigns, political parties serve to safeguard the freedom so highly prized by Americans. No matter how much the American people may differ in their opinions, it is now generally agreed that the strength of their democracy lies in the two-party system. It is a system that provides the voters with a choice of candidates and issues and, once the excitement of a campaign is over, the disappointed candidates usually accept the verdict of the people with good grace.

The defeated or minority party— sometimes called "the loyal opposition"— still has a useful function to perform. Watchful criticism by the "outs" can serve as a brake on the temptation of the "ins" (the majority party) to take advantage of their position. The "ins" therefore are inclined to be more careful in the exercise of power. Meanwhile the "outs" are hard at work, hoping for a return to power at the next election, and the country benefits from the competition.

The Democratic Party and the Republican Party are the two major national political parties in the United States today. Though third, or minor, political parties have been organized from time to time and sometimes are influential locally —in cities and states—they have never won a major national election.

Presidential Medal of Freedom, the highest civilian award in the United States, is bestowed each year by the President on an "honors list" of persons who have made outstanding contributions in the fields of culture and public service. The design of the medal shows a white star mounted on a base of gold eagles, with a center ring of thirteen smaller stars against a buff background.

George F. Ball, Under Secretary of State (1961–66), addressing a group of distinguished men and women who received the annual award, said:

Each nation rewards achievement in its own manner and in its own style. Fiercely committed to the democratic principle, the drafters of our Constitution forbade titles of nobility. But they made clear by their acts as well as by their words that democracy, God forbid, should never imply mediocrity, and they knew that a society would be unworthy that did not pay homage to its elite.

The Presidential Medal of Freedom Award was instituted by President John F. Kennedy, and the first awards were made July 4, 1963, a few months before his death. He himself was awarded the medal posthumously in a special ceremony at the White House (Dec. 6, 1963) by President Lyndon B. Johnson.

Press, Freedom of. *See* EXPRESSION, FREEDOM OF.

Press and Other Forms of Communication. When the American Revolution began, two-thirds of the colonial newspapers favored the cause of the patriots and helped to unite them in their struggle for freedom. Important in fostering a desire for independence was the publication of such pamphlets as *Common Sense* by Thomas Paine, and numerous proclamations and resolutions written by other leaders and circulated in leaflet form. The influence of the printed word was recognized by such leading patriots as Dr. Benjamin Rush (see separate entry) during the Constitutional Convention. Newspapers, he said, were "not only the vehicles of knowledge and intelligence but sentinels of liberties of our country."

Thomas Jefferson was well aware of the importance of newspapers in maintaining a free government. Though bitterly and often unjustly criticized by the press, Jefferson was convinced that, if the press were kept free, truth would prevail in the end. If voters were to form intelligent opinions, he maintained, they must be provided with full information concerning public affairs, and this could best be accomplished through newspapers distributed to the mass of the people. He said:

Were it left to me, to decide whether we should have a government without newspapers, or newspapers without a government, I should not hesitate a moment to prefer the latter. But I should mean that every man should receive those papers and be capable of reading them.

What has been called the public's "right to know" may be satisfied today, not only by numerous newspapers, but by thousands of magazines and books that pour from the presses. Radio commentators tell of important events, and television programs bring pictures of these events, almost as soon as they happen, into millions of homes.

Though government officials may withhold information if, in their opinion, national security is involved, and at times have been accused of "managing the news," American newscasters and newspaper writers do not hesitate to criticize governmental policies or officials.

The situation is quite different in nations controlled by dictators. There the public is given only such information as government officials want them to have. In contrast, American men and women are doubtless as well informed as any people in the world, due to their free press. It has helped the voters to form the judg-

ments essential for the success of a democratic form of government.

Even the American press, though, is subject to pressures. Pressure may be exerted by advertisers who furnish a large part of the revenue, and sometimes influential persons or groups demand that certain facts be withheld. On the other hand, there have been countless instances when crusading newspapers have exposed crime and corruption; when they have influenced the electorate to vote for the better of two candidates in an election campaign; and when they have championed worthwhile causes.

Progressive Movement. Abraham Lincoln had called the American government "a government of the people, by the people, for the people," but during the half century following the Civil War many Americans feared this was no longer true. A comparatively few rich men had managed to get control of many forests, mineral supplies, sources of water power, and other natural resources, which they exploited for their own advantage. The so-called "Big Business" leaders formed large corporations, and some of these corporations combined to form even bigger organizations called "trusts." When they became so powerful that they could force their rivals out of business, the public was at their mercy. Once competition was done away with, the big industrial firms could charge whatever they wished for the products and services they sold.

Some of those same leaders made large contributions to the campaigns of men they wanted elected to office. This meant that many members of Congress and state legislatures felt obliged to pass the kind of laws Big Business wanted. The result was that a few Americans profited at the expense of the many. As conditions worsened, the great mass of Americans became restless and angry.

Public indignation was further aroused by a flood of magazine articles and books by well-known authors who exposed corruption in business and government alike. When Theodore Roosevelt became President (1901) he, too, condemned "the malefactors of great wealth," as he called some of the unscrupulous business leaders who considered themselves more important than the government. President Roosevelt did not object to corporations just because they were big, but he did object to business leaders who considered themselves above the law. The fact that the nation was founded on the idea of freedom, he said, did not mean "freedom for the strong to wrong the weak."

Theodore Roosevelt was the first President to realize how much the country had changed during the years since the Civil War. On his recommendation, Congress passed several progressive measures, but T.R.'s great talent was in molding public opinion. He felt one of the duties of a President was to educate the public, and because of his colorful personality and popular following he succeeded admirably. The American people began to realize that changes were needed to meet new conditions.

Several years after T. R. left the White House, he decided to run again for the Presidency and was bitterly disappointed when the Republican Party refused to nominate him. He then became the candidate of the new Progressive Party, but the Republican vote was split, and the Democratic candidate, Woodrow Wilson, was elected. The two men were political rivals and different in personality and approach, but they were agreed on a number of fundamental principles.

In his first Inaugural Address (1913), President Wilson reminded his audience that their great system of government had sought to set liberty upon an enduring foundation. He then continued:

But the evil has come with the good. We have been proud of our industrial achievements, but we have not hitherto stopped thoughtfully enough to count the human cost. The great government we loved has too often been made use of for private and selfish purposes, and those who used it had forgotten the people.

President Wilson called his program of reform "The New Freedom," after the title of a book he had written. The "forgotten people" he had mentioned in his Inaugural Address greatly benefitted from the new laws he recommended to Congress. These laws included legislation to help the farmer and to stop unfair trade practices. A Federal Reserve Board was set up to improve the nation's banking system. Though the entrance of the United States into World War I (1917) interrupted Wilson's program of reform, more reform legislation was passed during the first three years of his administration than at any previous period in American history.

The laws stayed on the books, but they could not prevent the disasters that followed World War I. The European nations involved—victors as well as nations that had been defeated—were in a pitiful condition. In some countries farms had been overrun, crops destroyed, cities gutted by fire. Many people were without work; many were hungry.

During this same period, the United States seemed prosperous enough—for a while. In 1929 Herbert Hoover, the great humanitarian and wartime administrator who had literally kept thousands of Europeans from starving, became President. He felt confident, as he said in his Inaugural Address, that the United States was "nearer the final triumph over poverty than ever before in the history of any land."

Unfortunately, the hard times in Europe meant that Europeans could no longer afford to buy U.S. products; but many

Americans were lulled by a false sense of prosperity and spent more than they could afford. They bought shares of stock in big industrial firms, often paying more than the stock was actually worth. As the prices of stocks went up, more and more people invested, hoping to make a big profit.

And then the prices of stocks began to go down. President Hoover had been in office only a few months when the stock market crash (1929) marked the beginning of the worst depression in the nation's history. The investors lost a great deal of money; many lost their life savings. Banks closed. Factories and stores had to shut down because they no longer had customers. By 1932 more than twelve million Americans were out of work.

In the beginning, neither the President nor other leaders then in the government believed that the depression would last for more than a few months. Time proved them wrong, and during the next two years conditions grew steadily worse.

The President finally asked Congress to pass several measures which he hoped would help, but the number of needy people increased. President Hoover, much as he regretted the suffering of his fellow citizens, felt they should be cared for either by private charity or by authorities in each community. Though local organizations did not have the funds that were available to the federal government, Hoover sincerely believed the government had no right to interfere.

Not so Franklin Roosevelt, who was the candidate for President on the Democratic ticket (1932). During the election campaign he proposed what he called a "New Deal" for the American people, and in November they voted for it in overwhelming numbers.

The New Deal brought about great changes in American life. Like his distant cousin, T. R., who had been President a quarter of a century earlier, the younger Roosevelt wanted to conserve the best of the old order, but correct the abuses that had brought the nation close to disaster. He said:

Nowadays we have a different kind of society. The Industrial Revolution changed the way people live....I am trying to see how democracy can be applied in a different kind of environment from that in which it was born.

Gradually the nation began to recover from the depression. The principle was established, as F. D. R. said in his Message to Congress (1937), that "the deeper purpose of democratic government is to assist as many of its citizens as possible."

The Progressive Party that had been organized by Theodore Roosevelt's admirers lasted only four years (1912–16), but the progressive movement continues. Nor is it confined to one political party. The need for progress remains constant, for new problems arise each year. Finding answers that will protect citizens from abuse and help them preserve their liberty remains the goal of American government.

worship according to the dictates of his own conscience.

Religion, Freedom of. When the Bill of Rights was added to the U.S. Constitution, the First Amendment read: "Congress shall make no law respecting an establishment of religion, or prohibiting the free exercise thereof. ..." The conviction that the way a person worships is his own affair had its roots deep in the past. For a century and a half before the United States became a nation, Europeans had been crossing the Atlantic in search of religious freedom. What has been called

Reformation. Even before the settling of what is now the United States, the spirit of inquiry sparked by the Protestant Reformation resulted in a ferment of ideas that was to have long-lasting results. No longer did many people feel they must submit blindly to authority in either religious or civil matters. This new spirit of independence made possible the development of a democratic form of government in which the voters have the right to make the decisions.

The Reformation, which began in Germany under Martin Luther during the 1500's, eventually resulted in the formation of a number of Protestant sects. It also stimulated a reform movement already well under way in the Roman Catholic Church. In neither case was the word "reformation" necessarily synonymous with religious liberty. For many years Catholics, when they were a majority in a country, persecuted Protestants. Protestants, when they were in control of a government, were cruel to Catholics, and Protestants of one sect often oppressed other Protestants who held contrary views.

The result was that thousands of Europeans of various religious opinions and practices fled to America, so each might

"the great migration" of thousands of Puritans, who fled England, accounted for the founding of Boston, Salem, and other New England towns. Jews found a refuge in Rhode Island and Georgia; Catholics in Maryland, though Protestants also were welcomed; and Quakers, as well as other persecuted groups, came to Pennsylvania.

Oddly enough, the Puritans, who crossed the Atlantic to worship as they thought right, discriminated against anyone who disagreed with them or who refused to attend a Puritan church. In Virginia, and in several other southern colonies, the Church of England was established by law as the state church, and the colonists were expected to support it, regardless of their personal preferences. It was due to the courage of a few leaders, including Roger Williams, William Penn, Thomas Jefferson, and James Madison,

that such narrow and bigoted practices came into disrepute.

By 1787, when the Constitution was adopted, there was such a diversity of religious beliefs in the new nation that only by guaranteeing liberty of conscience to all could the people be expected to live in harmony. Time has proved the wisdom of that decision. The fact that each person in the United States may worship (or not worship) as his conscience dictates remains one of the most prized of American liberties.

Revere, Paul (1735–1818), a Boston silversmith and engraver, was one of the early heroes of the American Revolution. He was a member of the Sons of Liberty, a messenger for the Committees of Correspondence, and one of the leaders in the Boston Tea Party. "Paul Revere's Ride,"

the poem by Henry Wadsworth Long-fellow, tells the story of his historic adventure before the battles of Lexington and Concord (see separate entry).

Roosevelt, (Anna) Eleanor (1884–1962), from the time her husband, Franklin D. Roosevelt, entered public life and even before, was active in helping other people. To her, social welfare did not mean philanthropy or charity, but the right of every human being—because he *was* a human being—to the fundamental freedoms mentioned in the Declaration of Independence and guaranteed by the U.S. Constitution and Bill of Rights.

Because President Roosevelt was crippled, he depended on his wife to visit and report to him on some of the poverty-stricken regions in the country. Like him, she wanted all Americans to share in the benefits of freedom. In the depression years, when some young people thought Communism might provide an answer to their problems, Mrs. Roosevelt—through her writings, her speeches, and her personal contacts—renewed their faith in democracy. To the Negroes who had long been denied their rights she was a special friend. During World War II she traveled thousands of miles to visit American soldiers overseas. By helping them to understand that the President cared about them and that the government was interested in their welfare, she greatly strengthened their morale.

There had never been a First Lady quite like Eleanor Roosevelt. In her seemingly unlimited energy, she resembled her uncle, Theodore Roosevelt. At one time she was criticized for being so active, but later her activities brought her wide acclaim and she became known as "the First Lady of the World." In her trips abroad she had met many downtrodden and mistreated men and women. She had seen their unfortunate children, and she considered it her responsibility to help them.

After Franklin Roosevelt died, his widow was appointed a U.S. delegate to the United Nations (Dec., 1945) by the new President, Harry S. Truman. In this position Eleanor Roosevelt came into closer contact with representatives from Communist countries whose ideas about life and government were radically opposed to hers. Because she believed in the right of people to differ, she listened to them with her usual courtesy, but she also made them listen to her.

"In a democracy," she said, "you must be able to meet with people and argue your point of view. ... That must be part of the freedom of people in the United States."

Probably Eleanor Roosevelt's greatest service came after her appointment as the first chairman of the Commission on Human Rights.

The task of this committee was to work out a list of fundamental human rights that would serve as a standard of achievement for all peoples. Under the chairman's patient guidance, and after frequent meetings, the list was finally ready. It was submitted to the UN General Assembly and formally adopted (Dec. 10, 1948). This was not a legal document, but Mrs. Roosevelt put her confidence in the pressure of public opinion in the different countries represented to enforce its provisions. She said:

We hope this proclamation by the General Assembly will be an event comparable to the proclamation of the Rights of Man by the French people in 1789, the adoption of the Bill of Rights by the people of the United States, and the adoption of comparable declarations at different times in other countries.

The year after Mrs. Roosevelt's death, the Eleanor Roosevelt Memorial Foundation was chartered by Congress (1963) to perpetuate her ideals.

See also UNIVERSAL DECLARATION OF HUMAN RIGHTS.

Roosevelt, Franklin Delano (1882–1945), the thirty-second President, began his career in the New York State Senate (1911–13) and as Assistant Secretary of the U.S. Navy (1913–20). He was well on his way to a brilliant political future when he was stricken with poliomyelitis (1921). Though he was never able to walk again unaided, after several years of intensive treatment he returned to politics. In 1928 he was elected Governor of New York State, then reelected. He was interested— as his distant cousin, Theodore Roosevelt, had been—in having laws passed that would help the people.

By the time Franklin Roosevelt's second term as governor began (1931), the effects of the worldwide depression were being felt in the United States. There were some government officials who said the situation would right itself in time, but Governor Roosevelt insisted the facts must be faced. With many New Yorkers out of work and in actual need, he believed it was the duty of their government to help them until such time as they could help themselves. New York was the first state to use funds from its treasury to set up temporary relief stations and to start a system of public works that would provide jobs for the unemployed. The governor's success in handling the problems of the depression made him a national figure, and he was elected President.

The day of his inauguration (Mar. 4, 1933) was a critical time in the nation's history. Hundreds of banks had failed, and thousands of Americans had lost their life savings. They had lost their homes and their farms. Factories and stores had been forced to close, which meant their employees were out of work, and thousands were left without money even to buy food for their families. When the new President stood on the platform erected before the east front of the Capitol, he looked down at the crowd that had gathered to hear his Inaugural Address. Despair was written on many of the faces.

Franklin Roosevelt sounded stern when he began to speak. There was no lack of substance, no lack of plenty in the land, he said. It was the "unscrupulous money changers" and "self-seekers," who through incompetence and greed for high profits, had caused the depression. Yet the American people need not distrust "the future of essential democracy." The voters, in electing him, had delivered a mandate that they wanted action—"direct, vigorous action"—and that was what he intended to give them. He proposed to ask Congress for the necessary legislation and authority to bring about the recovery of "a stricken nation in a stricken world."

"This great nation will endure as it has endured," he said confidently, "will revive and prosper. The only thing we have to fear is fear itself."

The   new   President's   confidence

brought a renewal of hope to the American people. On his recommendation, Congress enacted into law a number of measures (that came to be known as "the New Deal") for dealing with the depression. F.D.R., as he was called, believed that government should be strong enough to protect the freedom of the people. He also believed that none should be free to injure others and that government must impose limitations on those who tried to do so—a point of view that brought him both praise and bitter criticism. His answer to his critics was that he was not for a return to that interpretation of "liberty under which for many years a free people were being gradually regimented into the service of the privileged few." Slowly the country began to recover from the depression. What especially gratified F.D.R. was that important reforms had been accomplished without loss of liberty.

This had not been true in parts of Europe where the people had suffered even more than the Americans during the previous few years. In Germany and Italy dictators seized control of their governments, promising to solve all the problems of the two nations. On the other side of the world, a small military clique was the real ruler of Japan. Once the dictators had subdued their own people, they set out to conquer neighboring countries, and their dreams of world conquest brought on World War II.

Many Americans realized that they, too, might have to fight for freedom and, confident that President Roosevelt would be an able leader in a time of great danger, they elected him to a third term. Four years later (Nov., 1944) they elected him a fourth time, for the situation was even more critical. The United States had been brought into the war by the Japanese attack on Pearl Harbor (Dec. 7, 1941), and American forces were fighting around the globe.

If Franklin Roosevelt ever had inner doubts about ultimate victory, he did not let anyone know. His spirits always seemed high, and he inspired others with his courage. He was determined not only to win the war but also the peace that would follow. The failure of the League of Nations after World War I had made him realize that the same mistakes must not be repeated.

In the midst of the fighting, the President went abroad several times to confer with other Allied leaders. At some of these meetings, both war plans and peace plans were discussed. The final conference in which F.D.R. took part was held in Yalta, a town in the Crimea. This region was a part of the Soviet Union, which was then an ally of Britain and the United States.

One accomplishment at Yalta that gratified the President was an agreement to hold another conference at San Francisco, to which fifty nations would be invited to send delegates. There final plans would be made for a permanent United Nations organization to keep peace when the war was over.

After his return home, President Roosevelt appeared before a joint session of Congress (Mar. 1, 1945). Instead of standing with the aid of heavy steel braces around his legs, as he usually did when he made a speech, he spoke from his wheelchair. He looked tired and ill, but he sounded confident as he reported on the Yalta Conference. One purpose of the Conference, he said, was to bring defeat to Germany with the smallest possible loss of Allied lives. The second purpose was to continue efforts to lay a foundation for lasting peace, with "guarantees of tolerance and freedom." He continued:

The structure of world peace cannot be the work of one man, or one party, or one Nation . . . . It cannot be a structure of complete perfection at first. But it can be a peace —and it will be a peace—based on the sound and just principles of the Atlantic Charter—on the concept of the dignity of the human being.

The President planned to attend the San Francisco Conference scheduled to open April 25. Earlier in the month he went to Warm Springs, Ga., for a brief rest. He died there very suddenly, worn out by overwork, but with the knowledge that he had defended liberty both at home and abroad. Through his New Deal he had proved that the democratic process could be made to work for the benefit of the people. Under his leadership his nation was helping to restore liberty to the conquered peoples of Europe. In planning the United Nations he had tried to make it possible, both for his own generation and posterity, to enjoy the freedom that comes only with security and peace.

Roosevelt, Theodore (1858–1919), the twenty-sixth President, was a fighter all his life. As a young man of twenty-three he was elected to the New York State Assembly from his district in New York City. Shortly after his arrival in Albany, the state capital, he was shocked when a lawyer friend told him the legislature was controlled by "an inner circle of power." This inner circle was made up of big businessmen and politicians, and Theodore was advised that he would need their backing if he hoped to get ahead.

"It was the first glimpse I had," he said later in his *Autobiography*, "of that combination between business and politics which I was in after years so often to oppose."

He began by opposing the "political bullies" who controlled the state legislature, but in spite of their opposition the public liked him, and he was reelected twice. Later, as Civil Service Commissioner in the federal government (1889–95) and as police commissioner of New York City (1895–97), he continued to oppose the men he called "crooked politicians," and to enforce laws that would help the people.

While Roosevelt was Assistant Secre-

tary of the Navy (1897–98), his belligerent attitude helped to bring on the Spanish-American War, in which he promptly enlisted. As colonel of a regiment popularly known as the Rough Riders, he joined the American forces fighting for the independence of Cuba from Spain, and the American newspaper war correspondents soon found that he made good "copy." Some of his daring activities were widely reported in the press back home, and he returned to the United States a popular hero (Aug., 1898). Later that same year he was elected Governor of New York State.

As governor (1899–1900), Roosevelt's accomplishments, though less spectacular than his exploits in Cuba, were more important for the cause of freedom and democracy. He brought about some much-needed reforms, including the passage of several laws to preserve the forests and minerals and other natural resources in the state for the people to whom they rightfully belonged.

These reforms won the approval of the people, but not of the bosses in Theodore Roosevelt's own political party. They were interested in helping the wealthy men in the big corporations, and they called the governor "a dangerous man"—dangerous because he refused to take orders. They knew he doubtless could be elected to a second term, and decided that the best way to get rid of him was to work for his nomination and election as Vice President of the United States. This was a dignified position but, at that time, one with little power. The bosses reasoned that by "kicking Roosevelt upstairs," so to speak, he could cause them no more trouble.

They could not have been more wrong. A few months after the inauguration, the President, William McKinley, was shot. Then "that wild man," as Senator Mark Hanna had once called the Vice President, was suddenly thrust into the Presidency (1901).

The new Chief Executive was certainly not a wild man, but he was enthusiastic, and he was determined—and also very popular. For his motto, he had taken an old African saying, "Speak softly and carry a big stick." By "big stick," he meant the power of the Presidency, and he intended to use that power for the "general welfare" of the people, as stated in the Preamble to the Constitution.

Probably not since the time of Andrew Jackson had the people felt so interested in a President while he was still in office. But "Teddy" or "T. R.," the nicknames by which he was affectionately known, did not inspire much affection among the leaders of some of the big business corporations. Though he recognized that corporations were a necessary part of the industrial system in the new century, he had only contempt for the business leaders who put profits ahead of human welfare. Big business, he said, must give the people a square deal. He was just as firmly resolved, though, that anyone in business who tried to do right was equally entitled to a square deal. By this term he meant fair play, and the phrase became the popular slogan of his administration. He said:

Here in America, we the people have a continent on which to work out our destiny. . . . Nowhere else in the world is there such a chance for the triumph on a gigantic scale of the great cause of democracy and popular government . . . . We believe this country will not be a permanently good place for any of us unless we make it a reasonably good place for all of us to live in.

One way the President hoped to bring this about was to try to stop the shameful waste of natural resources. He succeeded in setting aside, before it was too late, some millions of acres of timberland as national forest reserves. Among other measures he recommended to Congress were laws providing for the erection of huge dams in the western part of the country, with the result that regions once too dry for raising crops were turned into rich farm land.

There was not time in one administration to do all that needed to be done in conservation, and the work would have to be carried on by others in later years. But it was Theodore Roosevelt who first made people realize how rapidly their natural resources were being depleted. One of his great contributions, for which Americans are still grateful, is that he alerted the public to the need for action.

Runnymede is a meadow in England twenty miles southwest of London on the south bank of the Thames River. It was there (some say on a nearby island) that tyrannical King John yielded to the demand of his barons and placed his seal (June 15, 1215) on a great document of English liberty (see MAGNA CARTA).

Almost 750 years later (May 14, 1965), three acres of land on an adjoining hillside were dedicated as a memorial to an American President, John F. Kennedy. The land was given to the United States by the people of Britain, who, as Queen Elizabeth II said at the dedication ceremonies, had loved and admired the late President.

A path leads up the hillside to a simple monument of white stone on which are inscribed these words from President Kennedy's Inaugural Address:

Let every nation know, whether it wishes us well or ill, that we shall pay any price, bear any burden, meet any hardship, support any friend or oppose any foe, in order to assure the survival and success of liberty.

Rush, Benjamin (1745?–1813). This Philadelphia physician and signer of the Declaration of Independence realized—much better than most people of his time—the real significance of the American Revolution. He said:

There is nothing more common, than to confound the terms of the American Revolution with those of the late American War. The American War is over: but this is not true of the American Revolution. On the contrary, nothing but the first act of the great drama is closed. It remains yet to establish and perfect our new forms of government.

Dr. Rush recognized the need for a strong central government and, as a member of the Pennsylvania Convention (1787), urged that his own state approve the recently adopted Constitution. He felt confident the required number of states would ratify the new plan of government, and that it would soon become the supreme law of the land.

"Then to be a citizen of the United States . . . ," he said, "will be to be a citizen of the freest, purest, and happiest government upon the face of the earth."

Schurz, Carl (1829–1906), one of America's best known immigrants, had been forced to flee Germany as a young man because of his part in fighting for freedom in the German revolutionary movement of 1848–49. After his escape he lived in France and Switzerland, then in England for a while, but he was restless and dissatisfied. He wanted to do something worthwhile with his life. But where and how? He dared not return to his old homeland. Years later when he wrote his autobiography, *The Reminiscences of Carl Schurz,* he told how he happened to come to the United States. He had said to himself:

> The ideals of which I have dreamed, and for which I have fought, I shall find there, if not fully realized, but hopefully struggling for full realization. In that struggle, I shall perhaps be able to take some part. It is a new world, a free world, a world of great ideas and aims. In that world there is perhaps for me a new home.

After his arrival in America (1852) Carl Schurz continued to uphold the cause of freedom. Vigorously opposed to slavery, he campaigned for Abraham Lincoln as President, and later served as a general in the Union Army. In 1869 he was elected to the U.S. Senate—the first American of German birth to be so honored. As Secretary of the Interior (1877–81) he brought about needed reforms in the government's treatment of the Indian.

In all, Carl Schurz served his adopted country for more than half a century—as political leader, editor, writer, and orator. As an orator he is probably best remembered for his speech on "True Americanism" (1859) in which he spoke out against the efforts to curb the voting rights of men who were not native born.

The advocates of despotism, he said, maintained that people not experienced in self-government were not fit for self-government, yet the despots offered them no opportunity to acquire the experience. In contrast, Schurz reminded his audience, the fathers of the American Republic had believed that "liberty is the best school for liberty, and that self-government cannot be learned except by practicing it."

"That, sir," he went on, "is a truly American idea; that is true Americanism, and to this I pay the tribute of my devotion."

Self-Determination is the right of the people in a country to choose the form of government under which they live. This principle was first defined by President Woodrow Wilson in his address to Congress (Apr. 2, 1917), asking for a declaration of war against Germany. Among other principles for which Americans would be fighting, he said, was "the privilege of men everywhere to choose their way of life and obedience." By "obedience" he meant the government which they would be expected to obey and support.

In a later speech (Feb., 1918) President Wilson spoke of self-determination as one of the basic principles for a just peace to follow the war. When changes in national boundaries must be made, he asserted, the changes must be in accordance with the wishes of the people who would be affected.

Separation of Church and State is the principle, now firmly established in American life, that any and all religious groups are free from political control and that no church or churches shall be granted any special favors by the government. This was not true in colonial days, when the colonists were often penalized if they did not attend and support a certain church.

In the Massachusetts Bay Colony, for instance, the Puritan Church was in control for many years, and it was Roger Williams who led the protest against the narrow Puritan point of view. In Virginia, the Church of England was the established church. Thomas Jefferson, convinced that alliances between church and state had been responsible for much bigotry and cruelty in the past, worked for years to persuade his state legislature to enact the Virginia Statute for Religious Freedom (see separate entry). Religion, he said, was "a matter between every man and his Maker, in which no other, and far less the public, has any right to intermeddle."

This point of view prevailed by the time the Bill of Rights was added to the U.S. Constitution, and the first amendment states that "Congress shall make no law respecting an establishment of religion, or prohibiting the free exercise thereof." This means that in the United States, a country which has a variety of religions, every person is free to believe whatever he considers right—or not to subscribe to any religious belief. The principle of the separation of church and state is considered a necessary protection for one of the fundamental American liberties.

It was this principle, backed by the guarantee of the First Amendment, which prompted a 1963 decision of the U.S. Supreme Court. It was the majority opinion of the justices that specified prayers should not be used in public schools, since such prayers might be contrary to beliefs some pupils are taught at home.

Said Associate Justice Tom C. Clark:

The place of religion in our society is an exalted one . . . the inviolable citadel of the individual heart and mind. We have come to recognize through bitter experience that it is not within the power of government to invade that citadel. . . . In the relationship between man and religion, the state is firmly committed to a position of neutrality.

Sons of Liberty was the name of a number of patriotic societies that were organized to protest the Stamp Act nearly ten years before the American Revolution.

The name was suggested by a phrase in a speech by a member of the British Parliament, Colonel Isaac Barré (1765), in which he defended the rights of the colonists, and referred to them as "Sons of Liberty." When a report of the speech reached America, the name immediately caught on and was used for a number of organizations that seemed to spring up almost simultaneously in New York, Boston, and other colonial towns and cities. The members were usually impatient young men who held parades and meetings to stir up popular feeling. Sometimes, when ships arrived with supplies of stamps, there were riots in the streets,

and the "Sons" saw to it that the stamps were burned in public bonfires. Some of the agents appointed to collect the tax hastily resigned, rather than risk being tarred and feathered.

Though the Stamp Act was repealed

(1766), later taxes levied by Parliament aroused spirited opposition, and the Sons of Liberty helped to keep the spirit of rebellion alive. In nearly every town a "Liberty Pole" was erected, or a special tree dedicated as a "Liberty Tree," where the members held rallies. Laws passed by Parliament, or acts of local British officials, if the members thought they interfered with the people's rights, were denounced in fiery speeches.

Because the Sons of Liberty occasionally resorted to violence, they were often referred to as "the mob." Yet their membership included such highly respected men as Paul Revere. Samuel Adams, well-known Boston politician, was convinced that the societies were the "strength of every community . . . that must finally save the country."

Sovereignty of Nations. Any country is called a sovereign nation if it is independent and if the decisions of its government are not subject to outside control. For instance, the nations of eastern Europe that are subject to the control of the Soviet Union are classified as satellites and cannot be called sovereign.

The United States has been called "a sovereign Nation of many sovereign States." This means that each state in the Union has authority, or sovereignty, in local matters. It has a right to pass laws for the state, but such laws must not contradict, or tend to nullify, any federal law. On entering the Union, each state gave up a certain degree of sovereignty, so that the United States might have a stronger and a more effective federal government.

Sovereignty of the People. In a democratic government such as that of the United States, sovereignty (the supreme power or authority) rests with the people. The voters, by means of elections, delegate their power for a limited time and for certain limited purposes to their officials and representatives in government.

Said Chief Justice John Marshall (1819):

> The government of the Union . . . is emphatically and truly a government of the people. In form and substance it emanates from them. Its powers are granted by them, and are to be exercised directly on them, and for their benefit.

Speech, Freedom of. *See* EXPRESSION, FREEDOM OF.

Stamp Act (1765). This law, passed by the British Parliament, marked the beginning of serious trouble between Great Britain and her thirteen colonies in America. It was a new form of taxation requiring the purchase of stamps to be used on newspapers, almanacs, and all legal documents, and would work great hardship on all classes of Americans. Though most Americans were still loyal to the mother country, they were accustomed to having their own colonial legislatures levy taxes, and they protested that the Stamp Act was both illegal and a threat to freedom. Many merchants signed agreements to buy no more goods in England, and patriotic societies called Sons of Liberty sprang up in several colonies, determined to resist the new tax.

In October, the month before the Stamp Act was to become law, nine of the thirteen colonies sent delegates to a Stamp Act Congress in New York. Here they adopted a series of resolutions, one of which stated that it was "essential to the freedom of a people that no taxes be imposed on them without their consent. . . ." These resolutions were sent to England, together with petitions addressed to Parliament and to King George III, asking that the unpopular law be set aside.

Though the law went into effect (Nov. 1) as scheduled, the colonial protests did not go unnoticed in England. William Pitt, leader in Parliament, said he rejoiced that America had resisted. English merchants, however, did not rejoice over the loss of American trade, and Parliament finally gave in to their demands that the Stamp Act be repealed.

When the news reached America, there were joyful celebrations in Boston and other towns. Bells were rung and streets were gay with flags. In their enthusiasm many people overlooked the fact that, on the same day that Parliament had repealed the Stamp Act (Mar. 18, 1766), it had passed the Declaratory Act. This new Act, asserting that Parliament had the *right* to make laws "of sufficient force . . . to bind the colonies . . . in all cases whatsoever," was to bring new threats to freedom in the days to come.

See BOSTON TEA PARTY.

Stanton, Elizabeth Cady (1815–1902), was chiefly responsible for calling the first women's rights convention ever held in the United States; and the meetings in a little church in Seneca Falls, N.Y. (July 1848) marked the beginning of her fifty-year struggle to gain the right for members of her sex to vote.

"The ballot," she once told a committee of the U.S. Senate, before whom she appeared to urge the adoption of a woman suffrage amendment to the Constitution, "is the scepter of power in the hands of every citizen. Woman can never have an equal chance with man in the struggle of life until she too wields this power."

Mrs. Stanton, wife of a well-known antislavery reformer, was convinced that not only slaves but women had been forced to endure much injustice. An eloquent speaker and writer, she worked for equal opportunities for women in both education and industry and for their right to control their own property. Throughout most of her career she was closely associated with her friend Susan B. Anthony, another pioneer suffrage leader.

"Star-Spangled Banner (The)," by Francis Scott Key. This song was declared to be the American national anthem by Act of Congress in 1931, but it had been a national favorite long before that. It was composed during the War of 1812, shortly after the enemy had invaded and set fire to Washington, D.C., capital of the new republic. There was good reason to fear that the neighboring city of Baltimore might suffer the same fate when a British fleet sailed into Chesapeake Bay (Sept., 1814).

Francis Scott Key, a Baltimore attorney traveling under a flag of truce, was rowed out to one of the ships to arrange for an exchange of prisoners. Though his request was granted, he was told that he could not return to Baltimore that night. The reason became clear when under cover of the darkness the British began to bomb Fort McHenry, a fort important for the defense of the city. For Key, the suspense was almost unbearable as he stood on deck, watching the bombing. After it stopped, he had no way of knowing if the Americans had been forced to surrender.

Then, with the coming of dawn, he saw the American flag still flying over the fort. In the intense feeling of relief that surged over him, the words of a song began forming in his mind, and he set them down on the back of a letter he was carrying in his pocket.

The British, after their failure to capture Fort McHenry, sailed away. Key, having been put ashore before the British left, wrote several additional stanzas for his song, to be sung to an old English tune, "To Anacreon in Heaven." His brother-in-law had it printed in the form of handbills, and it was widely reprinted in newspapers in towns and cities throughout the nation. Soon, not only the people of Baltimore, but Americans everywhere were singing the stirring song which ended with the words:

> *And the star-spangled banner in*
> *triumph shall wave,*
> *O'er the land of the free and the*
> *home of the brave.*

Today the mammoth flag, partly shot away, which inspired Francis Scott Key to write his famous song, is prominently displayed in the Museum of History and Technology in Washington, D.C.

Statue of Freedom. This tall statue, which is also called "Armed Liberty," surmounts

the great white dome of the Capitol and appears to be standing guard over the nation's capital city. At its base are the Latin words *E Pluribus Unum* ("One out of many"), the motto of the United States.

The present cast-iron dome of the Capitol, replacing an earlier dome of wood covered with copper, was begun in 1856 and finished several years later. The country was in the midst of the Civil War when, in the presence of a large crowd and to the booming of cannon, the Statue of Freedom was hoisted into place by ropes and pulleys. The mammoth figure had been cast in bronze from a plaster model which was designed by Thomas Crawford, an American sculptor then working in Rome.

Statue of Liberty. This impressive statue in New York harbor, long considered a symbol of welcome, may be seen from far out at sea by travelers to America. The tall figure of a woman with uplifted torch was a gift from the people of France to the people of the United States, and it was hoped it would be ready in time for the centennial celebration (1876) of the adoption of the Declaration of Independence. The outbreak of the Franco-Prussian War made it necessary to postpone these plans, and it was October 28, 1886 when the statue was finally unveiled.

Originally called the Statue of Liberty Enlightening the World, it was designed and constructed by the French sculptor, Frédéric Auguste Bartholdi. Made of thin copper sheets over a steel framework, it was so large it had to be shipped across the Atlantic in sections, then mounted on a giant pedestal. The pedestal was built with money contributed by Americans, but the funds for the statue itself were raised by subscription in France. This impressive figure of Liberty, which on its pedestal is 300 feet tall, has been declared a national monument and the island on which it stands is now called Liberty Island.

The Statue of Liberty was erected during the period when thousands of immigrants, many of them in desperate straits, were seeking freedom or better opportunities in America. On a tablet inside the pedestal is engraved Emma Lazarus's famous sonnet, ending with the words:

> *Give me your tired, your poor,*
> *Your huddled masses yearning to*
> *   breathe free,*
> *The wretched refuse of your*
> *   teeming shore.*
> *Send these, the homeless, the*
> *   tempest-tost to me.*
> *I lift my lamp beside the golden*
> *   door.*

Stevenson, Adlai (1900–65), the liberal governor of Illinois (1949–53) and twice an unsuccessful candidate for President (1952 and 1956), was honored in his later years as one of the world's most dedicated champions of freedom. He served as the U.S. Ambassador to the United Nations (1961–65), a post in which his eloquence and integrity, his wit and kindly spirit, won him the trust and admiration of people in many parts of the world.

Whatever discouragements Ambassador Stevenson faced—and they were many —he never despaired of the future of democracy. He said:

After 150 years of uninterrupted expansion of the idea of government by consent of the governed, it has recently met with mounting and formidable challenges all over the world— from Fascist, Nazi, Communist authoritarians and a variety of dictatorships. But the important thing is that it has survived, because it is, as Jefferson said, "the only form of government which is not eternally at open or secret war with the rights of the people."

I have therefore no doubt that it can withstand the wild winds that are blowing through the world, if—and I repeat if—we who are its custodians continually re-examine and adapt its principles to the changing needs of our changing times.

Stowe, Harriet Beecher (1811–96), wrote her book *Uncle Tom's Cabin* because she had been deeply moved by the plight of Negro slaves. During the eighteen years (1832–50) she lived in Cincinnati, on the Ohio River, she met many fugitives who had escaped across the river from the slave state of Kentucky, and heard stories about others.

When her husband, Calvin Stowe, took a position teaching at Bowdoin College, he moved his family to Maine (1850), the same year the new Fugitive Slave Law was passed. This law, requiring that fugitive slaves, no matter what state they were found in, should be arrested and returned to their masters, caused violent controversy. Mrs. Stowe, though she had seven children to care for, including a newborn infant, determined to write a novel based on her own observations.

This story, *Uncle Tom's Cabin, or Life Among the Lowly,* was published first as a serial in an antislavery magazine, *The National Era.* Two of the characters were based in part on information the author had gathered about real people. A young Negro woman named Eliza Harris, with an infant in her arms, had actually crossed the Ohio River when it was filled with floating cakes of ice, as did Eliza in the story. The character of Uncle Tom was inspired by a narrative Mrs. Stowe had read about Josiah Henson, who had escaped to Canada and then had become a Methodist minister.

When *Uncle Tom's Cabin* came out in book form (1852), to everyone's surprise, including that of the author, it was an immediate sensation. Eight printing presses were kept busy supplying the demand, and within a year it had sold 300,000 copies. Later it was translated into more than twenty languages, and dramatic versions were produced a countless number of times upon the stage.

Though Mrs. Stowe did not pretend to be a literary craftsman, her book aroused the emotions of readers who seldom listened to a political speech, and more and more of them began to demand freedom for the slaves. In her story the author had tried to be fair. She had portrayed kind masters as well as those who were cruel, but it was the more sensational scenes that made the most vivid impression on her readers. Most Southerners condemned the book as inaccurate and unjust, and the furor it caused in both North and South undoubtedly contributed to the tension that finally erupted in the Civil War. After the war began President Lincoln invited the author to the Executive Mansion. "So you're the little woman who wrote the book that made this great war," he said.

HENRY WARD BEECHER, Mrs. Stowe's brother, probably the most popular preacher of his time, was also deeply involved in the antislavery movement. Though he did not believe that the Constitution authorized interference with the institution of slavery in states where it already existed, he advocated—as a moral right—disobedience of the Fugitive Slave Law. During the Civil War he was a strong supporter of President Lincoln.

Suffrage, or the right to vote, has been extended to more and more Americans as the years have gone by. In colonial times, though many colonists had come to America in search of freedom, comparatively few of them were permitted to vote. In the Massachusetts Bay Colony, established by the Puritans, the government was called a "theocracy," or rule by the church. Its purpose was to enforce what the Puritan leaders considered "God's laws," and only men who belonged to the Puritan Church could vote or hold office. John Winthrop, the first governor, a remarkable leader in many ways, was shortsighted in others. He called democracy the "meanest and worst of all forms of government."

This point of view was challenged by Roger Williams and Thomas Hooker, who left Massachusetts and founded more democratic colonies. Eventually there was so much opposition to the narrow Puritan policies that, by 1700, the suffrage had been extended to all freemen in Massachusetts, regardless of church membership.

"Freemen" were white men who owned property, and in most of the colonies only freemen were allowed to vote. Usually the property requirement specified real estate or land, but sometimes personal property could be substituted. A story has been told about Benjamin Franklin, one of the most enlightened of colonial Americans, who could usually be counted on to win an argument in an amusing way. What if a voter owned a mule, and then the mule died? he asked. Who had had the vote—the man or the mule?

Franklin, who played an important role in the Constitutional Convention, expressed his faith in the people—"the common people" who had helped to win the American Revolution. He believed they should have the suffrage, but some of the other delegates argued that men of property would be "the best guardians of liberty." Under the Constitution that was finally adopted (1787) the decision as to voting qualifications was left to the states. And the state constitutions adopted since the colonies had declared their independence granted the suffrage only to property owners.

This situation changed after more pioneers began going West to live. The pioneers braved hardship and danger to establish new homes in a part of the country where land was cheap and almost any man could own a farm if he was willing to work hard. When new states were formed out of the territory west of the Allegheny Mountains, the new state constitutions made no mention of property requirements for voting.

Just as the pioneers wanted to have

something to say about the way they should be governed, so did the plain people back East. Whether or not they owned property, they began to agitate for the franchise, and one by one the state legislatures had to give in. By 1850, all of the older states, as well as the newer ones, had passed laws that made it possible for every white adult male citizen to vote.

Even then the nation was far from living up to the promise of the Declaration of Independence. More than half the population still had no voice in their government. Not until after the Civil War did the Fifteenth Amendment (1870) impose a requirement on the states not to deny a citizen the right to vote "on account of race, color, or previous condition of servitude." The result of the Nineteenth Amendment (1920) was the extension of suffrage to all the women of the nation.

Local requirements may still keep some citizens from voting. But the day is much closer—many Americans believe—when they can make good the boast that they live under a government that derives its power from the consent of the governed.

Supreme Court of the United States. *Equal Justice under Law* reads the inscription over the main entrance of the impressive white marble Supreme Court building in the nation's capital. This inscription was inspired by a phrase in the Fourteenth Amendment to the Constitution: "Nor shall any state ... deny to any person within its jurisdiction the equal protection of the laws."

A visit to the Supreme Court is an interesting experience. On days when the Court is in session, the spectators are seated in the handsome room facing the long mahogany desk on a raised dais. Promptly at ten, everyone stands when the marshall of the Court announces, "The Honorable, the Chief Justice and the Associate Justices of the Supreme Court of the United States." The red velvet curtains back of the dais are parted, and the justices enter in their long black robes. They take their places behind their chairs, while the marshall calls for silence, using an old-time English word that means, "Hear ye!" He says:

Oyez! Oyez! Oyez! All persons having business before the Honorable, the Supreme Court of the United States, are admonished to draw near and give their attention, for the Court is now sitting. God save the United States and this Honorable Court.

An important function of the Supreme Court is to interpret the meaning of the Constitution in cases of dispute about laws, and thus make it possible for a written document to meet the changing needs of the nation. It reviews cases already passed on by the lower courts, both federal and state. Since there is a limit to the number of appeals the Court has time to consider, the justices accept only those cases that will test the validity of a law passed by Congress or by a state legislature.

If the Court decides a law is contrary to the Constitution, it can declare that law null and void, which means that it is no law at all. This decision is final, unless a law is rewritten or a Constitutional Amendment is passed that brings a law (which the Court had considered unconstitutional) within the framework of the Constitution. This "power of judicial review" was established many years ago by Chief Justice John Marshall, who asserted (in the case of Marbury *v.* Madison, 1803) that it is the duty of the judicial department "to say what the law is."

Many rulings of the Court have been controversial. Future events proved some of the rulings unwise, but in the main the Supreme Court has protected the guarantees provided by the Bill of Rights. De-

cisions are reached by a majority vote, for the justices often disagree. Their guiding principle, according to one former Chief Justice, is "harmony of aims if not of views." Each justice, before assuming office, repeats the following oath:

I, _____, do solemnly swear that I will administer justice without respect to persons, and do equal right to the poor and to the rich, and that I will faithfully and impartially discharge and perform all the duties incumbent on me as Associate Justice [or as Chief Justice] of the Supreme Court of the United States, according to the best of my abilities and understanding, agreeably to the Constitution and laws of the United States, so help me God.

Today the Supreme Court is administered by a Chief Justice and eight Associate Justices appointed by the President and confirmed by the Senate. In the past the number has varied from time to time, depending on legislation by Congress. Yet when President Franklin Roosevelt recommended that the number of justices be increased, in the hope that he could appoint additional justices more favorable to some of his New Deal legislation, the suggestion met with vigorous opposition. The report of the Senate Judiciary Committee (1937) was also an expression of the veneration in which the Court was held by the American people!

Let us, of the 75th Congress, the report read,

...declare that we would rather have an independent court...that will dare to announce its honest opinion in what it believes to be the defense of the liberties of the people, than a court that, out of fear or sense of obligation to the appointing power...approves any measure we may enact. We are not the judges of the judges.... We declare for the continuance and perpetuation of government and rule by law, as distinguished from government and rule by men, and in this we are but reasserting the principles basic to the Constitution of the United States....

See INDEX for references to individual justices.

Taft, William Howard (1857–1930), was the only man ever to serve both as President and as Chief Justice of the United States. Yet undoubtedly his most important contribution to the cause of freedom had been made earlier, as the first civil governor of the Philippines. For three years prior to his appointment (1901), the islands, which had come into the possession of the United States as a result of the Spanish American War, had been ruled by the U.S. Army. The new governor —a big handsome man, weighing more than three hundred pounds—was regarded with awe by the small muscular Filipino people. "The little brown brothers," as Taft called them, soon realized that he came, not as a conqueror, but to help them learn the difficult art of self-government.

As governor (1901–04), "Big Bill Taft" brought about many needed reforms. Twice during his term of office he was offered an appointment as an associate justice of the U.S. Supreme Court. To serve on the Supreme Court bench had long been his ambition and he realized such an opportunity might not come again. Yet he declined, because he felt he needed more time to complete his program of reform in the Philippines. "I have a deep affection for the Filipino people," he said, "and I mean to do everything that in me lies for their benefit."

After he left the Philippines, Taft served his country in several important offices, including the Presidency. As President (1909–13), he was neither very happy nor very successful, and he was not reelected. Several years later, when a vacancy occurred (1921) in the Supreme Court, another President, Warren G. Harding, appointed him, not an associate justice, but Chief Justice of the United States. To William Howard Taft, that was the most satisfying office in the world, and he served (1921–30) until a few weeks before his death.

Chief Justice Taft is remembered not so much for his legal decisions as for the Judges' Bill which he urged Congress to pass (1925). Until then, the Court had been overloaded with routine cases, but the new law made it possible to accept only those appeals that would settle some constitutional question or an important point in federal law.

It was also due to Taft, more than any other man, that Congress finally passed a bill providing funds for a new Supreme Court building. He did not live to see it completed, but the handsome marble structure patterned after an ancient Greek temple was—in the words of his successor, Charles Evans Hughes—"the result of his intelligent persistence."

Tecumseh (1768?–1813) was a Shawnee Indian chief who took a determined stand against the sale of Indian land for the use of white settlers in what is now called the Middle West.

After William Henry Harrison became governor (1801) of Indiana Territory, he began to make treaties with the chiefs of a number of Indian tribes. In exchange for gifts, they agreed to give up thousands of acres and find new hunting grounds farther west.

But Tecumseh refused to acknowledge the treaties. He exclaimed during a conference with Governor Harrison:

Sell a country! Why not sell the air, the clouds and the great sea, as well as the earth? White men are taking our hunting grounds. They do not have the right to buy land from one tribe, for all tribes own the land. The Great Spirit has appointed this place for us, and here we will remain.

In spite of his boast, Tecumseh realized that no one tribe was strong enough to hold out against the white soldiers. He hoped to form a confederacy made up of many tribes that could combine to drive the settlers back across the Appalachian Mountains. A short time after his meeting with Governor Harrison, he left on a long journey to try to persuade other chiefs to cooperate in his plan. While he was away the bloody battle of Tippecanoe (1811) took place near the juncture of the Wabash and Tippecanoe rivers. When the chief returned, he found his Shawnee village destroyed. All of his braves were either dead or had been forced to flee.

Tecumseh then realized that his dream of a confederacy could never come true. During the War of 1812 he joined the British and was killed in battle the following year. Today he is remembered as one of the bravest and most tragic figures in Indian history.

Texas, Republic of. The only state in the Union ever to have been an independent republic was Texas. At one time it was a part of Mexico, and for a while the Mexican government had encouraged settlers from the United States to come there and make their homes. By 1830, though, so many had arrived that further immigration was forbidden. Santa Anna became the dictator of Mexico, and the Texans considered his policies so oppressive that they resolved to secede. At a convention (Mar. 2, 1836) in a town on the Brazos River, the delegates issued a declaration of independence, set up a provisional government, and started to work on a constitution, modeled after that of the United States.

While the convention was meeting, Santa Anna crossed the Rio Grande with a force of several thousand and laid siege to the Alamo. This Franciscan mission, which the Texans had turned into a fort, had a garrison of only 187 men. Though outnumbered almost twenty to one, they refused to surrender, but Colonel William Travis, their commander, managed to send out a message. "In the name of liberty" he made a plea for reinforcements, but he must have realized that no help could reach them in time. For eleven days the little band of defenders fought desperately, until only a few wounded men were left alive. When the fort was finally captured (Mar. 6) the wounded were ruthlessly slain by order of Santa Anna.

After the siege, the diary of one of the defenders, the popular frontiersman Davy Crockett, was found. It described some of the frightful details. The final entry, written before he went down fighting, read:

Bom! Bom! Bom! throughout the day. No time for memorandums now. Pop! Pop! Pop! Liberty and independence forever!

The cry "Remember the Alamo!" swept through Texas and strengthened the determination of the Texans to be free and independent. Santa Anna was on the march, but Sam Houston, who had been appointed commander of a Texas army of four hundred men, managed to induce others to join. In less than six weeks after the tragedy at the Alamo, Houston surprised the Mexican forces on the banks of the San Jacinto River, defeated them, and took Santa Anna prisoner. The independence of the Republic of Texas was assured. In the meantime, the delegates holding their convention on the Brazos River had unanimously adopted their constitution (Mar. 17), together with a Declaration of Rights.

More than to any other man, the Republic of Texas owed its freedom to Sam Houston, and he was elected its first President. Nine years later, after Texas was admitted to the Union as a state (1845),

he represented it in the U.S. Senate. That Texas should become a part of the United States was regarded as an unfriendly act by the Mexican government and led to the Mexican War (1846–48)—a war that many Americans regretted.

Today Texas is known as the "Lone Star State" because the red, white, and blue flag it adopted after it gained independence showed a single star against the blue background. The Alamo, where a few brave men made such a gallant defense, has been preserved as a museum in the city of San Antonio.

Thomas, Norman (1884–   ), six times candidate of the Socialist Party for President, has been called "the conscience of America," and lived to see many of his ideas incorporated into law. His proposals concerning social security, minimum wage laws, unemployment insurance, a shorter work week, and the abolition of child labor seemed radical to many people at one time, but are generally accepted today. To the man who had begun his career as a Presbyterian minister, they offered a way of dealing with the waste and inequalities

The Alamo

and what he considered the "unnecessary poverty" he saw all around him. Believing he could accomplish more as a Socialist, he joined the Socialist Party in 1918. Through the years he has consistently advocated the right to protest what he considered wrong. The purpose of dissent, he once said, was "to tear a question open and riddle it with light."

Again and again Norman Thomas contrasted his own brand of democratic socialism with the Communism of the Soviet Union, and continued to put his faith in the democratic theory that "the good life is for all men." An enlightened, democratic socialism, flexible enough to meet changing needs, could, he felt, provide many answers for the problems of the United States and of the world.

His talks on world peace and civil rights, lightened with humor, were especially popular with students on college campuses. Many of his listeners were impatient with conditions in the modern world, but he warned them that it was not enough merely to be against something. They must be prepared to make constructive suggestions for improving the conditions they condemned. He himself had often criticized his country, because he hoped and wanted to make it a better country. But he had been just as quick to praise, because he knew there also was much that was right with America. The words of a speech he delivered on his seventieth birthday summed up his point of view:

There has been a saving commonsense about our democracy. The American story contains many pages describing the rise of a dangerous demagoguery from Aaron Burr to Joe McCarthy. But the end has always been victory for comparative reason and decency.

Tocqueville, Alexis de (1805–59), was a Frenchman who was convinced that the idea of democracy was bound to spread to the Old World, and wanted to see for himself how it worked in the New World. A young man, still in his twenties (1831), he traveled extensively through the eastern part of the United States, observing, asking questions, and taking notes for the book he planned to write. This two-volume work, *Democracy in America,* published after his return to France, is considered the most impartial analysis yet written about the influence of democracy. He said:

I confess that in America I saw more than America. I sought the image of democracy itself, with its inclinations, its prejudices, its passions, in order to learn what we have to fear or to hope from its progress.

What especially impressed De Tocqueville was the degree of equality among the Americans. "They are born equal, instead of becoming so," he wrote. This was possible because the country had been settled mostly by Europeans who thought they saw a chance to better themselves. Since most of the settlers had once been victims of poverty or misfortune, they had had no feeling of superiority, one above another. Unlike a European, no person in the United States, De Tocqueville continued, seemed to feel that his place in society was unalterably fixed. What the Frenchman feared was that absolute equality might lead to too much uniformity, stifling "independence of mind."

Yet he realized that it was this feeling of equality which caused most Americans to take such a zealous interest in both local and national affairs. They seemed to feel deeply involved in whatever happened in the country.

Town Meetings. In early New England, it was the custom for citizens in a community to meet at least once a year to discuss matters relating to the welfare of the people, to vote on new laws, and to elect officials to carry on the town government. Even residents who could not vote had an opportunity to express their opinions, and the meetings provided the New England colonists with excellent training in the practice of democracy.

Though a few towns and villages still have town meetings, most government today, including that of local communities, is handled by representatives elected by the voters.

Truman, Harry S. (1884–   ), the thirty-third President of the United States, had the task of leading his country through the difficult years that followed World War II. This task he performed with courage and energy and with firm devotion to the cause of freedom in America and throughout the world.

As a boy in Independence, Mo., Harry Truman became fascinated with the study of history. Though he could not attend college, for financial reasons, his constant reading gave him a thorough knowledge of history and government that was to serve him well as a U.S. Senator (1935–45). As Vice President he succeeded to the Presidency (Apr. 12, 1945), following the sudden death of Franklin Roosevelt toward the end of World War II. Many problems faced the new Chief Executive, and an understanding of the past and a vision of the future in the light of history were invaluable in those troubled times.

In less than a month after Truman took office, Germany acknowledged defeat, but at that time no one knew how much longer the struggle with Japan would continue. To the new President fell the awe-

Japanese surrender

some decision of whether a secret and highly destructive new weapon, the atomic bomb, should be used to cut short the war. When his military advisers assured him that without the bomb an invasion of the Japanese islands would undoubtedly be necessary and would cost a quarter of a million American lives, the President ordered that the bomb should be used.

After atomic explosions had been set off over two Japanese cities (Aug., 1945), causing horrible destruction, Japan also surrendered. At last World War II was over, but there were other momentous problems to be solved. It soon became apparent that the Soviet Union was trying to extend Communism throughout western Europe as well as in other portions of the world. President Truman was determined that the countries wishing to remain free from Communist domination must be helped to maintain their independence, lest the peace of the world be endangered again. In a speech before a joint session of Congress (Mar., 1947) he urged that financial aid and military advice be given to Greece and Turkey, two countries under heavy Communist pressure. "I believe," he said, "that we must assist free peoples to work out their own destinies in their own ways."

Congress gave its approval to the "Truman Doctrine," as the President's policy was called. It also voted for the Marshall Plan, a program strongly supported by the President that greatly reduced the impact of Communist propaganda in western Europe (see MARSHALL, GEORGE C.).

Harry Truman's domestic program, known as the "Fair Deal," met with less success in Congress. Many Republican members of the House and Senate vigorously opposed the reform measures he suggested, and many Southerners in Congress turned against him because of his civil rights proposals. When Harry Truman ran for election in his own right (1948), the

public opinion polls indicated that he would be decisively defeated.

But the President conducted a whirlwind campaign and surprised the nation (and stunned the pollsters) by winning. He then set to work once more to urge Congress to pass his Fair Deal program. In his State of the Union Message (Jan. 5, 1949), he stressed the need for legislation that would protect civil rights. He pointed out that faith in democratic institutions was the driving force behind the nation's progress:

That faith is embodied in the promise of equal rights and equal opportunities which the founders of our Republic proclaimed to their countrymen and to the whole world. The fulfillment of this promise is among the highest purposes of government.

Though the President still had an unfriendly Congress to deal with, some important legislation was passed on his recommendation: laws that provided for an increase in minimum wages (1949), construction of low-cost housing (1950), and an expanded social security coverage (1950). His suggestions concerning civil rights and medical insurance were not enacted into law at the time, but they laid the groundwork for future legislation, including the Equal Employment Opportunity section of the Civil Rights Act of 1964 and the Medicare legislation of 1965.

The outbreak of war in Korea in June, 1950 turned the American people's attention from matters at home, and for the rest of his term in office President Truman had to devote most of his thinking to that struggle. The war began when a Russian-equipped army from Communist North Korea invaded South Korea, a free republic. This armed aggression against a small independent nation must be stopped, the President was convinced, or it might lead to World War III. So when the North Koreans ignored a cease-fire resolution of the United Nations Security Council (which at that time the Russians were boycotting), President Truman ordered United States air and naval forces to assist the South Koreans. A few days later, in response to a UN request that member nations help drive back the aggressors, he ordered American ground forces into the struggle. His decisive action prompted other free-world nations to follow America's lead, and within a short time a United Nations army, composed of forces from a number of independent nations, was fighting the Communist aggressors.

The United Nations army was meeting with success when Chinese Communist "volunteers" entered the struggle (Oct., 1950) in support of the North Koreans. The fighting then continued with renewed intensity, and the war was not over when President Truman finished his term in office (Jan., 1953). Peace negotiations, however, were underway, and a truce was signed some six months later, after Dwight D. Eisenhower became President. Neither side had won an overwhelming victory. But the aggressors had been prevented from taking over a free nation by force, and that had been Mr. Truman's main objective.

"We [Americans] seek only a universal peace," he said in a speech shortly before he left the White House, "where all nations shall be free and all peoples shall enjoy their inalienable human rights."

Underground Railroad. This was the name given the system of helping Negro slaves escape to freedom. The term is believed to have come into use first in the early 1830's when a Southern slave owner in pursuit of some runaway slaves suddenly lost track of them after crossing the Ohio River. The Negroes must have disappeared, he exclaimed in disgust, on an Underground Railroad.

What had doubtless happened was that some kindly disposed people opposed to slavery had hidden the runaways until they could be transported under cover of darkness to the house or barn of some other sympathizers. These people, who came to be known as "conductors," would help the runaways continue their journey to another "station" on the Underground Railroad.

Within a few years there was a network of such stations covering fourteen Northern states and reaching all the way to Canada, where slavery was illegal. Many of the fugitives were captured by former owners or professional slave catchers sent to pursue them, but many more were saved. It has been estimated that the Underground Railroad helped more

than 75,000 Negro fugitives on their way to liberty.

The big increase in the "business" of the "railroad" came after the passage of the Fugitive Slave Law of 1850. Much stricter than an earlier law, which had never been rigidly enforced, it gave federal agents the power to arrest runaway slaves even after they had escaped to a free state. The law was vigorously opposed by many leading citizens, including Ralph Waldo Emerson and the Reverend Theodore Parker, whose home was always open to fugitives. Like many others, Parker gladly risked arrest because he was convinced that slavery was morally wrong.

Even greater risks were run by workers in the Underground Railroad who ventured into the South, including many Negroes. Of these there was none braver than Harriet Tubman, an escaped slave, for whose capture a reward of $4,000 had been offered. Though she was a frail-looking young woman, she returned again and again to the South on her rescue missions. It was her boast that she had guided more than three hundred slaves to safety and never once run her "train off the track."

"I never lost a passenger," she said.

United Nations (UN). This name, originally used for a wartime alliance, was retained for a world peace-keeping organization when representatives of fifty Allied nations assembled for the San Francisco Conference (Apr. 25, 1945).

Much preliminary work had already been done. President Roosevelt and Prime Minister Winston Churchill had issued the Atlantic Charter (Aug., 1941) stating the principles which they believed would furnish a foundation for an enduring peace. On New Year's Day, 1942, the United Nations Declaration was signed (see separate entry). In August, 1944, representatives of the leading Allies met at Dumbarton Oaks, an estate in Washington, D.C., to draft a tentative charter. Their Dumbarton Oaks plan offered many suggestions for the permanent charter later worked out in San Francisco.

President Roosevelt, who had been primarily responsible for the idea of a United Nations, did not live to attend the San Francisco Conference. It was his successor, Harry S. Truman, who addressed the final session in June:

Upon all of us, in all our countries, is now laid the duty of transforming into action these words that you have written. Upon our decisive action rests the hope . . . for a world of free countries.

The charter adopted at San Francisco provided that the purposes of the United Nations should be carried out by several organs or divisions, among them the General Assembly and the Security Council. The General Assembly, made up of representatives from all the member nations, has been called "the town meeting of the world," and its chief function is to discuss and suggest peaceful means of settling the numerous problems that arise. The function of the Security Council is to keep the peace. Unlike the General Assembly, it may vote to use force if suggestions alone fail to avert a war.

The Security Council has five permanent members—France, the Republic of (Nationalist) China, the Soviet Union, the United Kingdom, and the United States. Six additional members are elected by the General Assembly to serve in the Security Council for two-year terms. The Council has been handicapped in its peacekeeping mission by the veto rule, on which the Soviet Union had insisted. Any permanent member may veto any proposal by the other members, and during the first twenty-two years the UN was in operation, the Soviet Union used the veto ninety-four times. During that same period the other nations combined used the veto only seven times.

In spite of some failures, due mostly to the use of the veto power in the Security Council, the United Nations has a number of important accomplishments to its credit. UN troops preserved the independence of South Korea after it was invaded (1950) by forces from Communist North Korea. Among other, at least temporary, successes, was the armistice arranged by a General Assembly representative (1949) between Israel and its Arab neighbors. UN troops preserved the independence of the Republic of the Congo (1962). A UN force was sent to Cyprus (1964) to prevent further violence after civil war broke out between the Turkish minority and the Greek majority. When quarrels between India and Pakistan erupted into war (1965), a cease-fire was arranged at the request of the Security Council.

Certainly an impressive record of UN accomplishments must be credited to some of the specialized agencies. These agencies include UNESCO (United Nations Educational, Scientific and Cultural Organization) ; WHO (World Health Organization) ; FAO (Food and Agriculture Organization) ; ILO (International Labor Organization) ; and the World Fund (International Monetary Fund). They have increased the social and economic well-being of many people throughout the world.

The chief UN officer is the Secretary-General whose name is suggested by the Security Council, then voted on by the General Assembly. He holds office for five years and oversees all of the UN departments and the several thousand workers they employ. His most important duty is to settle disputes between nations, if possible, before an appeal must be made to the General Assembly or the Security Council. Perhaps no executives in the world have been faced with greater difficulties than have the men who have served the United Nations as Secretary-General.

The difficulties have multiplied with the admission of additional members representing the newly independent nations of Asia and Africa. There are now more than twice as many members as there were in 1945. In spite of many new problems, free people still consider the UN the greatest hope for maintaining peace.

Said Adlai Stevenson, the U.S. Ambassador to the United Nations (1961–65):

The UN is not a magic lamp. Perhaps it is only a candle in the window. But its spirit is that of . . . give and take. . . . Its method is . . . debating, voting . . . discussion and careful listening.

This was the method that had proved so successful in the United States, and the ambassador believed it would work in a community of nations, each independent

but bound together by a sense of common humanity. "In such a community," he went on, "every nation and every man . . . will have the greatest chance to develop the unlimited possibilities of freedom."

Since 1949 the principal headquarters of the United Nations have been located in New York City, on land overlooking the East River. In the courtyard, formed by several strikingly handsome buildings, may be seen the flags of all the member nations. The UN flag, which flies above the others, shows a white olive branch, the traditional symbol for peace, against a blue background.

United Nations Charter, Preamble to (1945). The Charter of the United Nations, adopted by the San Francisco Conference (1945), begins with a Preamble that sums up the purposes of the organization as follows:

We, the people of the United Nations, determined to save succeeding generations from the scourge of war . . . and

To reaffirm faith in fundamental human rights, in the dignity and worth of the human person, in the equal rights of men and women and of nations large and small, and

To establish conditions under which justice . . . can be maintained, and

To promote social progress and better standards of life in larger freedom, and . . .

To practice tolerance and live together in peace with one another as good neighbors, and

To unite our strength to maintain international peace and security, and

To ensure . . . that armed force shall not be used, save in the common interest, and

To employ international machinery for the promotion of the economic and social advancement of all peoples, have resolved to combine our efforts to accomplish these aims.

Accordingly our respective governments, through representatives assembled in the city of San Francisco . . . have agreed to the present Charter of the United Nations and do hereby establish an international organization to be known as the United Nations.

United Nations Declaration (1942). Two weeks after the United States entered World War II, Prime Minister Winston Churchill of Great Britain arrived at the White House (Dec. 22, 1941) to discuss war strategy with President Franklin D. Roosevelt. Together the two heads of state drew up a declaration of war aims to be signed by representatives of the Allied countries. The name "United Nations" was used to imply that the Allies were united in a common purpose.

The United Nations Declaration was signed in a New Year's Day (1942) ceremony at the White House by the President, the Prime Minister, and representatives of the Soviet Union and China (Nationalist China, now on Formosa). The next day other signatures were added by representatives of twenty-two other nations. They agreed to abide by the principles of the Atlantic Charter, and not to make a separate peace with the enemy. Complete victory was essential, the Declaration read, "to preserve human rights and justice" both in their own and other lands.

Universal Declaration of Human Rights. Soon after the United Nations was established, the question arose as to what exactly were the "fundamental human rights" mentioned in the Charter. A commission, made up of delegates from eighteen nations, was appointed by the UN General Assembly to draft a list of those rights that would apply to people everywhere. During the ensuing months, the Commission, with Mrs. Franklin D. (Eleanor) Roosevelt acting as chairman, met again and again to carry out their difficult assignment.

The delegates, coming from different parts of the world, represented widely different points of view.

"The rights of the individual," a representative from Panama reminded the others, "do not spring from the fact that he is a citizen of a given state, but from the fact that ... he is a member of the human family."

Listing the rights of *members of the human family!*—that was what the Commission was trying to accomplish. After many heated discussions, the members finally decided on a list of thirty articles, or provisions, to be presented to the UN General Assembly for approval.

When the issue came to a vote (Dec. 10, 1948), the delegates from the Soviet Union and several other nations abstained —that is, they did not vote. The representatives from all the other member-nations voted "yes." The Universal Declaration of Human Rights, as it was decided to call the document, was then formally adopted.

"The General Assembly," reads the Preamble, "proclaims this Universal Declaration of Human Rights as a common standard of achievement for all peoples and all nations. ..."

Some of the statements in the thirty Articles following the Preamble reflected the influence of the U.S. Bill of Rights and other American precedents. Several of the Articles listed privileges the majority of Americans simply take for granted, but which many people in other parts of the world have never known. The most important rights specified in the document (but here grouped by related points) are:

"All human beings are born free and equal in dignity and rights. They are endowed with reason and conscience and should act towards one another in a spirit of brotherhood.

"Everyone is entitled to all the rights and freedoms set forth in this Declaration, without distinction of any kind, such as race ... or other status.

"Everyone has the right to life, liberty and security of person .... No one shall be held in slavery .... No one shall be subjected to torture or to cruel, inhuman or degrading treatment or punishment."

All are entitled "to equal protection of the law .... Everyone has the right to own property ....

"Everyone has the right to freedom of thought, conscience and religion . . . to freedom of opinion and expression . . . to freedom of peaceful assembly and association."

"The authority of government" is dependent on the will of the people, as expressed in "periodic and genuine elections," based on "universal and equal suffrage . . . .

"Everyone, as a member of society, has the right to social security . . . to free choice of employment . . . to equal pay for equal work . . . to form and to join trade unions for the protection of his interests.

"Everyone has the right to rest and leisure, including reasonable limitation of working hours . . . to a standard of living adequate for the health and well-being of himself and of his family.

"Everyone has the right to education. . . ."

The Universal Declaration of Human Rights was neither a law nor a treaty, but the moral standards it set up have proved an inspiration to people throughout the world. The Declaration represents a goal not yet reached. What was significant, said Mrs. Roosevelt, was that for the first time in history fifty-eight nations (the number then represented in the UN) had

. . . found such a large measure of agreement in the complex field of human rights . . . . This must be taken as testimony of our common aspiration . . . to lift men everywhere to a higher standard of life and to a greater enjoyment of freedom.

Human Rights Day (Dec. 10) is now celebrated in many parts of the world in commemoration of the day in 1948 when the Universal Declaration of Human Rights was adopted by the UN General Assembly.

Virginia Statute for Religious Freedom. After the Continental Congress adopted the Declaration of Independence, Thomas Jefferson, the author, resigned from the Congress and returned (Oct. 1776) to Virginia. As a member of the state legislature and later as governor, he worked for the repeal of some of the old laws that existed when Virginia was a colony. Some of these laws he considered very undemocratic, and he hoped to bring the new state into line with the ideas he had expressed in the Declaration of Independence.

One of the laws to which Jefferson objected forbade attendance at any church except the Church of England. "The care of every man's soul belongs to himself," he said, and he introduced a bill into the legislature (1779) that would grant complete liberty of conscience to all of the people. The legislature failed to adopt it, but his friend James Madison continued to work for its passage after Jefferson was sent abroad as U.S. Minister to France.

Finally in December, 1785, the Virginia Statute for Religious Freedom was enacted into law. It stated that no person was to be compelled to attend or support any church; that all people would be free to express religious opinions; and that no

Monticello

one was to suffer any loss of civil rights because of his religious beliefs.

The guarantee of religious freedom later inserted in the American Bill of Rights was in large part inspired by the Virginia Statute for Religious Freedom. This statute, for which Thomas Jefferson had been primarily responsible, was one of the accomplishments of which he was most proud. Before he died he wrote his own epitaph and directed that the words "Author . . . of the Statute of Virginia for Religious Freedom" be included in the engraving on his tombstone. This may be seen today at Monticello, his mountaintop home in Virginia.

Voltaire was the pseudonym of François Marie Arouet (1694–1778), a brilliant French writer and philosopher. With acid and witty pen, he attacked the tyranny, injustice, and religious intolerance that existed in the France of his time. Though Voltaire personally disliked the "masses,"

he insisted that all men have natural rights to liberty, to fair trial, to religious freedom, and above all, to freedom of thought and expression.

"I may not agree with a word you say, but I will defend to the death your right to say it," is a quotation often attributed to Voltaire. In reality, the words were written by one of his biographers as an illustration of Voltaire's strong feelings about freedom of speech.

For more than sixty years, in plays, essays, novels, pamphlets, and letters, Voltaire assaulted despotism and defended liberty. His writings helped to awaken the minds of his countrymen and to bring on the French Revolution. In America his works were read by Thomas Jefferson and other political leaders. Voltaire's thinking contributed to the concern for the rights of the individual as expressed in the Declaration of Independence, the Virginia Statute for Religious Freedom, and the Bill of Rights.

Want, Freedom from. *See* FREEDOM FROM WANT.

Warren, Earl (1891–   ), who served for three successive terms as Governor of California, resigned (1953) to accept the appointment as Chief Justice of the United States. Since that time several decisions handed down by the Supreme Court have made Earl Warren one of the most controversial leaders in American history. Some of the decisions made under his leadership, especially those concerned with equality for the races, have caused a few extremists to declare he should be impeached. To other Americans he has been an outstanding modern spokesman for the principles on which the nation was founded, as expressed in the Declaration of Independence and the Bill of Rights. The Constitution, he once said, had weathered a variety of crises as acute as those we face today.

Washington, Booker T. (1856?–1915), an American educator, has been called "the Moses of his people" because of his leadership during the critical years after their release from slavery. He was born a slave on a Virginia plantation. When he was about seven years old, all the Negroes were summoned to the "big house" where the master lived. There they found a stranger waiting who read them a rather long paper. When Booker T. Washington told the story many years later in his autobiography *Up From Slavery,* he said the man was probably a Union officer and the paper was the Emancipation Proclamation. All he remembered clearly was that the stranger had told the Negroes they were free.

Then Booker's mother leaned down and kissed him, and he saw that she was crying. He had often heard her pray that some day she and her children would be free, and he realized that at last her great dream had come true.

The memory of that day stayed with him throughout a long and remarkable life. Booker got his education the hard way. After the family moved to West Virginia, Booker's stepfather put him to work in the mines. Somehow, his mother got hold of a spelling book for him, and he found a teacher who gave him lessons at night. When he was about sixteen he hitchhiked five hundred miles to Hampton, Va., where a school had been opened for Negroes and Indians. By working as a janitor to pay his expenses, he managed to graduate (1875), and then he himself became a teacher.

Finally, in 1881, came his great opportunity. A Negro school was being started at Tuskegee, Ala., chartered by the state, and Booker T. Washington was offered a position as principal.

The school, later to be known as Tuskegee Normal and Industrial Institute, opened on the Fourth of July, 1881 with forty pupils. The first classes were held in an abandoned church and a dilapidated shanty with a leaky roof. When it rained, one of the students was obliged to hold an umbrella over Washington's desk while he—the only teacher—listened to the recitations of the others. As soon as possible he borrowed money for an adequate building, for which the students furnished the labor. He interested men of wealth in his school, and as time went on money poured in to erect other buildings and to hire more teachers.

Through contributions, both large and small, Tuskegee grew into a flourishing institution with a number of fine buildings on an attractive campus. In addition to regular school subjects, boys were taught a trade and girls learned to cook and sew. Land was purchased for a farm where the students raised their own vegetables and tended livestock. Their principal was convinced that what they needed most—with conditions as they were at that time—was a practical education that would enable them to earn a living and be economically independent. Tuskegee was to become the model of several similar institutions in the South.

By 1895 Booker T. Washington had become a leader of nationwide importance. That was the year he was asked to deliver an address at the Cotton States Exposition in Atlanta, Ga.—the first time a Negro had spoken from the same platform with Southern whites.

He said, in his deep resonant voice:

No race can prosper till it learns that there is as much dignity in tilling a field as in writing a poem. It is at the bottom of life that we must begin, and not at the top. Nor should we permit our grievances to overshadow our opportunities.

The speech was quoted in newspapers throughout the nation. It pleased the majority of white people, but a rising group of young Negro intellectuals called it "the great Booker T. Washington compromise." Though these Negroes realized how much Washington had done for their people, they were disappointed that he failed to take a firm stand against such evils as lynching and the terror tactics of the Ku Klux Klan. By overemphasis on industrial training, to the exclusion of liberal arts education, his critics maintained that he was limiting the opportunities for talented members of his race. It was not enough, in the words of William E. B. Du Bois, for "black men to believe that if their stomachs are full, it matters little about their brains."

Du Bois, the brilliant young author of *The Souls of Black Folk* (1903), was a Harvard graduate and the first Negro to receive a Ph.D. degree from that university. In his opinion, Mr. Washington was at fault in not coming out forcibly for equal rights and Negro suffrage. "By every civilized and peaceful method," said the younger man, "we must strive for the rights that the world accords man."

In contrast, Booker T. Washington summed up his philosophy in the words, "Let down your buckets where you are." He meant that Negroes must take advantage of such limited opportunities as were then available to them, and he adopted the only policy which, in his own time, had much chance of success. He believed it more important for the Negro to have economic opportunity, a chance to earn a living, than to be able to vote—a point of view that continues to be challenged by modern members of his race.

But the fact that Negroes have made remarkable progress in recent years does not lessen their debt—or the debt of white Americans—to the man who brought about a better understanding between the two races in the difficult half century following the Civil War.

Washington, George (1732–99). "The liberties of America depend upon him in a great degree," said John Adams of George Washington.

Both men were delegates to the Second Continental Congress (1775), and the forty-three-year-old Virginian had just been elected commander in chief of the new Continental Army. In order to accept this assignment, he had to give up the life he loved—that of a prosperous Virginia

Mount Vernon

planter living at Mt. Vernon, his gracious home overlooking the Potomac River. He knew that the leaders then in control of the British government would consider him a traitor, but he risked everything— his property, his reputation, his life—because he believed that the rights and liberties of Americans were in danger. He insisted that, except for his expenses, he would serve without pay.

Few generals in history have faced greater difficulties than George Washington did. He had to drill an untrained army, recruit new soldiers, and literally beg for money—to pay and feed and clothe them —from the Continental Congress. The next few years were a time of almost incredible hardship for his ragged troops, but by sheer force of character Washington held an army together. To him must go the major credit for finally winning the war that forced Great Britain to acknowledge the independence of the United States (1783).

After the siege at Yorktown, Va. (Oct., 1781) ended in an overwhelming defeat for the enemy, Washington could easily have made himself a dictator. There were grave doubts at the time that the war was really over, and the army could not be disbanded until a treaty of peace was signed. Many of the soldiers who had not been paid for months were close to mutiny. They felt they had been shabbily treated by the Continental Congress and that only General Washington was interested in justice for the army. One group of officers decided that the army would be better off under a monarchy, and one of them wrote their commander, hinting that he make himself king.

Instead of being flattered, the general was shocked and angry that anyone should think he would even consider such a proposal. Yet he realized the soldiers had cause for complaint. After the treaty of peace was signed, he sent a circular letter to the governors of the different states, urging justice for the men who had won the war. In this same letter he called attention to the fact that the citizens of America were now "the proprietors of a vast tract of continent" and that the rights of mankind were better understood than ever before. It was an auspicious period for the United States to come into existence as a nation.

"If their citizens," he said, "should not be completely free and happy, the fault will be entirely their own."

After the formal recognition of the United States as an independent nation, George Washington resigned his commission in the army and returned to Mt. Vernon. He expected to spend the rest of his life as a private citizen, but the liberties of America were still in danger. Once the war was over, the states no longer seemed to feel the need for united action. Washington was among the first to see the need for a strong and stable central government. Other leading patriots shared his concern, and a federal convention (later known as the Constitutional Convention) met in Philadelphia (May, 1787) to consider what measures must be taken. Washington, one of the five delegates from Virginia, was asked to preside over the meetings.

As president of the convention, the former general took no part in the proceedings, but his calm presence and reputation for integrity were important factors in the adoption of the U.S. Constitution. After it became the supreme law of the land, George Washington—one man in the new nation in whom everyone had confidence—was unanimously elected first President of the United States.

He accepted with reluctance; but he knew he was still needed. In his address when he was inaugurated (Apr. 30, 1789) in New York City, the new nation's temporary capital, he reminded his listeners that "the preservation of the sacred fire of liberty" was their responsibility. The destiny of the republican form of government, he said, was "staked on the experiment intrusted to the hands of the American people."

During George Washington's two terms as President he set the government on a strong and sturdy foundation. Though some of his policies were severely criticized, the majority of his countrymen were grateful. They would gladly have elected him to a third term, but all he wanted was to be plain Farmer Washington again. After serving his country for so many years, he wanted to live out the rest of his days at Mt. Vernon.

The only reward he asked, as he had said when he resigned as commander in chief, was the approval and "affections of a free people."

Webster, Daniel (1782–1852), the foremost American orator of his time, is best remembered for his efforts to prevent disruption of the Union. While he was serving in the U.S. Senate, another senator, Robert Y. Hayne of South Carolina, made an eloquent plea (1830) for nullification—that is, the right of a state to set aside a law of the federal government. Webster had only one night to prepare an answer, but his speech, known as the "Reply to Hayne," presented ideas that are now a part of American political belief.

Calmly, deliberately, Daniel Webster demolished the arguments of his opponent. The government of the United States, he maintained, was not the creature of the state governments. It was the *people's* government, and the people had declared the Constitution to be the supreme law of the land. If each of the twenty-four states (the number in the Union at that time) were to decide which acts of the national government they chose to obey, then Congress "would be the servant of four and twenty masters of different wills and different purposes." The idea of "Liberty first and Union afterwards" was folly

and delusion, Webster pointed out. He went on, in his deep voice:

While the Union lasts, we have high, exciting, gratifying prospects spread out before us and our children . . . . Liberty and Union, now and forever, one and inseparable.

During the next twenty years the quarrels between North and South became even more serious. The Mexican War (1846–48) resulted in the addition of a vast new territory to the United States— territory that some day would be divided into states. Since each state elects two members to the Senate, an effort had been made to please both North and South by admitting one slave state for each free one. Then the desire of California to come in as a free state threatened to destroy this balance. Many Southerners talked openly of secession, unless the South had its proper share in the new lands, and by 1850 Civil War seemed inevitable.

To avert this calamity, a fellow sen-

ator, Henry Clay, suggested that the only way to avoid a disastrous civil war was for both sections of the country to make further concessions. Clay was called "the great peacemaker," because thirty years earlier he had worked out a compromise plan (known as the Missouri Compromise) that had settled the quarrel about slavery —at least temporarily. In 1850 he worked out a new plan—to become known as the Compromise of 1850, which he hoped would satisfy both North and South. To secure the passage of his bill by Congress, Clay urgently needed the support of an orator with the persuasive powers of Daniel Webster. In order to preserve the Union, he asked Webster to support the Compromise and to speak in its behalf.

For "the great Daniel," as he was sometimes called, it was a difficult decision. Especially distasteful to him was one provision of the Compromise for a stricter Fugitive Slave Law which would forbid, under pain of arrest, any person aiding a runaway slave. For years Daniel Webster had been an outspoken foe of slavery, and most of the people in his native New England were as fervently antislavery as he was himself. If he offended them, his cherished ambition to become President might never be realized.

But what if he refused to support Senator Clay? What was the alternative? The two men agreed that there could be no greater tragedy than disunion. On March 7, 1850, the Senate chamber and galleries were packed, everyone waiting to learn what stand Senator Webster would take.

"I speak today," he began, "for the preservation of the Union. Hear me for my cause."

The Seventh of March speech lasted for more than three hours. Webster's staunch supporters were amazed when he urged the Senate to vote for the Compromise in order to avoid secession. "Peaceable secession" was impossible, he said. "The dismemberment of this vast country" could never be accomplished without war.

Due in large part to Webster's eloquence and influence, the Compromise of 1850 was passed. Neither North nor South was entirely satisfied, but it averted an immediate conflict. For Daniel Webster, it was a bitter victory, for he lived to hear himself reviled as "the enemy of freedom." Even the kindly Quaker poet John Greenleaf Whittier condemned him, in the poem "Ichabod" that began:

> *So fallen! so lost! the light with-*
> *drawn*
> *Which once he wore!*
> *The glories from his gray hairs*
> *gone*
> *Forevermore!*

Many of Webster's antislavery friends believed the worst—that he had tried to conciliate the South because of his ambition to become President. Webster knew that his speech, on the contrary, had hurt his chances, yet he was determined to try again. Though his party, the Whigs, refused to nominate him (1852), he never regretted the stand he had taken. He had said, in his final speech (1850) to the Senate:

> What are personal consequences . . . in comparison with the good or evil which may befall a great country in a crisis like this? . . . No man can suffer too much, and no man can fall too soon, if he suffer or if he fall in defense of the liberties and Constitution of his country.

Westward Movement. When Henry David Thoreau, New England nature writer and philosopher, said, "Westward I go free," he was only putting into words what thousands of Americans had felt in their minds and hearts since the nation began. Even before the colonies declared their independence, a few hardy colonists had sought new homes farther west, and during the next century more and more people pushed farther and farther west across the continent.

When a settled region became less democratic, with influence concentrated in the hands of too few people; when it was no longer possible for a poor man to own a farm in the East; and when he had to work for whatever wages might be offered him, the West held out the lure of free land—or at least land that was very cheap. The pioneers who cleared this land to build new homes often endured great hardships. Living on the frontier as they did, they learned to depend on themselves and on one another. As a rule, the residents of a pioneer community in the wilderness were equally poor, and most of them wanted to better their condition. What has been called "frontier democracy" was a feeling that no man was better than any other, so long as he was willing to work hard and could be trusted by his neighbors.

The development of the American ideas about freedom and democracy owes much to the westward movement across the continent, but what Americans meant when they talked of "the West" changed from time to time. In the late 1700's and during the early years of the next century, Kentucky and the Northwest Territory were called "the West." After those regions became more settled, the vast territory on the far side of the Mississippi River was referred to in the same way, and in time "the West" was interpreted to mean the country bordering the Pacific Ocean. The pioneers on each new frontier, facing similar problems, developed the same independence of spirit and the same convictions about equality. Before their territories were admitted into the Union as states, they adopted democratic constitutions which extended the suffrage to all white men.

Such measures were not without effect in the older states of the East. Many people who had never had much influence before began to demand equality, and they

demanded the right to vote. The frontier, by fostering the idea that every man has a chance to rise in the world, had vitalized all American democracy. This was the opinion of Frederick Jackson Turner, well-known historian and author of *The Frontier in American History*.

In one article, he said:

Each frontier did indeed furnish a new field of opportunity, a gate of escape from the bondage of the past . . . . Men would not accept inferior wages and a permanent position of social subordination when this promised land of freedom and opportunity was theirs for the taking.

Whitman, Walt (1819–92), known as "the poet of democracy," published his first collection of poems (1855) under the title *Leaves of Grass*. Written in free verse, an innovation at that time, and expressing some unconventional ideas, the book brought him more ridicule than praise until a fellow American, Ralph Waldo Emerson, voiced his enthusiasm. Emerson wrote the new author that he had found great joy in the "free and brave thought" of the poems and in the "incomparable things said incomparably well."

To Walt Whitman himself, his book was an expression of his faith in democracy, and of his belief that through the practice of democratic principles the American people could become "the most splendid race the sun ever shone on." To him these principles applied not only to politics, but to every aspect of daily living.

As a nurse with the Union forces during the Civil War, Whitman witnessed many distressing scenes. At the end of the war the generous terms of surrender offered by General Ulysses S. Grant, as well as the equally generous efforts of the defeated general, Robert E. Lee, to bring about a better understanding, caused Walt Whitman to exclaim, "Affection will solve the problems of freedom yet." Following the assassination of President Abraham Lincoln, Whitman wrote his moving tribute, "O Captain! My Captain!" one line of which read, "The ship has weather'd every rack; the prize we sought is won."

The prize, as the poet saw it, was the triumph of democracy, which meant—as he said another time—"the realization of the age-long dream of the brotherhood of man." It meant also the triumph of the principle of equality, in which he had expressed his fervent belief in *Leaves of Grass:*

> *Each of us limitless—each of us with his or her right upon the earth,*
>
> ....
>
> *Each of us here as divinely as any is here.*

Williams, Roger (1603?–83), one of the earliest fathers of American democracy, advocated ideas usually taken for granted today, but which were considered radical in the 1600's. As a Puritan minister in England he offended the authorities by some of his sermons, and in 1631 he sailed for the Massachusetts Bay Colony in the New World. The Puritans who had settled there earlier had come in search of religious freedom, but Williams soon found that they wanted freedom only for themselves —not for anyone who disagreed with them. In 1635, while serving as pastor for the church at Salem, he had to stand trial before the General Court.

This court, made up of fifty magistrates representing both the church and the civil authority, accused the outspoken young minister of having "dangerous opinions." Magistrates were chosen exclusively from among members of the Puritan church—a practice Williams considered unwise. Moreover, he said, they had no right to interfere in matters of religion, and to persecute a man "because of conscience" was "contrary to the doctrine of Jesus Christ." He had also made himself unpopular by condemning the practice of taking land that rightfully belonged to the Indians without proper payment.

Though Williams defended himself eloquently, the verdict of the court was that he be banished from the colony. It was bitter cold when later he made his way through the snowy woods. After many weary days he reached the wigwam of an Indian friend. Here he was joined by

several men from his Salem congregation who were in sympathy with his views, and when spring came they set out to find a location for a settlement where they could bring their families. The place they found was so beautiful that Roger Williams decided to buy the land from the Indians and start a town. He called it Providence, in gratitude, he said, "for God's merciful providence," in his distress.

Within a few years several other settlements were started close by, and they united to form what was later called the colony of Rhode Island. It attracted many people from both Massachusetts and England, for Roger Williams promised that his colony was to be a place where all men might "walk as their consciences persuaded them." He called his government "a democracy," maintaining that it should be "by free and voluntary consent of all the inhabitants," and the heads of families met regularly to decide what laws were needed.

No law was ever made, though, about what a man should believe or what church he should attend. Baptists, Catholics, Jews, Quakers, and others who had been cruelly treated elsewhere were invited to Rhode Island. Though Williams himself did not always agree with the newcomers, all that he asked of them was that they "be loyal and keep the peace."

Under his wise leadership Rhode Island prospered, but Roger Williams's influence was not confined to his own colony or to his own time. His belief that the purpose of all good government was "to promote the happiness" and "the rights and liberty of all" was shared a century later by the author of the Declaration of Independence.

Our present-day ideas regarding religious liberty and the separation of church and state owe much to Roger Williams, and Americans also are indebted to him for proving that democracy can be a practical form of government.

One noted historian, George Bancroft, summed up Roger Williams's contribution in these words: "More ideas that have become general have emanated from the little colony of Rhode Island than from any other."

Williamsburg, the capital of colonial Virginia during the stirring days before the American Revolution, has been restored to look as it did when Washington, Jefferson, Patrick Henry, and other patriots walked the streets. Colonial Williamsburg, a unique museum of eighteenth-century America, was financed by John D. Rockefeller, Jr. and consists of more than five hundred restored or reconstructed public buildings, homes, shops, and dependencies, as well as gardens and greens.

"That the future may learn from the past" has proved an appropriate motto. The more than a million visitors who come to Williamsburg each year not only learn about the everyday life of the 1700's, but come to realize what a difficult decision had to be made by the patriots at that time. For many who had always considered themselves loyal subjects of the mother country, it was not easy to demand their rights and take a stand for liberty. The film *The Story of a Patriot* which is shown to visitors, sums up what freedom really means: it is the right to choose.

"We have made our decision . . .," says the hero at the end when he and his son are about to join the Revolutionary forces. "It wasn't an easy choice, but it was a free one. And if one wants to be free, one must learn to choose. May God help us always to make the right choice."

Wilson, James (1742–98), a Scottish-born American lawyer who settled in Philadelphia as a young man, was a signer of the Declaration of Independence. He also served in the Constitutional Convention, but perhaps his most important service was as a delegate to the Pennsylvania

Ratifying Convention. A farsighted man, he foresaw the time when "myriads of citizens" living in states still unformed would inhabit "the vast uncultivated regions of the continent"; and he warned against a point of view that would consider the needs of only one state.

Later, James Wilson was appointed (1789) an associate justice of the U.S. Supreme Court by President George Washington, and he has been called one of the most profound "political thinkers of his age."

Wilson, (Thomas) Woodrow (1856–1924), the 28th President, once said the beauty of democracy is that no matter how humbly a youngster is born, he has a "chance to master the minds and lead the imaginations of the whole country."

Tommy, as Woodrow Wilson was called as a child, was not humbly born, but he grew up to lead the imaginations of his countrymen and of many people in the rest of the world. Too frail to go to school, he had his first lessons with his father, Joseph Wilson, a Presbyterian minister. The Reverend Wilson encouraged Tommy to write, and emphasized that the purpose of words was to express the exact meaning of what one had to say. The boy never forgot that advice. Years later he was to take his place beside Jefferson and Lincoln as an eloquent spokesman for the ideals of democracy and freedom.

Another circumstance of Wilson's youth that was to influence him as a man was his close-up view of the destruction caused by the Civil War. As a boy in Augusta, Ga., he knew some of the soldiers who had returned home wounded. The war was over by the time his family moved to Columbia, S.C., a town that had been set on fire by invading Union forces, but the results of that invasion could still be seen on every side. Woodrow, as he now preferred to be called, felt sick at heart when he walked through the business dis-

trict where only the charred ruins of a few buildings remained.

Woodrow Wilson grew up to study law, to teach, and to write books on government and history. He became a professor at Princeton, formerly the College of New Jersey, from which he had graduated (1879). Later, as president of the college, he tried to make student life more democratic by doing away with exclusive undergraduate clubs, but his ideas were not approved by the trustees nor by many of the alumni.

The same ideas, though, made him famous throughout New Jersey as a champion of democracy, and he was elected governor of his state. As governor (1911–13) he brought about the passage of a number of laws that would help, not just a few rich business leaders, but the majority of the citizens, and his success in New Jersey led to his election as President of the United States.

The speeches Woodrow Wilson had made during the campaign were published in book form under the title, *The New Freedom,* and summed up what he proposed to do for the nation. "A new economic society has sprung up, and we must effect a new set of adjustments," he said. Congress agreed and, during the early part of the Wilson administration, more reform laws were passed than at any previous time in the nation's history (see PROGRESSIVE MOVEMENT). Unfortunately, after World War I began in Europe (1914), the President's domestic program had to be dropped because of new challenges that faced the country.

Woodrow Wilson, a man who profoundly loved peace, was finally forced to ask Congress (Apr. 2, 1917) to declare war on Germany, and the American nation entered the war on the side of the Allies. During the dark days that lay ahead, the American armed forces fought with guns, and the President fought with ideas. His speeches were printed and

dropped by airplanes behind the German lines. Many German soldiers came to feel that the American President spoke for all downtrodden peoples, themselves included.

One speech widely read in Germany was the President's Message to Congress (Jan. 8, 1918) outlining Fourteen Points as the basis for a just and lasting peace. To Wilson, the most important of these points was the Fourteenth, providing for "a general association of nations" (later to be called the League of Nations) that would guarantee "political independence and territorial integrity to great and small states alike." On the basis of the Fourteen Points, Germany finally asked for an armistice, which was signed Nov. 11, 1918.

The news brought rejoicing to all of the Allied countries that had suffered through several years of bitter warfare. In Washington, D.C. the President made a formal announcement to Congress that

the war was over, but with this announcement went a warning:

"To conquer with arms," he said, "is to make only a temporary conquest."

A few weeks later, President Wilson, as head of the American Peace Commission, sailed for France to take part in making a final treaty. As his carriage rolled through the streets of Paris, enthusiastic crowds shouted, *"Vive Wilson! Vive l'Amérique!"* Europeans who had read his speeches called him "Wilson the Just"—a man they hoped could save them from the horror of future wars. Could he possibly live up to their faith in him?

As it turned out, he could not. The Peace Conference met at Versailles, a suburb of Paris, and the President soon found that the leaders of the other victorious countries were more interested in revenge than in justice. The conference was forced to adopt a policy of "give and take" in order to come to an agreement. Though bitterly disappointed, Wilson agreed to some provisions in the treaty of which he disapproved in order to have his way about the League of Nations (see separate entry). He declared it was "the first real step forward" in settling disputes between nations before the disputes could lead to war.

After the Versailles Treaty was signed (June 28, 1919), Woodrow Wilson sailed for home. On July 10, he presented the treaty to the U.S. Senate, which must approve all agreements made with foreign governments. The President said:

The united power of free nations must put a stop to aggression and the world must be given peace. Shall we or any other free people hesitate to accept this great duty?

A number of Senators did hesitate, and Henry Cabot Lodge, the chairman of the powerful Foreign Relations Committee, led the opposition to the treaty and the League of Nations. He was the President's political enemy, and both men could be stubborn. When it was suggested that reservations or changes in the treaty might make it more acceptable to the Senate, Woodrow Wilson refused to consider them. He maintained that if he asked for further changes at such a late date, then the representatives who had signed on behalf of all the other countries involved would have to be granted the same privilege.

By the end of the summer (1919), after many heated discussions in the Senate, the President realized the treaty was in grave danger of defeat. Though his health was failing, he embarked on a nationwide speaking tour, in an attempt to rally public support for the League of Nations. He was much heartened by the warm reception he received from crowds in city after city, as he made his way toward the West Coast. On his return trip, he stopped in Pueblo, Colo. (Sept. 25) to deliver what would prove to be his final speech. His audience was deeply moved when he told them that the liberty and salvation of the world might depend on the decision of the United States to join the League.

That night the President was stricken with paralysis, and for the rest of his life he was an invalid. Though the Senate voted against the United States joining the League, Woodrow Wilson never lost faith that some day his cause would triumph.

Woman Suffrage Movement. It did not seem to occur to the founding fathers who framed the Declaration of Independence and the U.S. Constitution that the ideals set forth in those two great documents should also apply to women. It did occur to a few outstanding women of the time, including Abigail Adams, during the period when her husband, John, was away serving in the Continental Congress. In a letter to a woman friend she suggested that they send a petition to Congress, in the hope that the new government to be formed would treat women more fairly than the laws of England did.

"I ventured to speak a word [to John] on behalf of our sex," she said, but evidently Abigail became discouraged by her husband's jesting reply. Perhaps it was because he did not take her seriously or perhaps she was too busy managing the family farm during his absence, but the petition was never sent. Seventy-five years went by before any decisive action was taken on behalf of women's rights.

In July, 1848, a group of determined ladies, deeply concerned about the plight of their sex, held a convention in Seneca Falls, N.Y. There was good reason for concern. Women could not vote, and they enjoyed few of the other privileges that most men took for granted. A girl was not supposed to need much education, so colleges were closed to her. After she married, if her husband proved unkind, she was at his mercy, and he could take charge of any property she owned. If she had to work, there were only a few positions she was permitted to hold, and she was paid a much lower wage than a man would have received.

At the convention in Seneca Falls—the first women's rights convention ever held in the United States—the suggestion was made that a Declaration of Sentiments be issued. Elizabeth Cady Stanton, author of the Declaration, listed the "repeated injuries" to which women had been subjected, and included a clause concerning a woman's "inalienable right to the elective franchise." Some of the ladies present were shocked. For women to demand the right to vote seemed going just a little too far. Even the gentle Quaker, Mrs. Lucretia Mott, who had cooperated with Mrs. Stanton in calling the convention, protested.

"Why, Lizzie," she said, "thee will make us ridiculous."

Mrs. Stanton persisted, for she was convinced that the franchise must come first, if women were to gain the other rights to which they were entitled. Her resolution, adopted by the convention, has been called a feminine Declaration of Independence.

A few years later Mrs. Stanton met Susan B. Anthony, who was active in reform movements of the day, and the two women became firm friends. For the next half century they worked together as a team for the cause of women's rights. In the beginning most men and many wives disapproved of their activities, but as the years passed the two dynamic leaders attracted many followers. The suffragettes, as the women working for equal rights were called, refused to be discouraged by sneers and insults. They made speeches, organized parades, wrote articles, and brought pressure to bear on legislators in various states to permit women citizens to vote.

The first breakthrough came in the territory of Wyoming, which granted suffrage to women in 1869, twenty-one years before it became a state. By 1913, eight other states had fallen into line, and suffrage leaders decided to spend more time and effort in working for the passage of a woman suffrage amendment to the federal Constitution. Suffragettes from all over the nation arrived in Washington, D.C. to urge Congress to take action. Again they held parades and demonstrations and made speeches, their campaign coming to a climax during World War I.

"We women of America voice our deep indignation," said one speaker, "that while efforts are being made to establish democracy in Europe, American women are being deprived of a voice in their government at home."

The suffragettes were finally successful. Both houses of Congress approved an amendment stating that the right of citizens to vote should not be denied on account of sex. Before the end of 1920, the Nineteenth Amendment had been ratified by the required number of states and went into effect in time for American women to cast their ballots in the Presidential election that November.

The pioneers of the suffrage movement did not live to see that day of triumph, but younger women just as dedicated had taken up the cause. Among them was Mrs. Carrie Chapman Catt, president of the National American Woman Suffrage Association. After the passage of the Nineteenth Amendment, that organization was no longer needed, and she founded the National League of Women Voters (1920) to take its place. The League was nonpartisan, and its purpose was to encourage good legislation, regardless of which political party passed it. Another purpose was to provide League members with the political education essential for the success of a democratic government. The League, Mrs. Catt believed, would show American women the way to use the suffrage for good citizenship.

"The vote is your symbol of equality," she told one audience. "Use it intelligently. Understand what it means and what it can do for your country."

World War I (1914–18). After the war, now called World War I, broke out in Europe (1914), Woodrow Wilson, President of the United States, asked the American people to remain neutral. His offer (1916) to mediate between the Allies (including England and France) and the Central Powers (Germany and Austria-Hungary) was not accepted, and as the months passed, the American people found it increasingly hard not to take sides. They feared the autocratic ambitions of Kaiser Wilhelm II, ruler of Germany, and were outraged by newspaper accounts of atrocities committed by German soldiers.

Feeling ran high when German submarines began sinking vessels on which Americans were traveling, and several hundred Americans were sent to their deaths. Pledges were made by the Kaiser's government that in the future passengers and crews would be warned in time for them to take to the lifeboats, but this promise was soon broken. Germany announced a policy of unrestricted submarine warfare, and in March, 1917, five American merchant ships were torpedoed by submarines. The first of that same month a note was intercepted on its way to Mexico, proposing that Mexico join Germany in a war on the United States.

The American people could remain neutral no longer. When the President spoke before a joint session of Congress (Apr. 2), he asked for a declaration of war against Germany. All of the important leaders in government were present, and the galleries were crowded with visitors. In the hushed silence, Woodrow Wilson reminded his listeners of the principles that had given the nation birth. In entering the war, he made it clear that the American purpose was to bring about "the ultimate peace of the world." The United States wanted no material rewards—no additional territory or indemnities. He said:

We shall fight for the things which we have always carried nearest our hearts, for democracy, for the right of those who submit to authority to have a voice in their own governments; for the rights and liberties of small nations, for a universal dominion of right by such a concert of free peoples as shall bring peace and safety to all nations, and make the world itself at last free.

The Allies were in desperate straits when the first U.S. troops arrived in Europe, but with the aid of more than two million American soldiers, the American Navy, and American money and supplies, Germany was finally defeated. The Kaiser was forced to flee the country, and a new German government asked for an armistice. The anniversary of the day the armistice was signed (Nov. 11, 1918) is now observed as Veterans' Day.

Thousands of American fighting men had believed the President when he said it was "a war to end war." He was determined to make good this promise, and when he attended the Peace Conference near Paris, early in 1919, he insisted that provision for a League of Nations be included in the Versailles Peace Treaty. The League was a plan to settle disputes by peaceful means, but the U.S. Senate (which must approve all treaties) refused to allow the United States to join.

To Woodrow Wilson this seemed a tragic decision. He knew the suffering that had been caused by the war—the homes and towns destroyed, the millions of soldiers and civilians who had been wounded and the many who had died. His prediction that without an effective method to prevent future wars there would be another even more terrible conflict in another generation was to prove all too accurate.

"The peace of the world cannot be established without America," he had said in one speech. "America is necessary to the peace of the world."

It took another tragic war to convince his countrymen that he was right.

World War II (1939–45) was brought about by the lust for world power of several dictators. Benito Mussolini, leader of the Italian Fascist Party, had already begun his conquests by invading Ethiopia in eastern Africa (1935–36). Adolph Hitler, fanatical leader of the Nazi Party in Germany, assured the German people they were a master race and all other races were subservient to them. After annexing several neighboring countries, he started World War II by invading Poland (Sept., 1939). On the other side of the world, a few autocratic military officers, the real masters of Japan, had invaded China. Their dream was to conquer all the lands and islands of the Pacific. In 1940, Japan entered into an alliance with Italy and Germany which became known as the Axis.

Less than a year after World War II began in Europe, Hitler's Nazi hordes had overrun most of western Europe, inflicting terrible hardships on the conquered peoples in the Allied countries. Only the British had kept their freedom, and in spite of repeated bombings England still held out against the savage foe. Until England was conquered, the Nazis could not extend their aggression to the Americas, but gradually the American people realized that their nation stood in great danger. Most of them agreed with President Franklin D. Roosevelt that their "greatest hope" of staying out of the war was to provide all possible aid "short of war" to those peoples that were still fighting the Axis.

In a Fourth of July radio speech (1941), the President said:

It is indeed a fallacy for any Americans to suggest that the rule of force can defeat human freedom in all other parts of the world and permit it to survive in the United States alone.

When war finally came to the United States, it was in an unexpected manner. While diplomats from Japan were in Washington, D.C. discussing ways of adjusting differences between the two countries, Japanese airplanes bombed the American naval base at Pearl Harbor, Hawaii. Several thousand people were killed or injured; U.S. planes that were grounded there at the time were destroyed; and heavy losses were inflicted on the U.S. fleet. The date of the sneak attack (Dec. 7, 1941) would "live in infamy," said President Roosevelt when he spoke to a joint session of Congress the next day to ask for a declaration of war against Japan. Germany and Italy then declared war on the United States.

The next three and a half years were filled with the pain and misery that are a part of war. American armed forces fought with the Allies in Asia, in Africa, in Europe, and on the oceans. After the Nazis were driven out of North Africa,

an attack was launched on Italy which by then had ousted its dictator. A new Italian government surrendered, but the Nazis still in control of large areas in Italy put up a fierce resistance before they were finally driven out. Meanwhile, General Dwight D. Eisenhower, who had commanded the Allied invasion of Africa, was appointed Supreme Commander of the Allied Expeditionary Forces. From England he launched a massive invasion of western Europe (June 6, 1944) to liberate the captive nations, but eleven months of hard fighting still lay ahead.

The Soviet Union was then an ally of Britain and the United States, and Soviet troops battered Germany from the east, while the Allies attacked from the west. Hitler's dream of world conquest was crumbling and, when faced with certain defeat, he committed suicide. May 8, 1945,

the day following the German surrender, was celebrated as V-E Day (Allied Victory in Europe) by the United States and other Allied nations.

Nearly four months later, September 2, would be officially proclaimed V-J Day (Allied Victory in Japan). This victory came much sooner than had been expected. At one time U.S. military authorities had believed the Japanese islands would have to be invaded, and they estimated that a quarter of a million American and British lives would probably be sacrificed, in addition to millions of Japanese who would be killed. By the first of August, the authorities knew the invasion would probably not be necessary. Experiments with the atom bomb, on which scientists had been working, proved successful. Two of the bombs, many times more powerful than any instrument of warfare invented before that time, were dropped on two Japanese cities, and the destruction they caused was so horrible that the Japanese surrendered.

The surrender ceremonies took place on board the American warship *Missouri* in Tokyo Bay. General Douglas Mac-Arthur, Supreme Allied Commander of forces in the Southwest Pacific, received the surrender, in the presence of American naval and army leaders, and representatives of several Allied countries. The Japanese representatives, looking white and tense, signed the surrender document, as hundreds of aircraft flew overhead.

The victory over the Japanese brought with it relief and also profound concern. In a radio broadcast to the American people, General MacArthur warned that the destructiveness of war now made it imperative that some alternative be found for settling international disputes.

"A new era is upon us," he said.

It was indeed a new era. As a result of the war, the United States and the Soviet Union had become the two most powerful nations in the world. They represented entirely different points of view, and the American people suddenly found themselves the chief guardians of liberty, with the chief responsibility for its preservation. It was not a role for which they had asked, and they assumed it reluctantly.

President John F. Kennedy, who had been a navy lieutenant during the war, said:

It is the fate of this generation to live with a struggle we did not start, in a world we did not make. But the pressures of life are not always distributed by choice. And while no nation has ever faced such a challenge, no nation has ever been so ready to seize the burden and the glory of freedom.

Zenger, John Peter (1697–1746), who had been an immigrant boy from Germany, grew up to become the printer and publisher of the New York *Weekly Journal*. Because he had the courage to publish a series of articles denouncing the corrupt practices of the royal governor, he indirectly laid the groundwork for the freedom of the press that Americans value so highly today.

The articles had been written by some of the outstanding citizens of the town, but because Zenger was the publisher he was held responsible and accused of seditious libel. For more than a year he was kept in prison while awaiting trial, and was allowed to communicate with no one but his wife. Talking with her through a small hole in the door of his cell, he gave her instructions about publishing the *Journal*, and she did not miss getting out a single issue. One day she brought the disturbing news to her husband that two local lawyers who had planned to defend him had been disbarred.

The judge, who was under the influence of the governor, then appointed another attorney for the printer, but Zenger's friends realized he could not expect a fair trial under the circumstances. They decided to seek the help of Andrew Hamilton, a well-known attorney of Philadelphia, but their visit to him was kept secret.

Hamilton, deeply moved by Zenger's plight, agreed to take the case without fee. The journey from his home was a real hardship for a man past eighty and in poor health, but on August 4, 1735, he suddenly appeared in the New York courtroom. The judge, taken by surprise, could find no reason to object. He could not very well disbar one of the most distinguished attorneys in the colonies.

According to the English libel law of that time, a statement was considered libelous if it was critical of the government—even if the statement was true. Hamilton, though, in his defense arguments, maintained that people have "a right publicly to remonstrate the abuses of power ... by men in authority."

Everyone in the crowded courtroom listened intently as the elderly lawyer appealed to the jurors for an impartial and uncorrupt verdict. They would then be honored, he went on, as men who had baffled an attempt at tyranny:

> The question before the Court and you, gentlemen of the jury, is not of small nor private concern. It is not the cause of a poor printer nor of New York alone which you are now trying. No! It is the cause of liberty ... the liberty both of exposing and opposing arbitrary power ... by speaking and writing truth.

The jurors realized they were expected to bring in a verdict of "Guilty." The court had made it clear that the question to be decided was not whether the statements in the *Journal* were true, but whether they were critical of the government. The members of the jury stood in some awe of the judge, but they had been completely won over by Hamilton's eloquence and logic. They voted to acquit

John Peter Zenger—a vote that went far toward establishing in America the right of free public discussion of the conduct of public men.

After his release, Zenger printed a book with a verbatim account of his trial, which was widely read both in Great Britain and throughout the colonies. His personal victory was hailed also as a decisive victory for freedom of the press.

Books for Further Reading

OF GENERAL INTEREST

Acheson, Patricia. *America's Colonial Heritage*, 1957, Dodd, Mead & Company.

Barth, Alan. *Heritage of Liberty*, 1964, McGraw-Hill Book Company.

Bontemps, Arna. *One Hundred Years of Negro Freedom*, 1961, Dodd Mead & Company.

Coit, Margaret L. *The Fight for Union*, 1961, Houghton Mifflin Company.

Commager, Henry S. *The Great Declaration*, 1958; *The Great Constitution*, 1961; *The Great Proclamation*, 1960, The Bobbs-Merrill Co., Inc.

Coolidge, Olivia. *Women's Rights: The Suffrage Movement in America*, 1966, E. P. Dutton.

Foster, Genevieve. *Abraham Lincoln's World*, 1944; *Birthdays of Freedom*, 1952, 1957; *George Washington's World*, 1941, Charles Scribner's Sons.

Fribourg, Marjorie G. *The Bill of Rights, Its Impact on the American People*, 1967; *The Supreme Court in American History*, 1965, Macrae Smith Co.

Galt, Tom. *How the United Nations Works* (rev. ed.), 1965, Thomas Y. Crowell Company.

Hall-Quest, Olga. *Bell That Rang for Freedom*, 1965, E. P. Dutton & Co., Inc.

Hodges, C. Walter, *Magna Carta*, 1966, Coward-McCann, Inc.

Kennedy, John F. *Nation of Immigrants* (rev. ed.), 1964; *Profiles in Courage* (Young Reader's Edition), 1961, Harper & Row, Publishers.

Lens, Sidney. *Working Men: The Story of Labor*, 1961, G. P. Putnam's Sons.

Meltzer, Milton (ed.). *In Their Own Words: A History of the American Negro* (2 vols.) 1964, 1965, Thomas Y. Crowell.

Miers, Earl S. *Billy Yank and Johnny Reb: How They Fought and Made Up*, 1958, Rand McNally & Company; *Freedom: The Story of Your Rights as an American*, 1965, Grosset & Dunlap, Inc.; *Yankee Doodle Dandy*, 1964, Rand McNally & Company.

Neal, Harry. *Diary of Democracy: Story of Political Parties in America*, 1962, Julian Messner.

Nolan, Jeannette C. *The Shot Heard Round the World: The Story of Lexington and Concord*, 1963, Julian Messner.

Price, Willadene. *Bartholdi and the Statue of Liberty*, 1959, Rand McNally & Company.

Savage, Katharine. *The Story of the Second World War*, 1958, Henry Z. Walck, Inc.

Sterling, Dorothy. *Forever Free, The Story of the Emancipation Proclamation*, 1963, Doubleday & Company, Inc.

Tunis, Edwin. *Pictorial History of the Indian*, 1959, The World Publishing Company.

LEADERS IN LIBERTY

Angle, Paul M. (ed.): *Lincoln Reader*, 1964, Rand McNally & Company.

Cammiade, Audrey. *Franklin and the American War of Independence*, 1967, Roy Publishers, Inc.

Campion, Nardi. *Patrick Henry: Firebrand of the Revolution*, 1961, Little, Brown and Company.

Cavanah, Frances. *Triumphant Adventure: The Story of Franklin Delano Roosevelt*, 1964, Rand McNally & Company.

Commager, Henry S. *America's Robert E. Lee*, 1951, Houghton Mifflin Company.

Cooke, David C. *Tecumseh, Destiny's Warrior*, 1959, Julian Messner.

Daugherty, James. *Abraham Lincoln*, 1943; *Poor Richard*, 1941, The Viking Press, Inc.

Deutsch, Babette. *Walt Whitman, Builder for America*, 1941, Julian Messner.

Douglass, Frederick. *Life and Times of Frederick*

Douglass (adapted by Barbara Ritchie), 1966, Thomas Y. Crowell Company.

Douty, Esther M. *Patriot Doctor, The Story of Benjamin Rush,* 1959, Julian Messner; *Under the New Roof: Five Patriots of the New Republic,* 1965, Rand McNally & Company.

Eaton, Jeannette. *Leader by Destiny: George Washington, Man and Patriot,* 1938; *Lone Journey: The Life of Roger Williams,* 1944, Harcourt, Brace & World, Inc.; *That Lively Man, Ben Franklin,* 1948, William Morrow.

Emery, Anne. *American Friend: Herbert Hoover,* 1967, Rand McNally & Company.

Fast, Howard. *Haym Salomon, Son of Liberty,* 1941, Julian Messner.

Forbes, Esther. *America's Paul Revere,* 1946, Houghton Mifflin Company.

Freeman, Douglas S. *Lee of Virginia,* 1958, Charles Scribner's Sons.

Galt, Tom. *Peter Zenger, Fighter for Freedom,* 1951, Thomas Y. Crowell Company.

Gray, Elizabeth Janet, *Penn,* 1938, The Viking Press, Inc.

Gurko, Leo. *Tom Paine, Freedom's Apostle,* 1957, Thomas Y. Crowell Company.

Hall-Quest, Olga. *Guardians of Liberty: Sam Adams and John Hancock,* 1963, E. P. Dutton.

Johnson, Gerald W. *Franklin D. Roosevelt, Portrait of a Great Man,* 1967, William Morrow & Co.

Judson, Clara I. *Mr. Justice Holmes,* 1956; *Theodore Roosevelt, Fighting Patriot,* 1953, Follett Publishing Company.

Lee, Bruce. *Boys' Life of John F. Kennedy,* 1964, Sterling Publishing Co., Inc.

Lisitzky, Gene. *Thomas Jefferson,* 1933, The Viking Press, Inc.

Lomask, Milton. *John Quincy Adams, Son of the American Revolution,* 1965, Farrar, Straus & Giroux, Inc.

Lovelace, Delos W. *"Ike" Eisenhower: Statesman and Soldier of Peace,* 1961, Thomas Y. Crowell.

Meyer, Edith Patterson. *Champions of the Four Freedoms,* 1966, Little, Brown and Company.

Nolan, Jeannette C. *Andrew Jackson,* 1949; *John Brown,* 1950, Julian Messner.

Peare, Catherine O. *William Penn,* 1958, Holt, Rinehart & Winston; *The Woodrow Wilson Story,* 1963, Thomas Y. Crowell Company.

Roosevelt, Eleanor. *Autobiography,* 1961, Harper & Row, Publishers.

Severn, William. *Adlai Stevenson, Citizen of the World,* 1966, David McKay Co., Inc.

Steinberg, Alfred. *James Madison,* 1965; *John Marshall,* 1962; *The Man from Missouri: The Life and Times of Harry Truman,* 1962, G. P. Putnam's Sons.

Sterling, Dorothy. *Freedom Train, The Story of Harriet Tubman,* 1954, Doubleday & Company.

Wibberley, Leonard. *Young Man from the Piedmont,* 1963; *Dawn in the Trees: Thomas Jefferson, The Years* 1776–1789, 1964; *The Gales of Spring: Thomas Jefferson, The Years 1789–1801,* 1965, Farrar, Straus & Giroux, Inc.

Wood, James Playsted. *Trust Thyself; A Life of Ralph Waldo Emerson,* 1964, Pantheon Books.

INDEX

Main entries are printed in boldface type, and the boldface numbers under these entries indicate the pages on which the main article appears. In some instances the subject of one main entry has been cross-indexed to another which may not specifically mention the subject or name of the first entry (see Hutchinson, Anne), but provides additional general information. Topics listed in regular type do not have main entries in the *Encyclopedia*, but refer the reader to an entry or entries where information about the subject may be found.

FRANCES CAVANAH, the author, is well known for her many books for young people in the field of American history and biography. One of her first books, *Our Country's Story,* has become a classic.

ELIZABETH L. CRANDALL, the author's collaborator, is an expert in the field of world history. She has written biographies for young people of Leonardo da Vinci and Benjamin Disraeli, and is a co—author of a world history textbook.

LORENCE F. BJORKLUND has illustrated more than 200 books, many of them on historical subjects.

PRINTED IN U.S.A.